The Federal Principle

S. RUFUS DAVIS

The Federal Principle

A Journey Through Time in Quest of a Meaning

If a man will study
how things arise from their beginning
and come to be, in this way
he will best perceive the truth of a thing.
ARISTOTLE

UNIVERSITY OF CALIFORNIA PRESS

BERKELEY · LOS ANGELES · LONDON

University of California Press
Berkeley and Los Angeles, California

University of California Press, Ltd.
London, England

ISBN 0-520-03146-6
Library of Congress Catalog Card Number: 75-32673
Printed in the United States of America

Designed by Theo Jung

To My Family

Anna

Stephen

Judy

Jennie

Contents

Preface

My purpose is to take stock of an idea that has lived a long life, to see from whence it has come and what it has become. Aside from a long-standing curiosity, there is cause for inquiry. Whereas federalism was once an ornament of political science, it has begun to show distinct marks of wear and tear. The signs are everywhere: in the many and different approaches to the subject; in the varying attempts to rectify its name; in the contradictory political programs urged in its name; in the alternating arrangements brought within its fold; in the minimal returns of comparative studies; and in the growing disinclination of many scholars to work with the concept. The subject has indeed fallen on hard times.

How to take stock? The ways are almost as many as the ways of looking at the subject; there is history, culture, practice, and language. Each, in its own way, is indispensable to the understanding of the whole, and none by itself is sufficient to grasp it all. But the principle of selection and the manner of arrangement spring from a single unargued hypothesis—that we can better understand what has taken place if we look to the early years of the federal idea, at the different ways it evolved, and the different ways it was adapted to different circumstances. This perspective—evolution, adaptation, and diversity—therefore dominates this exposition.

However, it is not my intent to undertake a journey as encyclopaedic as Sobei Mogi's _The Problem of Federalism_. Nor is it my purpose to attend to each and every genetic twist and turn, for I have deliberately mapped out a tight itinerary so that I would not linger and explore the byways, exciting and profitable as that might have been. I have chosen instead to journey

with history just far enough to bring federalism to its modern
launching point in 1787. And I have taken just enough of
particular practices to suggest the kind of diversity with which
theory has had to grapple, and must continue to grapple if it
wishes to renew the idea.

So much for intent and aim. But a preface is more than this.
And here I would like to acknowledge several people who have
given me the kind of help that one remembers for the length of
one's days. First and foremost, I wish to thank Mrs. Mary
Bradford, the administrative secretary of the Department of
Politics at Monash University, Clayton, Victoria, Australia. It
has been my good fortune to enjoy her counsel and disarming
forthrightness for some ten years. Not only did she lighten my
burden as chairman of the department, but her understanding,
integrity, and constancy have made her a tower of strength to
all who have enjoyed the privilege of her friendship. I am also
deeply grateful to my friend and colleague Dr. Denis White, a
political philosopher who enriches all his colleagues with his
insight and gentle wit. He read the whole of the manuscript,
and conveyed his comments to me more often by frowning and
pursing his lips than by words alone. I sought his help and
advice on numerous occasions, and was always rewarded by his
unfailing generosity and wisdom. My command of Latin,
French, and German is at best "law-school" Roman law and
high-school French and German; as for Greek, it was a great
mistake of my youth to have turned down the opportunity of
making some elementary contact with it. I am therefore much
indebted to Professor Guy Manton, Associate Professor Gavin
Betts, and Dr. Jack Ellis for their generous aid in translating
some passages in Althusius' *Politica* and Bodin's *Methodus*. I
am also grateful to Dr. Irmline Veit-Brauser and Associate
Professor Walter Veit for their translation of several sections of
Busolt's massive study, *Griechische Staatskunde*. And of others
who gave me unstinting help, I should like to thank Dr. Louis
Green for his advice on the medieval leagues of Europe, Mr.
Ken Horne of the Victorian State Public Library for assisting
my use of the splendid 17th- and 18th-century resources of the

Preface   xi

library, and Mr. Greg Walsh for his valuable research assistance. There are others whose help is the word of encouragement, advice, and friendship without which life is much poorer. I wish to mention Philip Siegelman, Nelson Polsby, Martin Landau, and Aaron Wildavsky of Berkeley, and Elie Kedouri of the London School of Economics. They will know best of all what I wish to say.

S.R.D.

The Federal Principle

1

In the Beginning
Or, Covenant is the Cell

How many times has it been said that concepts, abstractions, and words are like living things; they come into life, they grow, they change, they die like the humans that live by them. As men make facts and fashion concepts, so the facts and concepts fashion and possess men. As their masters migrate, and as their users mingle at home and abroad, so too the concepts, abstractions, and words mingle, miscegenate, interbreed, fuse with aliens, become interchangeable, displace each other, degenerate or atrophy. To know this alchemy is to call upon history, for as the identity of man is his history, so too his symbols and linguistic artifacts. Observe Richard Koebner's introduction to the story and significance of a political word, "imperialism":

> This is the biography of a political word and its rise to world power status. From its early beginnings in the 1840's until today it has changed its meaning no less than twelve times, and nobody of the present generation is aware of its first meaning or of subsequent meanings which that term possessed in the days of Palmerston and Disraeli. Few people realize how the word spread and what circumstances promoted its diffusion. Generations come into the possession of words and ideas as they come into the possession of public buildings. They call them "their own" and no longer remember who built them and for what purpose. Sometimes those buildings are put to new uses and their public function is altered. The fate of ideas and words often tells a similar story. Their use and function reveal the mind of each generation. Words do not change their meaning fortuitously; they often acquire specific connotations in connexion

1

with specific events and situations. And, just as words have an impact upon actions, so there is an impact of actions upon words. . . .[1]

So too with "federalism": If we wish to come to terms with this political concept, we must come to terms with its history, even if we reconstruct it imperfectly. Moreover, those who travel this precarious journey into the past must not expect to find a beginning, nor one simple coherent thing, nor a single path; human institutions are not like that, nor is the language which summates them. Neither must they expect to find all the scattered sherds that need only the potter's skill to bring them back to their original form. For despite the zealotry of those who search for the one and only holy meaning and avert their eyes from every solid find that will imperil their goal, or the ecumenism of those who search for a final compromise among the babel of scholarly voices, it is rare to find a single "root-meaning" waiting to be purified or compromised. And worse for the explorer, there is no register of birth for political ideas, no birth names, no book of dates.

More difficult still is the nagging thought that the whole enterprise of tracing the evolution of a political idea, like any other idea, may be a dubious undertaking. Not merely because of the imperfections of our records; but of what we can take to be the life record of an "idea."[2] For what science, indeed, can record every living second of a human mind, or trace every mutation of our thoughts; the infinite number of ways in which we communicate our meaning, or the infinite number of ways that meaning is received, translated, passed on, and received in turn by others, through generations of conversation, through the endless change of idioms, metaphors, facial expressions, and silences that attend human communication. All this imperils the journey; but this said, let us proceed as best we can.

The origin of the federal idea is wreathed in mist, as indeed is the origin of life itself. Various claims have been made for

1. In Richard Koebner and H. D. Schmidt, *Imperialism* (London: Cambridge University Press, 1964), p. xiii.
2. See J. N. Figgis, *Political Thought from Gerson to Grotius, 1414-1625*, p. 3.

specific discoverers or for specific periods of history. But there are no secure details of parentage, no reliable paternity tests. Where then do we begin to probe? We could begin as Edward Freeman did with a definition, and then scan the political life of man for things that are like or unlike. I prefer to begin with the word "federal" itself. For somewhere near the beginning of it all is the idea of *foedus*, the first traceable linguistic resemblance to the *foederal* phenomenon of Rome and after. And the lexicographic association of *foedus* with *covenant*, and of its cognate *fides* with faith and trust, provide us with the first crucial clue. Because in the idea of covenant, and the synonymous ideas of promise, commitment, undertaking, or obligating, vowing, and plighting one's word to a course of conduct in relation to others, we come upon a vital bonding device of civilization.

Thus, the idea of covenant betokens not merely a solemn pledge between two or more people to keep faith with each other, to honor an agreement; it involves the idea of cooperation, reciprocity, mutuality, and it implies the recognition of entities—whether it be persons, a people, or a divine being. Without this recognition there can be no covenant, for there can be no reciprocity between an entity and a non-entity. Further, covenant betokens the need for some measure of predictability, expectation, constancy, and reliability in human relations. Men desire whatever certainty they can obtain to ease the strain of survival. By committing themselves to each other through promises, pledges, contracts, vows, and treaties, and by calling upon the most potent forces or valued symbols in their society to give moral sanctions to their undertakings, they regularize or institutionalize their relations with others, and thereby hope to bring some stability into their lives.[3]

3. In the absence of civil law and its enforcement by the "state," people called upon pagan gods, or the God of Judeao-Christian religion to hold them to their vows. "I vow by Jupiter" . . . "I vow and attest by almighty God" . . . "I vow by my honour." Cf. "I swear to tell the truth, the whole truth, . . . so help me God." The contemporary forms of oathtaking prior to giving evidence in civil or criminal courts are interesting relics, relying as they do not merely on state punishment for perjury, but doubtless on a fall from

As a concept, "covenant" is not exclusive to politics, nor has it an exclusive role in politics, for the universe of covenant in the world of man is without end. Throughout recorded history, covenants have been made, promises given, obligations assumed for a multiplicity of reasons, in a multiplicity of circumstances, and between a multiplicity of people. Yahweh, the God of Abraham, may covenant with his people to obey his commandments if they are to be his chosen,[4] an emperor may covenant with his kings to acknowledge his primacy and come to his call, kings with their feudal barons to render fealty and service, tribes with tribes to render aid, cities with cities to observe boundaries, individuals with individuals to obtain property, chattels, or service. Covenant has all the appearance of the primary cell, the bonding block, the DNA molecule from which the simplest or the most complex double-helix relationships between people may be formed. Whilst we shall never know the first moment of covenant, yet, as an experience, it symbolizes a critical shift in social evolution, from a world of random, passing, accidental relations to an awareness of the immense potentialities of promise, trust, and obligation. It is, if

---

heavenly grace as further punishment. See Hannah Arendt, *The Human Condition* (New York: Doubleday Anchor Books, 1959), "Unpredictability and the Power of Promise," pp. 219-223: ". . . the power of stabilization inherent in the faculty of making promises has been known throughout our tradition. We may trace it back to the Roman legal system, the inviolability of agreements and treaties . . ., or we may see its discoverer in Abraham, the man from Ur, whose whole story, as the Bible tells it, shows such a passionate drive toward making covenants that it is as though he departed from his country for no other reason than to try out the power of mutual promise in the wilderness of the world. . . ."

4. Most federal scholars have neglected the constitution of early Israel, but the league of the twelve tribes of Israel and its institutions cannot be overlooked in the historiography of federalism. Certainly it casts as much light on the embryonic forms of "tribal" or "religious" associations as the amphictyonic leagues of early Greece. See, for example, John Bright, *A History of Israel*, pp. 156-175. See also, D. J. Elazar, "Government in Biblical Israel." Doubtless additional sources will be brought to light with the development of Oriental and Asian political history; see for example the reference to the Grand Union of Chinese States planned by Confucius in C. S. Rhyne, *International Law*, p. 11. The structure of the Islamic Caliphate is particularly relevant to this field of studies.

we heed Nietzsche, the Rubicon point which marks off human from animal life.[5]

To trace all the tributaries of "covenant" is a prodigious task; they course through so many different channels, theological doctrine, theories of the state, theories of society, private and public law. They are borne along by the momentum of a growing world of interdependency we have come to call "civilization"; the tributaries continue to multiply, move in different directions, and sometimes meet and mix. Indeed, as we pick at the federal idea we become quickly aware that we are exposing not one single idea but a whole intricate and varied network of interrelated ideas and concepts—of contract,[6] of partnership, of equity, of trusts, of sovereignty, of constitution, of state, of international law. And as we pick at these in turn we find that each of these concepts is in fact a multicellular constellation, a molecular compound of its own ideas and concepts.[7] Note, for instance, how the evolution of the idea of promise into private contract and public treaty has borne with it the notions of "breach" of promise, breach of trust, "compensation" for the injury that may result, or the right to "secede" from an obligation where one or the other party has breached its terms, the "arbitration " of its terms where the parties are not in accord, and so on and on.[8] To establish these relationships, to indicate

5. See Herbert Spencer's extremely interesting comment on the origin of political forms and forces in "Political Institutions," Part 5 of *The Principles of Sociology*, p. 310: "The conceptions of biologists have been greatly enlarged by the discovery that organisms which, when adult, appear to have scarcely anything in common, were, in their first stages, very similar; and that, indeed, all organisms start with a common structure. Recognition of this truth has revolutionized not only their ideas respecting the relations of organisms to one another, but also their ideas respecting the relations of the parts of each organism to one another.

6. See C. G. Weeramantry, *The Law of Contracts*, pp. 3-20, where the author discusses the beginnings of contract.

7. See Ernst Gellner in D. Emmett and A. McIntyre (eds.), *Sociological Theory and Philosophical Analysis* (London: Macmillan, 1970), pp. 115-149. See also, for example, the successive chapters on promises, on contracts, on the oaths of those who hold sovereign power, and on treaties in Hugo Grotius, *The Law of War and Peace*, Vol. II, Chaps. 11-15.

8. See, for example, in the work of Baron Samuel von Pufendorf, *Of the Law of Nature and Nations*, p. 682. Speaking of the *Lex Commissoria*, one of the

where each begins and ends, or where one has injected its language into the other, to point to the fossil remnants they have inherited from each other, is a task beyond the scope of this work. That there is an evolutionary and osmotic relationship in this extraordinary web of covenantal ideas is a profitable conjecture. But if there is a Great Chain of Being for political ideas and institutions as is argued for the evolution of man, it has yet to be shown. And certainly no suggestive diagrammatic representation of the movement from the first reproductive union of man and woman to the union of states can tell the truth.

The most convenient vantage, for our purpose, from which to observe the developing use of covenant is in the context of *treaty*; the means by which tribes, communities, cities, and empires regulated their conduct with each other. And here our focus of attention must be narrowed even more closely to only a segment of this genus—the treaties of "alliance." For the general uses of "treaty" encompass an immense variety of transactions between peoples. The records of antiquity inform us of practices, usages, customs, and treaties (or formalized agreements) to regulate boundaries, to end war, to qualify and confine war, to fix the time and place of battle, to call a truce so that the slain may be buried, to give passage to traders through the lines of the contending forces, to extend immunity to ambassadors, and so on.[9] These are the civilizing transactions

---

editors comments in a footnote: "By that is generally understood a conditional Clause added to a Contract, the not performing of which renders void or makes the thing in dispute to be forfeited. We have seen some Instances of it relating to the Contract of Sale . . . and of *Pawns* and *Mortgages* . . . so in that Place the *Lex Commissoria* or *conditional clause* is an Article imposed upon the King; by virtue of which, if he breaks the Engagement which that obliges him to perform, he forfeits *ipso facto* the Crown: Just so in *Manors*, when the *Vassal* does not do Homage, or does not pay the Rent due to his *Lord*, or becomes guilty of *Felony*, the Fee falls into *Lapse*, as the Law terms it; that is, is forfeited to the use of the *Lord*, and is reunited to the *Manor*."

9. See Arthur Nussbaum, *A Concise History of the Law of Nations*, Chap. 1. Nussbaum draws attention to a treaty concluded in approximately 3100 B.C. between Eannatum, the victorious ruler of the Mesopotamian city-state of Lagash, and the men of Umma, another Mesopotamian city-state. "The

which, according to Grotius, flowed from the natural relationships of men and are received into the body of what early came to be named "The Law of Nations," and later still "international law." It is in the treaty that extends beyond the simple regulation of conflict, however, the treaties of alliance which, by their very nature, draw communities into closer association with each other, that we begin to discern the faint shadows of new political entities, and hence come closer to our concern.[10]

Who it was that first entered into a treaty of alliance is unknown. Pufendorf tells us that Pliny in his *Natural History* gives "Theseus the Honour of being the first that made or used them. . . ." But he hastens to add that this claim cannot be allowed,

> . . . in any other Sense than that perhaps he might be the first in Greece that entered into League, or that perhaps annexed certain Rights and Solemnities to be observed at the making of them.[11]

Whatever the precise date or circumstances of origin, however, it appears that the purposes of the earliest treaty associations between communities are few and simple: to defend each other against attack, or to assist each other in attacking, plundering, or robbing a common enemy. Schwarzenberger, for instance, tells us that in the fourteenth century B.C., Pharaoh Rameses II of Egypt concluded a Treaty of Peace, Alliance, and Extradition

---

treaty expressed in the Sumerian language preserved in a prescription on a stone monument pronounces the inviolability of the boundary ditch and border stone, which is acknowledged by the vanquished men of Umma under an oath by six or seven of the most powerful Sumerian gods."

10. In *Of the Law of Nature and Nations*, one of Pufendorf's editors and translators from the Latin edition, a Mr. Barbeyrac, explains in a footnote why he has chosen to express the Latin term *foedera* by the word "Leagues" instead of "Treaties": "I could not find a more proper Word to express the *Latin* term *Foedera* by. *Treaties* would have been too general; for 'tis plain that the Author [Pufendorf] here excludes all *Compacts* made during the War, whether to moderate or suspend acts of hostility, or barely to treat of Peace . . . So that the Word *League* may not be very improper here, though it is generally restrained to Treaties, by which several Princes or States unite, confederate, or league together, to defend each other, or in Conjunction to attack the common Enemy." (P. 857.)

11. *Ibid.*

with the King of Cheta; and Suppiluliuma, King of the
Hittites, entered into an alliance with Nigmad, King of Egarit,
in words that catch the spirit of all alliances from that time on:

> Just as formerly thy ancestors were friends and not enemies of
> the Hittite country, now thou, Nigmad, shouldst be the enemy
> of my enemy and the friend of my friend.[12]

The scope, content, and modes of solemnifying treaties of
alliance doubtless change and vary in place, time, and complexity; as indeed do the tongues in which each society engaged
and attested the bonds of alliance—whether Sumerian, Baby-
lonian, Hebrew, Greek, or Roman. But the word that has
exercised such a profound, and yet paradoxically distracting,
influence on federal scholarship comes to us from Rome. For if
Rome conquered a world by the force of arms, it was by the
treaty of alliance, *foedus*, or the plurality of treaties (*foedera*),
and the aid of those sworn into an alliance (*con-federati*) that
Rome conducted its diplomacy of security and aggrandizement.
In what may be one of the earliest instances of an attempt to
classify the treaties that Rome transacted with foreign communities, adjacent or distant from its borders, Menippus, An-
tioch's ambassador to Rome, is reported by Livy to have
reduced them to three kinds:

> *Esse autem tria genera foederum, quibus inter se pasciscerentur*
> *amicitias civitates regesque. . . .*

> There were three kinds of treaties . . . by which states and kings
> (*civitates regesque*) concluded friendships; one, when in time of
> war terms were imposed upon the conquered; for when every-
> thing was surrendered to him who was the more powerful in
> arms, it is the victor's right and privilege to decide what of the
> conquered's property he wishes to confiscate; the second, when
> states that are equally matched in war conclude peace and
> friendship on terms of equality (*cum pares bello aequo foedere*
> *in pacem atque amicitiam venirent . . .*); under these conditions
> demands for restitution are made and granted by mutual agree-

12. G. Schwarzenberger, *A Manual of International Law*, pp. 5-6.

ment, and if the ownership of any property has been rendered
uncertain by the war, these questions are settled according to the
rules of traditional law or the convenience of each party; the
third exists when states that have never been at war come together to pledge mutual friendship in a treaty of alliance (*ter-
tium esse genus cum, qui numquam hostes fuerint, ad amici-
tiam sociali foedere inter se iungendam coeant*...); neither party
gives or accepts conditions; for that happens when a conquering
and a conquered party meet. . . .[13]

This tripartite classification, needless to say, has been the
subject of some dispute. Grotius, for example, accused Menippus of making the classification "rather for his own purpose
than according to the rules of his craft" (*Foedera Menippus
regis Antiochi ad Romanos Legatus, referente Livio magis ex
usu suo quam ex praescripto artis ita divisit*).[14] And contemporary classical scholars have not been at ease on this matter.
But in common with Renaissance scholars, they have generally
spoken of two forms of the Roman treaty of alliance, *foedus
aequum* and *foedus iniquum*; the first, according to Sherwin-
White, set both parties on an equal footing; the second gave
Rome a hegemonic role, *in foedere superior*, a patron-client
relationship with its allies, binding them to come to its aid in
defensive and offensive wars, and calling on them to respect the
might and dignity of Rome.[15] These early classifications of
Roman treaties, while of considerable importance to sixteenth-
and seventeenth-century "federal" taxonomists, need not detain us at this juncture. What is important to note is that Western scholarship has thus far elected to observe only two moments in history when treaties of alliance have been used to
associate communities in such a way that they take on the appearance of "new" political formations: the first is the period
which marks the alliances of the Greek city-states; the second

13. Livy, XXXIV, Lvii, 7-9, in the Loeb Classical Library translation by E. T.
    Sage (London: Heinemann, 1953), vol. IX, pp. 562-563.
14. Grotius, *The Law of War and Peace*, Vol. II, p. 393.
15. See A. N. Sherwin-White in the *Oxford Classical Dictionary*, the note entry
    of Foedus, p. 442; also see E. Badian, *Foreign Clientelae (264-70 B.C.)*,
    pp. 1-14.

the period, almost a millenium later, which marks the alliances of cities and the emerging nation-states of Europe. We will now look at each of these.

2

The Hellenic Experience
Or, is it true what they say
about the Achaean League?

If we are to believe the considerable work of such historians of the Hellenic civilization as Freeman, Ehrenberg, Busolt, Tarn, Rostovtzeff, and Larsen, it would appear that the properties of something like a federal arrangement were first articulated in the Hellenic world of religious, tribal, and city-state alliances.[1] To relate oneself to this world, however, is not easy, even if we pay due homage to the authority of these scholars. To begin with, they constantly warn us that the inscriptional and other historical evidence is often fragile and speculative.[2] Further, it is extremely difficult to get a feel of the matter at this great distance in time, especially where only the barest demographic and geopolitical details are given to us.[3] And again, there is the

1. Edward A. Freeman, *History of Federal Government*; Victor Ehrenberg, *The Greek State*; Georg von Busolt, *Griechische Staatskunde*, Vol. II, pp. 1310-1531; W. Tarn, *Hellenistic Civilization*; M. Rostovtzeff, *The Social and Economic History of the Hellenistic World*; and J. A. O. Larsen, *Greek Federal States*. These works will be referred to hereafter in this chapter by author's name only.
2. For example, see Larsen, p. xi; or R. Sealey, "The Origin of the Delian League," p. 233. Freeman is not only given to cautioning his readers on this account; he is equally ready to draw the reader's attention to the inadequacies of French and German classical scholarship! (E.g., Freeman, pp. 220, 260, 263, 280, 285, and 294.)
3. It is especially difficult for a twentieth-century being to accommodate himself to the idea of a federation of territories which are sometimes geographically smaller than, say, Brooklyn, Queens, the Bronx; or the London County Council and its Boroughs; or Melbourne and its metropolitan city councils. See H. D. F. Kitto, *The Greeks*, Chap. 5; and A. Zimmern, *The Greek Commonwealth*.

constant threat that our "political science," our own world of
abstractions and symbolic language, will misrepresent and
overwhelm these Hellenic arrangements with false allusions
and false categories: as indeed, one suspects, may be the case
with some historians of this period. Observe, for instance,
Larsen's reference to a "leftist revolution" in the Achaean city
of Dyme about 120 B.C., or Sealey's suggestion that the purpose
of the Delian League was not, as others have presumed, to
plunder their neighbours, but to conduct a War of Liberation,
or Rostovtzeff's reference to the "more or less socialistic and
communistic lines" of Sparta's reconstruction by Nabis.[4] More:
sensitive as Freeman, Busolt, and others may be to the language, idioms, and metaphors of the Hellenic dialects, they are,
if we are to judge by Larsen's relaxed interchange of the terms
"confederal" and "federal," less than sensitive to the taxonomic
struggles of their contemporaries. But be all that as it may, the
reputation of classical scholarship, and the force of a legacy
that has so deeply affected the study of politics for seventeen
hundred years, cannot be set aside. Let us therefore take a
glance at the way these historians try to translate the nature of
these alliances.

The idea of treaties is fully assimilated in the Hellenic world;
they are used extensively, possibly more so than at any other
time up to the nineteenth century; and their purpose and forms
bear a striking resemblance to the treaties of all other ages,
before and after the submission of Greece to Rome.[5] Political
treaties regulated peace alliances, and commercial treaties regulated such matters as imports, exports, and coinage. It is the use
of treaties, however, to create "unities larger than tribes or city-
states" which at once excites attention and poses problems for
modern scholars. Larsen, for example, tells us that in their
effort to secure a Panhellenic peace, the Greeks made use of four
types of organization. They are:

4. Larsen, p. 503; Sealey, p. 239; Rostovtzeff, Vol. I, p. 56.
5. See Zimmern, p. 185; also Sir Ernest Barker, *From Alexander to Constantine*, p. 68.

1. Amphictyonies, or associations for worship in connection with the cult of some god: for example, the Delphic amphictyony.
2. Symmachies, or semi-federal alliances of states theoretically free and autonomous.
3. Sympolities, or true federal states.
4. Treaties for a general peace negotiated between several states.[6]

Of these four, it is the *symmachia* and *sympoliteia* that are singled out for prime attention by Freeman, Busolt, and Ehrenberg. And this for two reasons: because so much of epic Grecian political history is taken up with the origins, growth, organization, merger, success, failures, and demise of these arrangements; and second, because they exhibit more positive traces of contemporary "federal" phenomena than at any previous time in known history.

What is their nature? Some sixteen to eighteen Grecian leagues spanning some five hundred years have been recorded and described:

Thessalian	Achaean	Lycian
Boeotian	Acarnanian	Epirote
Locrian	Euboean	Magnesian
Chalcidic	Arcadian	Lacedaemonian
		(or Peloponnesian)
Aetolian	Athenian	Phocian
Corinthian (Hellenic)		

Of these, some endured for only a brief moment, either because they were destroyed or their purpose had been fulfilled; some were aborted before birth; and some (e.g., the Achaean League) endured for over a hundred years, though never in their original membership or their mode of government. Most of these leagues have been classified as *symmachia*, and four or five of these, notably the Achaean League, as *sympoliteia*. Strictly translated, the word *symmachia* is a relatively simple concept to handle, meaning "fellowship in fighting"; but it came to be used with several meanings; informal cooperation in war, a

6. J. A. O. Larsen, "Federation for Peace in Ancient Greece."

treaty of alliance, and a confederacy of allies; or paraphrased into current language, a "military alliance" or "security pact."[7] *Sympoliteia*, on the other hand, is a more fascinating and difficult term. It is sometimes translated as "fellow citizenship," "membership of one state," "the sharing of citizenship or a common political life," and sometimes as "a union of several states in which there is an exchange of civic rights." Many contemporary scholars, however, for reasons that will become apparent, have simply identified the *symmachia* as a confederal, and the *sympoliteia* as a federal, system of government.

Let us now look at each of these a little more closely. The *symmachia* began, Ehrenberg tells us,[8] as a simple fighting alliance between neighbouring tribes, but in time, about the sixth century B.C., another kind of *symmachia* emerges. This later type is, in its basic aim and form of loose organization, a military alliance between a leading state (*hegemon*) with a number of others (e.g., the Lacedaemonian, Peloponnesian, and the First and Second Athenian leagues); and though the leadership (*hegemonia*) soon comes to extend into other civic functions, the alliance remains primarily concerned with offensive or defensive purposes. In Ehrenberg's account this hegemonial *symmachia* exhibits some of the following features.

The first is the fundamental duality of the alliance; that is, it consists of two parts, the hegemonial state and its allies, which were individually brought into alliance with the *hegemon* by solemn oaths or treaties proclaiming the duty of the *hegemon*

---

7. Note that the word *sym-machia* combines the noun *mache*, battle, fight, with the preposition *syn* (which becomes *sym* before "m" or "p") to imply togetherness of some sort, e.g., fight together with an ally against an opponent, travel together, bring together, etc.

8. See Ehrenberg, pp. 112-131. I have mainly relied on Ehrenberg not because he stands as a greater authority on the Grecian leagues than Busolt, Freeman, or Larsen, but simply because Ehrenberg, in my view, is somewhat less partisan and less pressing than Freeman to identify the later Grecian leagues, especially the Achaean League, with contemporary federal systems; slightly less rigid and possessed by the jurisprudential language of German *staatslehre* (public law) than Busolt and his editor, Swoboda; and his study is more easily given to synoptic treatment than Larsen's extensive account of the leagues.

to protect its allies, and the duty of the allies to follow the
hegemon in war. Secondly, the terms of these treaties often
varied with the political situation. Thus, for example, individual treaties might be drawn up for an unspecified time, and
like any other alliance, could be concluded by notice. In other
cases, where secession was made an offense by oath and religious ritual, the treaties, in effect, created a "permanent
alliance." Similarly, where some treaties might provide for
hegemonial protection only against external foes, in others
(e.g., the Corinthian League) the protection was extended to
internal revolution. Or again, we may see this variety in other
ways. For example, in some cases, the terms of the hegemonial
alliance permitted individual members to form an alliance
between themselves, or a member to wage its own war (e.g., in
the Peloponnesian League), or two allies of the hegemonial
state could even fight one another so long as the league itself
was not at war at the time. Indeed, it was only in the second
Athenian League that each member was simultaneously sworn
to alliance with the hegemonial state, and in alliance (*sym-
machos*) with every other member of the league. The third, and
crucial, feature of the hegemonial *symmachia* was that, unlike
the *sympoliteia*, there was no common citizenship of the
league; the individual was a citizen only of his own *polis* (city-
state). The fourth element is the familiar tendency in hegemonial relations, for the supreme power of the league to pass into
the hands of the *hegemon*, and with it the decline and eventual
disappearance of any autonomy for the members of the league.
As Ehrenberg puts it:

> The relations between the leadership of the *hegemon* and the
> autonomous allies were seriously affected by military necessities,
> which easily led onto political compulsion. When the hege-
> monial polis interfered in the internal affairs of the allies and
> demanded that they should adapt their constitutions to its own,
> the autonomy of the allies had virtually ceased to exist. But that
> happened only at the end of a long development, though this,
> one way or another, repeated itself for every League. Anyway,
> the two principles of hegemony and autonomy never reached a

final harmony. . . . In the Athenian empire, the tendency to move from the unquestioned autonomy of the allies to the complete hegemony of the leading state reached its perfection. Although, compared to the Peloponnesian League, the elements of federation were at the outset here much stronger, Athens from the first was in a much more powerful position over against her allies than Sparta to hers. . . . The most important step in the reduction of the allies to subjects was the removal of the League treasury to Athens. . . .[9]

Doubtless, some of the historical reconstruction and interpretation of the hegemonial *symmachia* is speculative. But given this, Ehrenberg, Busolt, Rostovtzeff, and Larsen seem agreed on three things: first, that the hegemonial *symmachia* was an attempt to create a structure which transcended the single city-state; second, that the hegemonial *symmachia*, though varying considerably in structure, scope, and aim was "confederal," not "federal," in form; and third, that at some time in the fourth century B.C. the hegemonial *symmachia*, under the pressure of political events, began to evolve into a new form of association. Such is the importance of this gradual change that for greater accuracy I will quote Ehrenberg directly:

> In general, the alliances under a *hegemon* showed very different structures and developments; the reason is that we are not dealing here with a uniform type of constitution, but with unions of a mixed military and political character, which may have been shaped and modified as the changing situation demanded. Accordingly, the aims of each of the Leagues was different. With Sparta, League policy was her method of political expansion . . . [whereas] the Lacedaemonian League . . . was a pure war alliance without any political organization. . . .
>
> Quite different was the picture in 378 B.C. The aim of the new Athenian League was peace, not war. This meant a reversal of the essential meaning of the Symmachy. Certainly peace was to be guarded against Sparta, but only in order to secure autonomy. . . . Even non-Greek states could join this League; for in its organization, for the first time, the idea of a real League of states

9. Ehrenberg, pp. 115-116.

was taken seriously by creating a strong federal authority apart
from the power of the *hegemon*. . . . The [Corinthian (Hellenic)]
League of 337 B.C., quite apart from its importance as a political
weapon in the hands of Philip II, was set on one purpose, to
ensure the common peace. . . . As before, the means employed
was the Symmachy, the armed alliance of autonomous states.
. . . What was new in 337 B.C.—apart from the political situation—was the fact that a Panhellenic combination of a League
of Peace and a Symmachy stood under the leadership of a monarch as *hegemon*. . . . To speak of a union of Greece under Philip
would be to mistake the nature of both the Polis and the Symmachy; but as a body that could administer justice to the citizens
of its member states, or could appoint a member as arbitrator
between two states, *the Corinthian League was something more
than a mere Symmachy. The building of the bridge that led to
the federal state had begun*. . . .[10]

And this "building" process continued in the third and
second centuries B.C., manifesting itself in the emergence of
leagues which differ from the *symmachia* by their greater tight-
ness, by the greater involvement of the central leaders in both
military and political affairs, and by the provision of dual
citizenship—of the *polis* and of the league. The term given to
this type of league, namely, *sympoliteia*, appears some two or
three hundred years later than *symmachia*. According to Larsen,[11] its earliest known use is in a Lycian inscription of about
180 B.C., and this is the term used by the Greek historian
Polybios to describe the Achaean League. Its later appearance
than *symmachia* is extremely interesting because it suggests a
crucial change, albeit gradual, in the nature and the development of the Grecian leagues. This change, if we read the term
literally, probably took place when a "common citizenship," or
a citizenship of the whole of a league, was made available to the
citizens of a single city-state, and when some of the rights and
privileges of citizenship as understood and practiced in the
single city-state were partially developed in the governing in-

10. *Ibid.*, p. 118. (My italics.)
11. See the entry *sympoliteia* under Larsen's initials (J.A.O.L.) in the *Oxford
   Classical Dictionary*, p. 872.

stitutions of the league. It is in this kind of league, for example, that a citizen could begin to define himself in the dual terms of an "Achaean from Corinth" or "Aetolian from Naupactus."[12]

Of the five or six leagues of this kind (reputedly, the Arcadian, Acarnanian, Aetolian, Thessalian, Phocian, and the Achaean), it is the Achaean League, "the union of all Peloponnesos . . . maybe all of Greece," that is held up as one of the most advanced examples of a Hellenic "federal" system. It is this very Achaean League (281-146 B.C.) that Freeman coupled with the United States of America as "the most perfect developments of the Federal principle which the world has ever seen."[13] We shall look at this claim in a moment, but first some details about this League. Again to Ehrenberg:

> The Achaean League was from ancient times a League of cities whose immediate reason for cohesion probably lay in their common tribal stock; they had, however, a religious centre in the temple of Zeus Homarius near Aegium. These Amphictyonic beginnings had little influence on the later development. It is probable that a political unity with common citizenship existed here as early as the fifth century. . . . [At one stage, it contained twelve cities, later, no less than sixty Poleis were members of the League, and at times it covered an area of 8000 square miles.] Nowhere else was the permanence of the federal bond to the League so strongly emphasized; withdrawal counted as revolt. . . . We can best characterise the structure of this federal constitu-

12. Would an American, Australian, or Canadian declare himself to be an American, Australian, or Canadian citizen from a "state"—e.g., Ohio, Tasmania, Ontario—or from a city—e.g., New York City, Melbourne, or Toronto? The order of locality in a citizen's identification is highly revealing of his political culture.

13. Whilst Ehrenberg, Busolt, and Larsen all give an account of the Achaean Constitution, none of them challenges Freeman's remark that "As usual we have to frame our account of it from incidental notices, from general panegyrics, and from records of particular changes in detail. We cannot lay our hands on any one document, on any Declaration of Independence, on any formally enacted Federal Constitution. . . . We may console ourselves with the thought that an enquirer at any equal distance of time will have to frame his picture of the British Constitution from information of exactly the same kind." (Freeman, p. 253.) Obviously Freeman had too little faith in the British gift for antiquarianism, otherwise he might have foretold that magnificent British institution, the Records Office!

tion by regarding it as an adaptation of the Polis constitution. As the constitutions of the single states still persisted, there was a duplication of all essential political factors. Here, too, the relation of the individual to the state rested on his citizenship; but now it was a federal citizenship [*sympoliteia*], and the citizenship of the single Polis existed beside it. The organs of the League, as of the Polis, were the citizen assembly . . . [and] the Council (*boulé*), a body very diversely appointed in the different Leagues, but generally of some independence. In this body the idea of representation, already suggested though never accomplished in the Polis Council, partially materialized; for here the Councillors did actually represent their states. . . . Finally, there were the officials, frequently called by the same names as Polis officials (*strategos, archon, damiurgos*, etc.), sometimes expressly marked as federal officials (Boeotarchs). . . . Beside the leading board [Freeman called it a "cabinet" and the officials in it "ministers"], which was not usually large in number [ten, according to Freeman], . . . stood a single man, the *strategos* [whom Freeman equated with the American President], as the leader in war and often enough in politics too. He was the decisive leader of the executive, who . . . held extensive . . . military and civil power. . . . Citizenship of the League gave the citizens of each member state full citizen rights, not only the private rights of freedom to own property and to marry, but also the essentially political rights of active and passive franchise within the whole League territory. . . . [Thus] here arose the citizen of a truly territorial state. . . .

Much more important was the division of competence and functions between central power and single states. Matters for the League exclusively were foreign affairs, including conferments of citizenship . . . and the decision on war and peace. So too was the army; but the contingents from the single states in the federal army usually stayed undivided and unmixed under their own commanders. The election of federal officials was made by the federal assembly. . . . Legislation and jurisdiction lay in the hands of the League so far as they actually concerned it, otherwise they were left to the members; if there were disputes among the members, the League had the power to arbitrate. It also had the supreme right of coinage; but in addition there was often coinage by member states, though always of one and the same standard. Political and administrative activities, then, were shared between the two groups of authority; but federal authority was always dominant, and, in case of doubt, decisive. This was even true in relation to the individual citizen, who was bound by the federal laws before those of his own Polis. In military service each citizen was bound to the League, not to the individual state. Accordingly, in financial matters, the League seldom relied on fixed quotas from the member states, rather on taxes levied directly on the citizens, whether regular or called for at special occasions.

Ehrenberg's concluding sentences are quite arresting.

> Outwardly it might look as though the organization of the Polis had been transferred to a federation; Polybios had seen in the Achaean League a "single Polis." . . . *But what did it really mean?*[14]

Indeed! What did it really mean? If Greece was to give mankind a practical "lesson in the way of free government on a more extended scale" than the *polis*, what was this lesson to be?

On any reading of the secondary sources, there are, if we use the broadest and most neutral categories we can find, three things which seem unmistakably clear: *First*, the gradual movement, by will or by force, towards "association," "fraternization," or indeed, "integration," rather than anything we call "fusion," "merger," or "unification." And the reasons[15] for this

14. Ehrenberg, pp. 125-128 and 130.
15. See Herbert Spencer: "One of the laws of evolution at large, is that integration results when like units are subject to the same force or to like forces; and from the first stages of political integration up to the last, we find this law illustrated. Joint exposure to uniform external actions, and joint reactions against them, have from the beginning been the leading causes of union among members of societies." Spencer goes on to illustrate this tendency by examples drawn from the Karens. "Each village being an independent community, had always an old feud to settle with nearly every other village among their own people. But the common danger from more powerful enemies, or having common injuries to require, often led to several villages uniting together for defense or attack." And he gives examples from the Hottentots, the villages of New Caledonia, Samoa, Israelites, Greek communities, the Teutonic races. (Spencer, *The Principles of Sociology*, p. 278.)

relate to the age, the culture, and the circumstances—always the urge of mutual protection, conquest, retaliation, peace, sometimes the attraction of common cults; and everywhere the move to association is tempered (if we are to believe the sources) by one of the most significant features of the Hellenic culture, pride of *polis*. *Second*, if the Hellenic experience begins with relatively simple forms of tribal and city-state associations bonded by sworn agreements ("treaties of alliance") and attested by bronze "tablets" or inscriptions on pillars of stone, rather than anything we can properly call a "written constitution," it is clear that in some instances these associations broadened and matured into more extensive, more complex, more "institutionalized" political systems, though the boundaries between them, as Ehrenberg tells us, were not always very clear: amphictyonies into *symmachia* and *symmachia* into *sympoliteia*, and on occasion it involved the disappearance of smaller communities that refused to cooperate. *Third*, there is, at all stages from their first appearance and throughout their growth and ultimate demise, a rich variety in their size, form, complexity, cohesion, symbols of commonalty, interaction, the individual strength of each *polis*, their relative power towards the central "authority," the power of the most important single figure in the league, the *strategos* or "general," and the extent to which military and and civil functions were mingled in his office.

After all, some five to six hundred years of Grecian history separate the first recorded case of tribal alliance from the later complex alliance of Achaea, a period far greater than the time separating the foundation of the American federal system and the dozen or more imitators in the nineteenth and twentieth centuries. And just as political change in the two-hundred-year span of modern federal states goes some way to explain the differences between the original American form and its early and later imitators, so too changing political circumstances over at least twice this span of time explain the conversion of the simple, or "rude," forms of federal alliance (e.g., Phocian League) as Freeman called them, where there is no assembly, no civil head, no common citizenship, no vestiges of military or

judicial power, into the more elaborate system of the Achaeans.
To compare the scale of change *within* and *between* the time
span of each world is probably impossible. To suggest, for
example, that the character of "alliance" changed more dramatically in the greater span of Grecian history than in the modern federal state in the time that separates us from 1787, is not
only too fanciful, but probably untrue. But we must at least
note the important remark of one modern scholar of Greece:

> During the fourth century Greece steadily moves towards new
> ways of thought and a new way of life; so much so that to those
> who were born at the end of the century the age of Pericles must
> have seemed as remote, mentally, as the Middle Ages do to us.[16]

To formulate a satisfactory concept for these heterogenous
phenomena, therefore, without understating or exaggerating
their nature, is not easy. Perhaps the easiest course of all would
be to speak of all of them simply as "associations" of tribes and
city-states, without discriminating between them. And such a
course would not be without some justification in the eyes of
the Hellenes; because, as one modern historian has suggested,
albeit complainingly, "it is unfortunate that Greeks only possessed one word for almost every form of public and private
association; they would have applied *koinon* equally to the
League of Nations, the Swiss Republic, a Cambridge College, a
Trade Union, and the village cricket club; and it is too late
now, in translating it, to avoid various improper uses of the
word League."[17] Alternatively, we may narrow the matter by
referring to all but the purely amphictyonic associations, that

16. Kitto, *The Greeks*, p. 152.
17. Tarn, p. 68. Also see Busolt: "Their member states were called poleis in the
    official language and in the literature. As the state organization of a polis is
    represented in the politeia, in the same way the constitution of several
    poleis united into a single federal community is represented as *Koinopoli-
    teia* or *Sympoliteia*. The federations called themselves *Koina*. The concept
    Koinon comprises every political or nonpolitical association and commu-
    nity. Similarly, a polis was a *Koinon*. In a narrow sense a polis as a unified
    subject must be distinguished from a *Koinon* as an association of a number
    of poleis. In this way Koinon took on the meaning of a federal commu-
    nity." (Busolt, pp. 1315-1316.)

is, the *symmachiai* and the *sympoliteiai*, again simply by one word, *"alliances"* or *"leagues,"* distinguishing only between "alliances" for offensive or defensive war ("military alliances"), and the more complex "alliances" which extend to both military and civil purposes, e.g., common citizenship. In this way we may keep faith with the Roman and early medieval practice of referring to all those in alliance, whether Greek or Roman, as *foederati* or *confoederati*, and the states in alliance as *civitates foederatae*. And indeed, if we wish, we can go further with Roman practice and subdivide these alliances into two classes, *foedus aequum* and *foedus iniquum*, that is, equal and unequal alliances.

As we shall see, however, when we come to consider the practices of the medieval taxonomists, neither of these easy choices is readily available to us now. Where once the simple concept of *foedus* or "alliance" gathered almost everything into its fold but the city-state and empire, since the fifteenth century at least, with the rise of the modern sovereign state and certainly after the adoption of the United States Constitution in 1787, some scholars began to use two previously undifferentiated terms, *foederati* and *confoederati*, to differentiate the Greek alliances; and as we noted earlier, they have done this by translating *symmachia* in the contemporary guise of a confederation, and identifying *sympoliteia* with a federation. The taxonomic perspective had changed, of course, with the emergence of the "sovereign" state model. Nevertheless, it scarcely behoves a modern historian to complain of the Greek failure to provide a language to separate the different "associations" of their own age, when we are able to order the political laboratory of some five hundred years of Hellenic experience—and indeed our own—with only three terms: military alliance, confederation, and federation. But this is the way of man and history, and the only question that concerns us at the moment is, how well do these current terms fit their cases?

To characterize the *symmachia* as a "confederation" whether in the antique or contemporary sense, probably does the least injury to its identity. For the notion of a "confederacy" has become a catchment area or reject basket which has grown in scale inversely to the rigor with which federalism became a priestly and exclusive cult after 1787. At various times it has harboured the simplest and the most complex, temporary and permanent, military and military/civil alliances, indeed any association of communities wherever primary emphasis is given to the autonomy of its members, or conversely to the relative impotence of any collective organ or titular head to act without the consent and participation of all or the majority of its members. It troubles the imagination no end, of course, to couple the simple military alliances of small walled towns and citadel fortresses perched on a mountain spur in Greece with the massive international organization and logistics of a NATO. But insofar as the common property of all these is what Bodin called the preservation of *majestie* by each member (whether *de jure* or *de facto*), logic if not their scale, their complexity, their aims, or indeed their history, will be satisfied if we include the *symmachia* within the same fold as the first Swiss confederation of 1291, the American Confederation of 1778, the Germanic confederacy of 1813-66, UNO, the British Commonwealth of Nations, and indeed the European Common Market! Only the hegemonic alliances trouble this classification; for if city-states placed themselves or were brought under the protection of another more powerful city-state, what became of their *majestie*? The answer doubtless is—it depends on the conduct of the *hegemon*. For whenever a tyrant *hegemon* reduced the *poleis* to handmaidens of his will, wherever he overpowered, dominated, coerced, or destroyed them, or indeed wherever two or more *poleis* commanded the actions of their allies, then (*pace* Freeman) the Greeks can hardly teach the world how to maintain "free government on a more extended scale than the *polis*." They teach us only a lesson in "empire," *de jure* and *de facto*, and this lesson is much older than the Hellenic civilization.[18]

However, the *symmachia* is not the source of the taxono-

18. See C. J. Hughes, *The Theory of Confederacies*; also, by same author, *Confederacies*.

mists' nightmares. It is the *sympoliteia* which presents difficulties of a greater order. Can we really equate the *sympoliteia*,
and notably the Achaean League, with a "federal" system in
any of its contemporary refinements? Observe Larsen's formulation, for example: "The great question is whether they (the
federal states) went so far beyond the *symmachies* as really to
deserve the name? Did the cities actually cooperate much except
in war? Or did they otherwise go their own way?" He answers,
albeit tentatively: "In general it can be said that institutions
were not uniform in all Greek federal states but that they were
unified and centralized far more than the *symmachies*."[19] And
Freeman, with lesser material, and later Busolt and Ehrenberg,
give an even more positive affirmation.

Yet it is very difficult to read their work, and particularly
Busolt's and Freeman's, without some sense of disorientation,
that one is travelling in the distorted shadows of time, uncertain where reality and unreality begin and end. Note, for example, Busolt:

> By contrast with the confederations, the federal power in federa-
> tions had not only sovereign rights over the member states but
> also over their subjects. The federation presents itself as a struc-
> tured political entity in which the state power becomes active on
> the one hand through the organs of the federal community, and
> on the other hand through their members in immediate domi-
> nation over the land and people. It is different from a unitary
> state in that its member states have sovereign power in their own
> right, while the communities and regions or tribal subdivisions
> into which the unitary state is structured can exercise such rights
> only on the basis of conferment or consent by the sovereign
> power. . . .[20]

And Freeman:

> The supreme power of the [Achaean] League was vested in the
> sovereign Popular Assembly. . . . The Athenian Assembly was
> sovereign in the very highest sense. . . .[21]

19. Larsen, *Greek Federal States*, p. xviii.
20. Busolt, pp. 1313-1314.
21. Freeman pp. 263-264.

Or note Freeman's cross-cultural leap across two millenia when he speaks of the Achaean constitution with the nomenclature of American and British constitutional practice. Thus, he equates the *strategos* or "general" in command of the Achaean League with the "President of the Union" (the United States); the *Hipparch*, or undergeneral, with the "Vice-President of the Union"; the *boulé*, or assembly with the "Congress of the Union"; and the small group of officials, elected annually by the *boulé*, who worked with the *strategos* as a "cabinet council."[22] Conceivably, neither the school of German *Staatskunde*, nor Austinian jurisprudence, nor indeed the contemporary structure-function analysts will be greatly troubled by Busolt's language or Freeman's comparison. But if it doesn't trouble the imagination, it troubles commonsense. For not only is their language impregnated with the time/space assumptions of another age, but on their own admission it rests on a fragile foundation of fact.

Why then is the *sympoliteia* identified with a federation? Certainly the American "Founding Fathers" did not make this equation. On the contrary: Madison and Hamilton were constantly at pains to distinguish all Grecian leagues (*symmachia* and *sympoliteia*), from their own national project, and to depreciate them indiscriminately as antiquarian examples of the defective genus—"confederacy." Why did they do this? Because they could see essential differences between the Achaean League and their own project, where later scholars such as Freeman and Busolt could not? Because it suited their political purposes to construe differences where there were none? Because the differences they saw between the most advanced *sympoliteia* and the United States Constitution flowed from an indifferent classical scholarship? Because their concern for national strength led them to attribute the decline of the Grecian leagues to their structural weaknesses instead of to the overwhelming power of Rome? However we explain it (and Freeman accuses them of defective scholarship),[23] the question is, what are the

22. *Ibid.*, pp. 264-285.
23. "The founders of the American Union were not scholars, but practical

elements that have enticed the bulk of nineteenth- and twentieth-century scholars, if not the American Founding Fathers, to regard the *sympoliteia,* and notably the Achaean League, as "true" federal states?

The accounts differ, often profoundly, in their detail and interpretation. But if we simply abstract and assemble the elements most frequently mentioned by Ehrenberg and others, it would appear that the model of "federal" Achaea, for example, consists of some seven elements. Enumerated, they are:

1. Common citizenship
2. "Division of competence"
3. A central legislature and full-time executive
4. Executive (and legislative) power to command the *poleis* principally (if not exclusively) in matters of war and peace
5. Autonomy of the *poleis* in all matters but war and peace
6. Equal representation of each *polis* in the central assembly
7. The "permanence" of the treaty which created the league

To abstract the elements in this fashion, however, to unmoor them, as it were, from their historical and linguistic anchorage, and thus validate, analytically, the genuineness of Achaean "federalism," is almost certain to falsify reality. Take some of these elements at closer quarters.

From such accounts as we are given, it would be foolish to expect, let alone to strain for, a close geometric correspondence between the Achaean League and any "federal" or purportedly federal system in our time. Indeed, with the possible exception of "common citizenship," there is hardly one of the seven elements that cannot be translated in such a way as to alter the entire character of the League, either towards or away from any

---

politicians. They were fully disposed to listen to the teaching of history, but they had small opportunity of knowing what the true and uncorrupted teaching of Grecian history really was. Those chapters of the 'Federalist' which are devoted to the consideration of earlier instances of Federal Government show every disposition to make a practical use of ancient precedents, but they show very little knowledge as to what those precedents really were. It is clear that Hamilton and Madison knew hardly anything more of Grecian history than what they had picked up from the 'Observations' of the Abbé Mably." (Freeman, p. 319.)

of the contemporary ideas of "federalism." Thus, for example, where Freeman refers to the *strategos* and the officials around him as a "Cabinet Council," Ehrenberg refers to them as a "board"; Busolt to a "Federal Council"; Larsen to a "board of ten *damiorgoi*" or a "body acting as a sort of cabinet"; and it would not be inconsistent with either their activities or their annual election to speak of them in the same sense that we refer to the executive organ of, say, the Federated Clerks' Union as the "Committee of Management," or the executive organ of NATO as the North Atlantic Council. Similarly, with the "division of competence" or "division of power," where today this concept evokes the familiar imagery of the eighteenth- and nineteenth-century attempts to "divide" the entire domain of "sovereignty," in the case of the League we would be entitled to speak not of a "division of power" but simply of an "assignment of responsibility" to a central body, without implying the creation of some executive organ with absolute power to act independently in the business of the League.

But names aside, what is at the base of all the attempts to approximate the Achaean League to a "true" federal system is the "duality" of its system of government: on the one hand the "sovereign" assembly, its elected commanding "general," the *strategos*, and its elected "board" to act for the League in matters of war and peace, and on the other, the individual "sovereign" city-state (*polis*) to act in all other matters. And what is asserted is that each is able to stand on its own feet in those matters that a "treaty" has made their concern, that the *strategos* is able to issue commands to the citizenry or the individual city-states, and that neither will defile the treaty—the *poleis* by refusing to obey, or the *strategos* by interfering in the internal affairs of the *poleis*. How does this assertion stand up to their own facts?

As to the *poleis*, Freeman, for example, tells us:

> The constitution of the League was strictly Federal. The Federal form of government now appears in its fullest and purest shape. Every city remained a distinct State, sovereign for all purposes not inconsistent with the higher sovereignty of the Federation,

> retaining its local Assemblies and local Magistrates, and order-
> ing all exclusively local affairs without any interference from the
> central power. There is no evidence that the Federal Govern-
> ment, in its best days, ever directly interfered with the internal
> laws, or even with the political constitutions of the several cities.
> . . . So little indeed did the Federal power meddle with the
> internal affairs of the several cities that it tolerated distinctions
> within their territories which seem hardly in accordance with
> the principles of universal equality on which the League itself
> was founded.[24]

This is hardly surprising, given the reputed ethos of the city-
state in the Hellenic political culture. Though one might also
note in passing that this was not always the situation in the
earlier and less developed leagues, where the autonomy of each
varied not only with its population and wealth, but more so
with the hegemonic influence of a leading city; for example,
Thebes in the Boeotian League, Olynthus in the Chalcidian,
and Demetrias in the Magnesian League.

But if we accept Freeman's account of the autonomy enjoyed
by the cities of the Achaean League, what of the "federal"
power? As a start we could distinguish the Achaean situation
from our own times by pointing to the fact, for example, that
the power of the Assembly rested on a "treaty," with its obvious
contractual implications, rather than on a "constitution" as we
commonly understand it, or that the power of the *strategos* was
derived from a non-elected aristocratic assembly rather than
direct election by the whole *demos*. But important as these
distinctions are, they do not go to the heart of the matter. For
the issue is not the source of power so much as the fact of
power—hence the question must be, did the Assembly and the
strategos, however they were constituted, possess the kind of
capability which, from the late Middle Ages at least, is given the
name of *"majestie"* or "sovereignty"?[25]

---

24. *Ibid.*, pp. 255-256.
25. See Hughes, *The Theory of Confederacies.* In discussing the nature of a
    confederacy, Professor Hughes draws attention to the importance of this
    issue in formulating federal theory.

To this question, there are a number of passages in Freeman and Larsen which create serious doubts. For example, while Freeman tells us that:

> No single city could, of its own authority, make peace or war, or commission Ambassadors to foreign powers.

He immediately qualifies this with the comment:

> But it would appear that the separate action of the several cities was not quite so rigidly limited in the last respect as it is in the American Union.

And he elaborates by remarking on a number of exceptions:

> The Corinthians, after their union with the League, received separate Ambassadors from Rome, before Rome was dangerous. They came indeed on a purely honorary errand; another embassy had transacted the political business between Rome and the League; still, whether of right or of special permission, the single city of Corinth did give audience to the Ambassadors of a foreign power. It is quite possible that for a single city to receive an embassy was not so strictly forbidden by the Federal Constitution as it was for a single city to commission an embassy. This last, it is clear, was forbidden by the general law of the League. just as it is forbidden by the Constitution of the United States. Cases however occur in the course of Achaean history alike of the law being dispensed with and of the law being violated.[26]

The thrust of Freeman's comment, of course, is to present the Corinthian and other cases as exceptions which are sometimes licensed by the "federal body"; but the practice of unlicensed independent diplomacy with Rome, especially by cities which had been forced to join the Achaean League, continued to its last days. Thus, he adds:

> In later times [circa 198 B.C.], when unwilling cities were annexed to the League by force, and when Roman intrigue was constantly sowing dissension among its members, we shall find not unfrequent instances of embassies sent from particular cities to what was practically the suzerain power. The old law now

26. Freeman, pp. 260-261.

needed special confirmation. It was agreed, in the first treaty
between Achaea and Rome, that no embassy should be sent to
Rome by any particular Achaean city, but only by the general
Achaean body. But this agreement was of course broken when-
ever its violation suited Roman interests. Sparta especially, and
Messênê, cities joined to the League against their will, were con-
stantly laying their real or supposed grievances at the feet of the
Roman Senate.[27]

Again, though Freeman and others speak of a "sovereign
Assembly," one must note—especially from Freeman, the most
ardent advocate of the federal purity of Achaea—that the Assembly had no capital and no court; that "it met barely twice a
year and its sittings were short, limited to three days"; that "the
League was for 359 days in the year, scattered to and fro over
all Peloponnesos"; that "it entrusted one man with all their
power"; and that "from the shortness of the Assembly's session
naturally followed certain restrictions on its power . . . certain
augmentations of the powers of the executive government." We
must note further that whilst in Freeman's view "it could admit
of no reasonable doubt that the Achaean League was essentially
a national government . . . [and] that its laws and decrees were
directly binding upon Achaean citizens," nevertheless, in its
"financial and military systems,"

> . . . it is not equally clear that it had in all cases advanced beyond
> that system of requisitions from the particular members, instead
> of direct agency on the part of the Federal power, which, in
> modern politics, is held, more than anything else, to distinguish
> an Imperfect from a Perfect Federation.[28]

Freeman, of course, is right to draw attention to the importance of the distinction between direct and indirect federal
action in the taxonomy of nineteenth-, and indeed, twentieth-
century federalists. But if our concern is with the efficacy of the
"federal" power rather than its machinery, then we obtain some
perspective of this power from his comment:

27. *Ibid.*, p. 262.
28. *Ibid.*, p. 309.

We once get a glimpse of the Federal system of taxation when we
find certain cities, and those too cities of the original Achaea,
refusing to pay the contributions which were due from them to
the Federal Treasury. . . . In military matters, we find the
Assembly sometimes requiring particular cities to furnish particular contingents, and sometimes investing the General with
power to summon the whole military force of the League. Beside
these citizen soldiers, the League, according to the custom of the
age, made large use of mercenaries, whose pay must have come
out of the Federal Treasury.[29]

And we obtain a further perspective from Larsen's description
of the "federal treasurer" and the mode of "federal finance":

There was a federal treasurer, but he is seldom mentioned and
seems to have been relatively unimportant. There must normally
have been a little money in the treasury to provide for minor
current expenses—a sort of petty cash fund made up of sums sent
to the treasury by the constituent cities. There is no proof that
there existed any tax which was collected directly by the federal
government. At most there were taxes or fees collected by the
cities that were destined for the federal treasury, but it is much
more likely that the cities merely sent sums of various sizes
depending upon the circumstances. To judge by the examples of
early Boeotian, the Aetolian, and the Lycian confederacies, they
simply paid a certain sum for each representative in the federal
boulé (council). This sum could be increased when the demands
were heavy and lowered when the demands were few. In the case
of a windfall [e.g., spoils of war!], payments might be completely eliminated. . . . In 219 B.C., when the three cities of Dyme,
Pharae, and Tritaea felt that they were not adequately defended
by the federal general, they decided not to pay their eisphorai
[contribution]but to engage mercenaries themselves.[30]

Even such slender evidence as this would bring a latter-day
federal inspector to protest the name "federal" for the Achaean
League. For it bears no greater resemblance to the arrangements
of the Philadelphia Convention of 1787 which later expropri-
ated the "federal" name, or indeed any of the imitative systems

29. *Ibid.*, pp. 309-310.
30. Larsen, *Greek Federal States*, pp. 232-233.

after 1787, than the prehistoric ancestors of man, *homo habilis* and *homo erectus*, to modern *homo sapiens*. Not only are its institutions barely like the phenomena of the eighteenth and nineteenth century, "federal" or indeed "con-federal," but they rest on the slenderest visible basis of duality, and more certainly on no articulate theory of duality as the medievalists and the moderns came to understand it fifteen hundred years later.

The *polis*, in truth, was the center and the reality of Grecian life; the League a protective artifact.[31] The League neither diminished the status of the *polis*, nor did the League challenge its authority except in war and diplomacy, and even then without finality or certainty. The *polis* did not exist for the League, the League existed for the *polis*. In these circumstances, what need then for Aristotle or anyone to explain the implications of a new center of power, or to justify it by erecting a theory of dual authority? And if Aristotle was aware of the distinction between the *symmachia* and the *sympoliteia*, which is highly probable, there is no sign of it in his *Politics*. To be sure, Polybios' remark that the whole of Achaea had become like a single *polis* without walls appears to be an early intimation of Bodin's later formulation of the one-sovereign Commonweale (*République*). But Polybios, unlike Bodin, did not address himself to the problem of two masters in the one state, for this is not the way the League presented itself to the citizens of the *polis*.

However, if it is foolish to strain for correspondence, it is equally foolish to deny the presence of federal traces in the Achaean arrangements. For even if these traces are shadowy, even if, at any moment in the Achaean history, it is uncertain whether we are looking at the emergence of a "nation-state," an "empire," a "confederation," a "federation," or an advanced kind of "military alliance," we can no more exclude the Grecian leagues from the evolution of the contemporary "federal" idea than we can exclude the "pipe of peace," or "treaty" inscribed on a pillar of stone, or indeed any primitive symbols

31. Kitto, *The Greeks*, p. 161.

of intertribal diplomacy from the evolution of international law. To be sure, vast interstellar cultural spaces separate the forms and the symbolic language of the two worlds. But some of the traces of modern federal theory were unmistakably present; even if the process of welding and articulating them into a coherent theory of duality did not begin until the close of the millenial empire of Rome. In that vast span of time, however, the circumstances and the questions of state underwent profound changes. If the leagues symbolized the Hellenic attempt to protect the *poleis* from empires and tyrant hegemony,[32] for the late medievalists and the early moderns the sovereign nation-state symbolized the means of regaining a territorial identity which had been lost to the Holy Roman Empire. The first was a response to what Bryce termed the centripetal, the second to the centrifugal, moments of history. Each instance forced new concepts and new rationalizations of state power into the conversations of statesmen and scholars. But from these two separate experiences, the pressure for unity on the one hand and the pressure for identity on the other, emerged the materials for a theory of duality that became so vital to the eighteenth- and nineteenth-century federalists.

32. Rostovtzeff, Vol. I, p. 36.

3

The Medieval Leagues
and the Germanic Empire of Rome
Or, the christening of the "Monster"
by the early "doctors of civil knowledge"

In a world where there is but one master, where all communities are brought into one dominion by force or by faith, there is little soil in which other forms of political life, and no soil at all in which a system of international relations, can grow. It is only when there are many masters and many beliefs that new forms of political association can arise, and rules to civilize the relations of separate communities can flourish.[1] Thus, for our purpose, one may write the history of the fifteen hundred years that span the sway of the Roman *imperium*, the spiritual and political hegemony of the Roman papacy, the decay of the *Respublica Christiana*, and the debut of the sovereign nation-state.

It is an immense period of time, the millenial length of which, if nothing else, may have inspired the evil fantasies of a pathological Austrian house-painter. Incredibly diverse in its experience of differing civilizations, in the ceaseless contests of emperors, kings, princes, and holy men for domination, dynasty, and spiritual virtue, in the ultra-mundane rationalizations of their scribes and "doctors of civil knowledge," it revolved around the eternal theme of universalism versus particularism, a theme held in a dialectic cohesion through this

1. See J. N. Figgis, *Political Thought from Gerson to Grotius*, Lecture 1, esp. p. 27; also Otto von Gierke, *Political Theories of the Middle Ages*; and W. Ullman, *A History of Political Thought in the Middle Ages*.

period by the belief in a *principium unitatis*, the one Supreme Being. If Rome superseded Greece, however, if it is Rome, not Greece, that directly affected the later history of mankind, the metamorphosis of the Western world is achieved not by force of Roman arms alone, or the example of its institutions, but also its language. For it is the tongue of Rome, pure or vulgarized, that dominates the prayers, the law, the polemics, and the thoughts of this time, as it is the tongue of Rome that translated the ideas and institutions of Greece for medieval, Renaissance and indeed Reformation Europe.[2]

It is difficult to set foot even into the shallows of the literature without being made increasingly aware that most of the abstract ingredients required to transmute the Hellenic experience of "alliance" into modern federal theory, and especially the idea of dual power, are nearly fabricated and packaged in this period. But to pluck out the relevant traces from this gigantic, almost seamless tapestry of events is again difficult. For while some traces are readily visible, others just as crucial can only be forced from their complex mould of institutions, actions, and argument by analogy, and some only by what Arthur Koestler called "symbiotic innovation."

Thus, if we were to focus only on the simplest and most obvious traces of territorial alliances, then like the hostile world of the Hellenes, so the age of Rome, both at the zenith and in the ebb of its power, abounds in a multiplicity of leagues and coalitions: the Etruscan, the Etrurian, and the Samnian Leagues in the early years of the secular Empire; later, in the travails of the Holy Roman Empire, where Church and State are fused in one *civitas dei*, the Lombard League, and the first Helvetic League—the *antiqua confoederatio*, 1292;[3] and later still, in the period of its slow dismemberment, the League of

---

2. See Sir John Sandys, *A History of Classical Scholarship*, Vols. I and II; also Hugo Grotius, *The Law of War and Peace*, Vol. II, Chap. 15, "De Federibus ac Sponsionibus," esp. p. 135, where Grotius gives an account of the *symmachia*.

3. Note the introductory paragraph of the Pact of 1292 between the three forest cantons of Uri, Schwyz, and Unterwalden: "It is a good thing for public utility if communities agree to preserve peace and order. Therefore,

Cambrai, the Guelph League, the League of Venice, the
Swabian League, the League of Cognac, the Schmalkaldic
League, the Hanseatic League, the Netherlands League, the
Polish confederacies, and the league that brought Norway,
Sweden, and Denmark together.

With a few exceptions, however, these leagues of popes and
emperors, emperors with kings, kings with cities, and city with
city, are, in form at least, little more than military alliances
indistinguishable from the simplest Grecian *symmachia*; few
possessed the rudimentary centralized features that might compare them with the developed *symmachia* such as the Second
Athenian League, and few, if any, could be compared to the
more highly developed *sympoliteia* such as the Achaean
League. Often these alliances are of noncontiguous territories.
And beyond the immediate purpose of restoring the one true
faith of Christendom, or resisting "caesaro-papism," of regaining territory, defending themselves against invaders, extending
the empire, protecting trading interests, or subduing rebellion,
these *foedera* (or *confoedera* to those who preferred the longer
term) were, in most cases, not intended to endure or to serve
other ends. There was no provision for a common council to
organize their policies, and only rarely (e.g., the Florentine
League, 1375) did they charge any single figure, a commander-
in-chief such as the Achaean *strategos*, to mobilize their arms
and conduct their forces in battle. Indeed, insofar as we may
wish to allocate the great majority of these military alliances or
foedera to a contemporary field of discourse, they are more the
property of international relations than of federal theory.[4]

---

let all know that the men of the Valley of Uri and the commune of those
who live within the mountains, considering the dangers that threaten them,
and in order to be better able to defend themselves and their possessions,
have, in good faith, promised mutually to assist each other with aid, counsel, and support, with their persons as well as with their possessions, . . .
against each and all who may try to molest, harm, or injure any of them in
their persons or in their possessions. . . . "

4. See M. V. Clarke, *The Medieval City-State*; also Heinz H. F. Eulau, "Theories of Federalism Under the Holy Roman Empire."

But the matter of international relations and federal theory is not so easily disentangled in the noncompartmentalized world of medieval and early modern thought, especially not to the scholars who first tried to explain the nature of these alliances. And it is through these scholars and their curiosity that we probably come closer, and certainly more easily, to the course of federal ideas. How did the contemporary world, the "doctors of civil knowledge" and the littérateurs, look upon these *foedera*?

Curiosity, one need hardly say, never begins in vacuo, and rarely before its time. And it is enticed more often by the need to explain the odd, the unusual, and the irregular than the normal and the regular; when it is called on to explain the normal, it does so mainly when the normal is under challenge; and in either case, it carries out its task of explanation in the language of its own experience. The curiosity of the Middle Ages, for example, is less possessed with theories of alliance than with the vindication of ultimate power and salvation. It is only in the Reformation and post-Reformation periods that we come upon sources that, in trying to compose and vindicate the nature of the new civil society, also turn their eyes upon the leagues.

It is not the simple alliances, however, that excite the curiosity of the "doctors," or vex them intellectually. For history has already informed them of the Grecian and early Roman leagues; Livy's tripartite classification of treaties of alliance is familiar to them; and with few modifications they found little difficulty in equating the Grecian alliance (*symmachia*) with its Roman counterpart (*foedus*), and then subdividing the bulk of all alliances (*foedera*) into one of two categories: they were either *foedera aequalia* or *foedera inaequalia*; those, in other words, which placed the allies on an equal footing, and those alliances in which one member is, by virtue of some condition, placed in a superior position to others.

What taxed their curiosity and their ingenuity—and indeed what plagues many to this day—was how to explain those "everlasting" alliances such as the Helvetic League or the

Netherlands League which possessed, either from their beginning or acquired over time, the kind of institutional features
that symbolized a more enduring and a more complete sense of
mutual commitment than a simple alliance (*foedus simplex*);
for example, a joint council, or the solemn individual bond of
each citizen of the three original Swiss cantons (Uri, Unterwalden, and Schwyz) to defend each other. And far more challen-
ging and urgent than this was the need to make sense, both
juridical and political, of the Germanic Empire, that internally
ambivalent, truncated remnant of the Holy Roman colossus; a
"phantom" empire that resisted every simple categorization.
Indeed, it is no accident that almost the whole of federal scholarship up to and beyond 1787 is obsessed with the nature of this
Empire. And it is more than fate that the plethora of theories
spun in the course of explaining the constitution of this Empire have so deeply conditioned and incarcerated the understanding of federalism ever since.

To see how the "doctors" dealt with the leagues and the
Empire, however, it is first necessary to orient ourselves, albeit
very briefly, to their world of ideas and concepts; in Foucault's
terms, their "grid of knowledge," or what Figgis called the
"furniture" of their minds. It is, of course, a prodigious task to
map the "furniture" of one mind, let alone the archetypal mind
of a whole culture. But we can come as close, and for our
purpose, as quickly as possible, to the learning of an age
through the questions asked, the answers given, and the mode
by which the concepts, imbedded in the questions and answers,
are used by its scholars.

What are the questions? For some four hundred years, during
the ascendance of papal power, its fusion in the Holy Roman
Empire, and finally the fragmentation of that Empire (circa
1400), the questions contended on the battlefield and in controversy between the two "Titans," the Pope and the Holy Roman
Emperor, and later the Holy Roman Emperor and the territorial monarchs, were: who was to be acknowledged as ultimate master of Europe and Byzantium, and what was the fount
of his mastery? If it was the Pope, the Vicar of Christ on earth,

what was the domain of his authority? Did he stand above the Emperor and the monarchs in all things, spiritual and temporal, or spiritual only? And if spiritual only, could there be two equal masters, or was one master to be the superior of the other? And if the masters were equal in standing, each in his own domain, whose word was to prevail when the demands of the body and the demands of the spirit could not be reconciled? And if the Emperor and the monarchs were in conflict on earthly matters, whose voice should the monarch acknowledge to be the final voice, the Emperor or the Pope?

The question, who is to be the ultimate master, is, as the Reformation scholars came to know it, the question of sovereignty.[5] It occupies a commanding place in the "civil knowledge," the conceptual furniture of medieval and early modern scholarship, and its jurisprudential overtones penetrate every question of state.[6] The idea of ultimate, supreme, or final power, of course, is hardly the discovery of either Rome, the Middle Ages, or the Reformation. For those who first commanded men on earth and received unquestioning obedience knew its nature. But whether the claim to ultimate power is made on behalf of the Roman Emperor, the Pope, the monarch, or later "the people," or in whatever language and phrases the claim is made, the attributes remain essentially the same. Ultimate power is omnipotence, omnicompetence, singleness, and indivisibility. Observe the phrases: the power of the Roman Emperor, for example, is *plena majestatis*, he possesses *summum imperium*; he is *dominus mundi*, Lord of the World; similarly, the papal power is *plenitudo potestatis*, *absoluta potestas*; his *imperium* is *indivisibile et inalienabile*; and similarly, though later, the monarch is *rex imperator in regno suo*, or *entier empéreur dans son royaume* (the king is emperor in his own kingdom), his power is *summa potestatis majestas*; he recognizes no superior, *rex superiorem non recognoscens*, and

---

5. For the historical development of this idea, see F. H. Hinsley, *Sovereignty*.
6. "We cannot overestimate the influence of this legal atmosphere on the development of political thought, even on into modern times." (Figgis, p. 11.)

he has no equal; he alone possesses *souveraineté*,[7] and the power of the king, like that of the Roman Emperor, is *indivisibile*.

What is the case, however, when there are two claimants to ultimate power? Plainly, if the power of a gun cannot resolve the matter, or if the force of arms and the force of belief are equally matched, then the ingenuity of a canonical jurisprudence, inspired by a remarkable instinct for survival, composed the rationalizations and the formula of reconciliation in a theory of duality. It is pronounced in the Gelasian doctrine of the "two swords," *regnum et sacerdotium*; in a recognition, that is, of *potestates distinctae*, two kinds of power, *regimen ecclesiasticum et saeculare*, and in the idea of an alliance between the papacy and the imperial rule, *summum sacerdotium et Romanum simul confoederatur imperium*. Here, in this diplomatic accommodation, we find the ingredients that may have fed the idea of "dual sovereignty," of "co-ordinate" and "co-equal" power; of two masters in the one realm, each responsible for a separate and distinct order, yet both drawing his title and his legitimacy from the one source: God for the medievalists, the "people" and the "constitution" for the Romans and the moderns.

But in the harsh experience of power and rivalry, the notion of duality was merely a temporary foil, a fiction, a counsel of mutual forbearance which sat as uneasily on the policies of the medieval contenders as it sat later in the contentions of the eighteenth- and nineteenth-century federalists. If it had been able to sustain both the ultramundane aspirations of an earthbound papacy, and the earthly aspirations of divinely oriented emperors and kings, it might have survived. But under the stress of exclusivist claims and jurisdictional conflicts, the theory and the diplomacy of duality proved impossible. And in the triumph of the secular monarchic sovereign nation-state, the state in which there is but one master and one only, drawing his right from God, the constitution, or the people, the doctrine of

7. Note, for example, that Bodin uses the term *souveraineté* as well as *majestas* and *summa potestas*. See Hinsley, p. 122.

duality was interred, faintly revived in the continued struggle of
the church for immunity and autonomy in the fourteenth century, and fully reconstructed in the federalist theories of the
eighteenth century.

This, briefly, is some of the furniture of the sixteenth- and
seventeenth-century civil learning. How did the "doctors" use
it? In a word, they used the idea of sovereignty with apparent
ease. A few flirted with the idea of "dual sovereignty," but they
skirted its implications because it was both logically obnoxious
and politically explosive. And some, in trying to establish the
identity of the Germanic Empire, found a compromise in the
feudal notion of a hierarchratic corporate state, where, though
there is but one sovereign to whom territorial princes owe
material and ritual fealty, and though the princes do not stand
as equals with the emperor in dignity or power, nevertheless
some of the attributes of mastery are invested in them by feudal
right and usage.

But let us now take a closer look at the way the inherited civil
learning of an age is applied to the analysis of the ancient and
contemporary *foedera*—the leagues, the coalitions, and notably
the Germanic Empire. To this end, I have chosen the relevant
portions of the work of Bodin (1577), Althusius (1603),
Pufendorf (1667), and Hugo (1661), because in so many ways
they not only reflect the analytical style of their time, but
because their ideas occupy a dominant place in the corpus of
European (and notably German) federal scholarship up to
1787.[8]

8. Note Mogi's comment that "No (British) political thinker up to the end of
   the eighteenth century—that is, until the formation of the North American
   federation of 1787—had dealt with the federal state in any treatise." (Sobei
   Mogi, *The Problem of Federalism*, p. 211.) Thus, for instance, when Locke
   speaks of the "federative power" of the commonwealth (i.e., any independent community, whether a democracy or not), he is simply referring to the
   external executive power of a state (as distinct from its legislative or internal
   executive power) which "contains the power of war and peace, leagues and
   alliances, and all the transactions, with all persons and communities without the commonwealth, and may be called 'federative,' if any one pleases.
   So the thing be understood, I am indifferent as to the name." (John Locke,
   Second Treatise of Civil Government, Book II, Chap. 12.) Or Hume's por-
   trayal of his "ideal of a perfect commonwealth" is simply a model of the
   Netherlands confederation.

First, Bodin: The relevance of this sixteenth-century French érudit to federal ideas is not immediately clear. Published in a period of sustained political crisis, war, and turbulence, the concern of his major work, *La République*, was "to meet the danger to France," to "preserve the royal form of government from destruction," and to compose the principles of a "well-ordered Commonweal" from the teachings of history and the experience of public affairs. The resulting prescription for order and safety is a classic rationalization of the unitary monarchic state. Paraphrased, it is this: Instability is a chronic condition of civil society, and all states are transitory. The best that one can do to preserve order and diminish the insecurity of political change, is to ensure first, that the authority of the state is centralized, absolute and indivisible; and second, that sovereignty—the ultimate authority, or supreme power of the state—resides in a monarch, answerable only to God and natural law.

This equation of order with centralized, undivided, and unlimited power, courses through the *République* and the earlier *Methodus*. It explains the strict hierarchical structure of the Bodinian state—the single pyramid of command and obedience. It conditions the logic and the properties of sovereignty. It accounts for the rejection of *mixed* constitutions. And it governs the taxonomy of states, leagues, and alliances. Note Bodin's treatment of leagues. For example, at a point immediately after a revealing discussion of the nature of citizenship in his lesser known work, *Methodus*,[9] Bodin asks the question: "Can allied governments create one and the same State; for instance, the city-states of the Swiss[10] and the towns of the Baltic?" (". . .

9. J. Bodin, *Methodus ad Facilem Historiarum Cognitionem*, Chap. 6, "De Statu Rerumpublicarum," pp. 249-253; English translation by Beatrice Reynolds, *Method for the Easy Comprehension of History*, Chap. 6, "The Type of Government in States," pp. 153-168. Bodin also considers the nature of alliance in his major work, *Les Six Livres de la République*; see the facsimile reprint of the English translation of 1606, *The Six Bookes of a Commonweale*, "The First Booke," pp. 72-84. See also M. J. Tooley's Introduction to his translation and abridgement of *Six Books of the Commonwealth*.

10. It is important to remember that when Bodin speaks of the Helvetic (Swiss) League, he is referring to the more extended and developed league of his own time, which consisted of thirteen cantons, not the original *antiqua*

*queri potest, utrum foederate inter se civitates Rempublicam
efficiant eandem, puta civitates Helvetiorum & Balticae ur-
bes.*") Observe his answer:[11] In the opinion of *other* scholars the
league of Swiss cantons constituted one state,

> . . . because the Swiss are allied together in the closest union,
> have furthermore the same assemblies, a town in Baden, and
> many places common to them all where they send common
> officials.

But Bodin rejects this view:

> to have exchange of goods, sanctity of contract, rights of inter-
> marriage and of mutual entertainment, finally a firm bond of
> friendship does not create one and the same state.

For if they had this effect,

> . . . the kingdom of the French and that of the Spanish, who have
> these things in common, would be the same. This is not the case,
> even if they use the same laws, as once upon a time the Romans
> and the Greeks did, after the Romans had accepted the laws of
> the Greeks. Finally, it is not true even if they had so close a
> union among themselves that they attacked the same enemies
> and welcomed the same friends, as often happens among princes
> of the greatest loyalty and sympathetic understanding.

Bodin then further justifies his rejection of the Swiss and Baltic
leagues as "states" on the ground that there is "no common
control" nor "centralization of power" in either of the two; and
he illustrates his point by referring to the Greek leagues.

> There remains, then, this common control and centralization of
> power to which I referred.

> Thirteen Swiss city-states, three of the Rhetians, and seventy of
> the Baltic area sealed a lawful alliance to the effect that they
> would not injure each other and that in their common peril they

---

confoederatio of 1292, formed by the personal oath-taking of all the citizens
of the three cantons.
11. English translation by Reynolds, pp. 165-168; the corresponding pages of
the 1566 Latin edition of *Methodus* are pp. 249-251.

would fight their sworn foes with mutual aid. But there is no
common authority, and no union.

The seven Amphictyonic cities used no other type of alliance,
nor the three Aetolian, nor the twelve Ionic, which, however,
had certain common assemblies that they might defend their
possessions and drive off the enemy. Yet each one of these city-
states was separated from the others by its sovereign rights. Thus
the separate city-states of the Helvetians are bound by the decrees
of the others only so far as they voluntarily agree, as in private
partnerships. On the contrary, in one and the same dominion
what pleases the majority binds all.

Then, to illustrate the contrary case, Bodin gives examples of
leagues and other arrangements which satisfy the requirements
of "statehood":

A different opinion must be given about the forty-seven states of
the Latins, twelve of the Achaeans, the same number of
Etruscans, and about the German imperial towns and provinces,
which compose a state because they are subordinated to the same
empire and the same emperor.

Achaeans, Latins, and Etruscans created an executive for each
separate year, . . . the Germans for life. The two Philips and
Antigonus, Kings of Macedonia, were once elected leaders by the
Achaeans, . . . the Spanish and the French kings were created
German emperors in the same way.

This judgment is not altered by the mere time-scale of the
alliance, whether it is temporary or permanent.

. . . the Swabian association, which was formed for forty years,
and the alliance of Baltic towns differ from the Helvetic association only in this respect, that the latter was made for all time the
"Everlasting Alliance," the former for only a stated period. . . .

Thus Bodin concludes:

. . . an alliance of diverse city-states, exchange of goods, common
rights, laws, and religions do not make the same state, but union
under the same authority does.

As one might expect, Bodin answered his opening question —"can allied governments create one and the same state"—in terms of the contemporary symbols of sovereignty: Is there *one* supreme master lawgiver, one ruler, one commander, or not? There is not the faintest hint of a middle-ground, and certainly the idea of co-ordinate, co-equal, or co-sovereign status is anathema to the Bodinian state. Indeed, the whole perspective of the *République* is so hostile to fractionalized systems of authority, so little capable of development, so rigid in categorizing deviant and false claimants to statehood, and so imbedded in the crustacean dichotomy of Roman and Medieval taxonomy,[12] that it could only impede the emergence of any dualistic theory of the state. To include Bodin in a study of federal ideas, therefore, would seem as incongruous as mating a monogamous saint with a polygamous sinner.

Such a conclusion, however, would be mistaken, and to omit Bodin would be a grave error. For whether by the force of repulsion or resistance, his catalytic influence on federal theory cannot be ignored. By defining the state in the exclusivist terms of sovereignty, he compelled all those who sought to legitimize the deviants, and principally the Germanic Empire, to come to terms with either his formulation of the concept or its application to particular cases. Their response varied with their objects, their circumstances, and the case in hand. If Bodin's concern was for France, the concern of other jurists was for the Germanic Empire. Hence some, for example, resolved the en-

---

12. Note, for example, the tight scholastic symmetry of this observation. In paraphrase: An alliance of states (*foedera civitates*) may be converted into one state (*respublica*) if there is one common authority; but if there is no one who can declare peace and war, who can command but not be commanded, then it is not a state, and remains an alliance; as an alliance, it may be of two kinds, equal and unequal (*foedus aequum* or *foedus iniquum*); if equal, it may be of two sorts, offensive or defensive; if unequal, it may be again of two sorts, "when the one acknowledgeth the other to be his superior for honour, and yet is not in his protection: or else the one receiveth the other into protection, and both the one and the other is bound to pay a certaine pention, or to give certaine succours; or else owe neither pention nor succours." (From the English translation, *The Six Bookes of a Commonweale*, pp. 72-73.)

counter by reinterpreting the facts of mastery in particular cases
(Bodin himself gave two different identities to the Empire at
different times), while others devised fresh concepts (the notion
of "powers *analogous* to sovereignty"), or proclaimed the existence of a *new* kind of state (though Bodin spoke of only one
possible form of state) with a new name (e.g., *composite* state,
or *state of states*, or *duplex* state). But whatever course they
took, whether one of denial or modification, the "doctors"
could no more evade Bodin than successive generations of
political jurists could free themselves from the questions—who
commands, and how many masters can there be in a stable state,
one, two, three, or more?

What of Althusius? His *Politica*[13] raises a difficult but ines-
capable phylogenetic puzzle: How far can we relate his corporate theory of the state to federal ideas? The suggestive richness
of his theory is considerable, and numbers of scholars, preemi-
nently Gierke, have declared Althusius the genetic fount of the
federal principle where others have denied it. Let us look at it.
To begin with, there is at least no question at all that Althusius'
theory of the state is essentially monistic: while he explains the
Holy Roman Empire as an all-inclusive association of associations which have contracted to live together (*consociatio symbiotica universalis*), nevertheless the state is identified by the
overarching power of the Emperor's sovereignty. In common
with Bodin, Althusius' notion of sovereignty in *Politica* is
exclusive and indivisible; but unlike Bodin, Althusius holds
that all those who exercise power, from the highest, the Emper-
or, to the dukes, princes, and those below them, do so on behalf
of the people; for ultimately sovereignty resides with them, and
only they can alienate it.

From this perspective, his treatment of the way in which
different territorial communities may elect to join together for
all or some of the benefits to be derived from larger and closer
associations is without any marked novelty. Thus, on the question *confoederatio quid* he writes:

13. Johannes Althusius, *Politica Methodice Digesta.*

> A political association may be created by the agreement of king-
> doms, provinces, cities, towns, and villages to become bonded
> together into the communality of the one State; and thus by
> being enlarged, the state (the all-inclusive political community)
> is made stronger and safer.
>
> This step [however] cannot be taken without the authority
> and the consent of the people belonging to each of these bodies,
> and the consent of those who administer their affairs.

And in accord with his maxims of *prudentia politica*, he coun-
sels those who would combine with others to form a political
association to pay heed to a number of prior considerations.

> In combining with others, considerations should be given to a
> number of matters; the reasons, the form, and the conditions of
> association; the nature of the parties with whom one is entering
> into a bond of association, their character, their power, and their
> interests; one should consider whether the reasons for associa-
> tion are good or bad, and whether the conditions of association
> are dangerous or false. There is a considerable difference be-
> tween entering into a bond (*fedus*) with a kingdom or a state
> [*consociatio universalis*, the all-inclusive German Empire]; for
> with the latter the bond is permanent, and with the former it is
> temporary, lasting only during the life of the king.

At this point he draws a distinction between two kinds of
confoederatio:

> A political association with a foreign people, or a people from
> another association, is of two kinds; either complete, or incom-
> plete in part or to any degree.
>
> A *complete* political association (*plena consociatio*) and a
> covenantal union (*confoederatio*) is formed when a foreign king-
> dom and its subjects, or a province, or some other State (*con-
> sociatio universalis*) integrates its basic laws and its rights of
> sovereignty with those of another power, and is freely taken by
> this power into full and complete rights and partnership in
> ruling; the two are, so to speak, joined together into one and the
> same body, and grow together like limbs of one and the same
> body.

As examples of the "complete" association, Althusius cites the cases of the Romans with the Albans, the incorporation of Judea into the Roman Empire, the Dukedom of Lithuania with Poland, Borussia with Poland, Silesia and Moravia with the kingdom of Bohemia, and Scotland with England.

The second kind of association he describes in the following way:

> The *incomplete* association is one in which separate provinces or kingdoms, while individually retaining their right of sovereignty, solemnly make a treaty together or enter into an agreement binding themselves to provide mutual help against enemies, or to observe obligations and maintain peace and friendship between each other, or to keep common friends and share expenses in coping with enemies; this kind of association can be for a definite period, which is the better way, or for an indefinite one.[14]

And as examples of the "incomplete" association, Althusius cites the treaty between the Swiss towns (*fedus inter Helvetiorum pagos*), the Netherlands provinces (*confoederatio inter provincias Belgicas*), the Hanseatic cities (*fedus inter civitates Ansaticas*), the treaty between Venice, Florence, and the Roman pontificate (*fedus inter Venetos, Florentinos, et Pontificem Romanum*), the treaty between England and France (*fedus inter Anglum et Gallum*), the treaty between the Pontificate, Spain and Swabia (*fedus inter Pontificem, Romanum, Hispanum, et Sabaudum*), and others. He also draws attention to the kinds of considerations which ought to be borne in mind by those who intend to engage in these "incomplete associations," and particularly to the manner in which these treaties should be written and attested.

To this point, we simply witness the customary sixteenth-century diadic taxonomy whereby all covenantal political associations are classed into two kinds: (a) those in which two or more "sovereignties" are merged into one to form a single state,

14. *Ibid.*, pp. 127-135.

and (b) "the rest"—a miscellaneous collection of alliances varying from the simplest examples of military alliance to the more
enduring and organizationally advanced arrangements of the
Swiss, Hanseatic, and Netherlands leagues. And if this were all
there was to Althusius, there would be little reason to enter his
name in the pantheon of federal theorists. The puzzle, however,
is: What are we to make of the power relations between the
different associations that have joined together (by consent,
pact, or treaty) to form the all-inclusive corporate state—the
Empire he conceptualized as *consociatio symbiotica universalis*? Was it a simple hierarchy, or not? And if one interprets the
Empire as a hierarchy, what is to be made of his account of the
power inhering in the head of the province (prince, duke, mar-
grave, landgrave)? He is entrusted with this office, Althusius
tells us, by the *"summa imperans"* of the Empire; yet while
remaining inferior, the prince wields precisely the same sovereign power in his estate as the Emperor himself: *tantum potest
in districtu quantum summus magistratus in regno.*

   Whatever reasons moved Althusius to compose the *Politica*—
whether to erect a pure theory of politics, as he himself suggested in the prefatory dedication of the work, or to rationalize
the existing power relations within the German Empire, or to
find a bonding and mediatory formula which would resolve the
chronic rivalry between the Emperor, princes, dukes, the
church, and the cities—it is clear that the theoretical options
open to him were limited. For any theory that would make
sense of the Empire would make nonsense of Bodinian sovereignty; and any theory that reinforced the separatist tendencies,
and bolstered the autonomous pretensions of powerful princes,
would imperil the Empire. The theoretical and the practical
question therefore, if the Empire was to survive, was how to
reconcile the exclusive sovereignty of the whole with the "separate and independent communal life of partial societies."[15]
Althusius' theory of *consociatio symbiotica universalis* was the
mediatory formula, and as Gierke notes, its "decisive factor was

15. Otto von Gierke, *The Development of Political Theory*, p. 263.

first and foremost the elaboration of the medieval theory of corporation by jurisprudence"—or the idea, in effect, that every commune and corporation (*universitas*) "has its own independent sphere of rights in public law." But with this one crucial difference, that "while the medieval construction was from the top downward, we have here by means of the social contract a reconstruction from the bottom upward."[16] Let Gierke put the matter fully:

> It was Althusius again who with creative genius embraced in a system and grounded on a theoretical principle the federalistic ideas fermenting in the world of events and in the opinions of his own religious and political environment. This he achieved by simply carrying the idea of the social contract, which was first erected into a principle by him, unreservedly into his fundamental scheme of resolving all public law into private law. This gave him a construction of society by pure Natural Law, in which the family, vocational association, commune, and province are necessary organic links between the Individual and the State; in which the larger society is always composed of smaller societies as corporative units, and only through them does it act upon their members; in which every smaller society, as a true and original community [e.g., family], draws from itself its own communal life and its own sphere of rights, giving up to the higher society only so much of this as is indispensably required for the attainment of its specific end; in which, lastly, the State is otherwise generically of the same nature as its component societies and differs from them only in its exclusive sovereignty.[17]

The genealogical line which links Althusius' theory of the corporate state (the association of associations) to Gierke's influential *Genossenschaftstheorie* (the theory of the corporation), and which persists through contemporary pluralist theory (for example, Harold Laski's argument that society and authority are "essentially federal in nature")[18] is well known, as indeed are the philosophical and empirical assaults on these

16. *Ibid.*, pp. 264 and 257.
17. *Ibid.*, p. 266.
18. Harold J. Laski, *A Grammar of Politics*, p. 270.

theories. But is this use of the "federal" idea an illicit analogy, a metaphoric illusion, an etymological bastard, or does it flow from the same historical source that links covenant, foedus, alliance, contract, and consent into a consanguineous family of ideas?

To do justice to Gierke at least, he makes it quite plain that he does not equate Althusius' "completely federalized conception of the State" with the idea of a "Federal State" in the strict nineteenth-century formal sense of the term.[19] What Gierke is concerned to point out, however, is that "Of all the distinctive features of the political system of Althusius, none is perhaps so striking as the spirit of Federalism which pervades it from bottom to top."[20] Whatever else Gierke means by this, there are at least three integral elements in Althusius' theory which relate unmistakably to the historic evolution of the federal idea: *first*, the notion of creating, in the tradition of the Hellenes, larger "unities" out of the villages, towns, cities, provinces, and estates of the Empire; *second*, the notion of a reciprocal covenant, *foedus*, to create, enlarge, and bond unities together for the advantages of greater cooperation and communality; *third*, the notion that the incorporation of a part into a larger whole does not entail the dissolution or the abandonment of any part—on the contrary, *foedus* assures each incorporated member its inherent right to existence and its freedom to engage in those activities which are the rationale of its existence, e.g., the family.

It is by no means obvious, of course, that these elements constitute "a *full-bodied* concept of federalism," as Friedrich claims;[21] nevertheless, they are profoundly important ingredi-

19. That is, *Bundesstaat*, as distinguished from *Staatenbund*, or Confederation. See Gierke, *The Development of Political Theory*, p. 39. What Althusius presents us with is the vision of protected plurality, or plurality as of right, rather than the idea of duality, dual sovereignty, or coordinate status. See also Eulau, "Theories of Federalism," p. 648.

20. Gierke, *The Development of Political Theory*, p. 257.

21. C. J. Friedrich, *Trends of Federalism in Theory and Practice*, p. 12. "The repeated attempts at federalism which were made to unite Greece against Macedonia and Rome failed. It was only in the Middle Ages, with its great city leagues, that the first vague hints at such a concept appeared. But not

ents. To ignore their presence in Althusius' theory is to close one's eyes to the suggestive power of *Politica* on federal ideas, and its influence on later theories of the Empire. More: to dismiss Althusius' corporate theory of the state because it may have bred an incongruous and sometimes ugly variety of progeny (e.g., state absolutism), and worse, because the identification of federalism with corporate and pluralistic theories introduces "an element of confusion" into the term "federal,"[22] is to close one's eyes to the power of an idea that has fed and proliferated nonterritorial associative life far more extensively than the territorial expression of *foedus* ever has. The most elementary proof of this matter is at every hand—simply glance at the pages of any telephone directory in any English-speaking city and count the number of associations (professional, industrial, commercial, trade union, etc.) which have prefixed their name with the words "federation" or "confederation." In all cases where the name symbolizes an organization of groups that have pooled a part of their strength to protect and advance the whole or part of their common interest, here are the perfect *nonterritorial* heirs of Althusius' idea of the *confoederatio non-plena.*

---

until the confederations of the Swiss and Dutch had come into being did a full-bodied concept of federalism make its appearance. This concept was formulated by Johannes Althusius (1562-1638) who, fully conversant with both these federal regimes, made the bond of union (*consociatio*) one of the cornerstones of his political thought. In contrast to Jean Bodin (1530-1596) —who is justly celebrated for establishing the concept of sovereignty, but for precisely that reason was hard put to give an adequate account of the emergent federal government of Switzerland or of the federally organized Empire—Althusius expounded a federal theory of popular sovereignty." Friedrich's statement is at some odds with his earlier interpretation. In his introduction to *Politica Methodice Digesta,* he writes: "In truth the system of governing by estates is, for Althusius, only a special form of the general consociational symbiotic nature of political life. But it was perhaps none too fortunate to characterize the relation of the less inclusive groups or symbiotic consociations to the more inclusive consociations as '*federalism*,' as has been customary since Gierke. For federalism is only a particular form of the general type of a symbiotic group which Althusius develops. *The word federalism is misleading,* I believe, because Althusius never wearies of emphasizing the unitary, collectivistic nature of any symbiotic group." (Althusius, p. lxxxvi; my italics.)

22. William S. Livingston, "A Note on the Nature of Federalism," p. 37.

Theoretical prescriptions, however, proceed differently according to different political needs and circumstances. The concern of the "doctors" in England, France, and Italy was either to vindicate the absolute monarch or to constitutionalize him. The concern in the German Empire was different; not with absolutism nor with caesaro-papism, but with an emperor and an empire standing on feet of clay. Althusius had offered one supportive formula: to reinstate the idea of sovereignty in the name of the people; to legitimize the Emperor as the pinnacle of popular sovereignty; and to confirm the established territorial interests in their historic status. But if Bodin's inflexible monistic (*indivisibile et inalienabile*) view of sovereignty was irrelevant to the facts of the German Empire, Althusius, by giving something to everyone—the Emperor, the princes, the church, and the people—nurtured the virus of atomization and anarchy. The problem for the Germanic "doctors," therefore, was to achieve Althusius' twin political purpose, strength and reconciliation, but to do so without accepting the absurdity of "double-sovereignty," without paying the excessive price of popular sovereignty and without encouraging a multi-centric empire.

Where there is necessity, political stake, and interest, scholarly ingenuity knows no bounds. In the two hundred years that separate Bodin and Althusius from the year of the Philadelphia Convention when "modern" federalism is said to begin, almost all but one of the possible variations on the sovereign theme were played out. Of the many who joined the search for a more fitting political jurisprudence and a more fitting identity for the German polity, two names, Samuel von Pufendorf and Ludolph Hugo, represent the contrasting formula of pre-1787 scholarship.

Pufendorf's treatment, "Of Different Forms of Government," is reminiscent of a clinical text in normal and morbid anatomy. In *De Jure Naturae et Gentium* (*Of the Law of Nature and Nations*), published in 1667,[23] he christened the German Em-

---

23. Pufendorf, *Of the Law of Nature and Nations*, "Of the Different Forms of Government," pp. 669-687. See also his *An Introduction to the Principal*

pire a "monstrous creature," an irregularity, a "bastard" mutant that answered to no form of government (*irregulare aliquod corpus et monstro simile*); it was neither a *foedus simplex* nor *unio*, a *confoederatio plena* nor *confoederatio non plena*, a *respublica simplex* nor *respublica composita*. It was a deformity that nothing less than a "surgical operation" would cure.

Why this morbific identification? To understand him, it is first necessary to grasp his pivotal distinction between "regular" and "irregular" forms of government. Thus:

> It may be useful . . . to observe, that most Authors who have treated of civil Knowledge, have imploy'd themselves in explaining the regular Forms of Government; as for the irregular Forms, many have not so much as thought of them, some few have very slightly touched upon them. Hence it came to pass, that if they happened to meet with a *civil body*, which did not exactly come up to one of those usually termed *simple* Forms, they had scarce any Word left to express it by, besides the Name of a *mixt* Government. But now, not to urge how very ill this *Mixture* is applied to some Commonwealths; it is weak to imagine, that besides these three *regular* Forms [Democracy, Aristocracy, and Monarchy] there are none other, which may be termed *irregular*. For all Men don't build their House just according to that Model which the Rules of Architecture prescribe.

The nature of the *regular* form of states presented no difficulties.

> The *Regularity* of a State we conceive to consist in this, that all, and each of the Members seem to be governed as it were by one Soul; or, that the supreme Authority is exercised through all the parts of the State by one Will, without Division or Convulsion.[24]

And of this kind of state there are three forms, corresponding to whether the "supreme power" resides in the populace, a coun-

---

Kingdoms and States of Europe, pp. 280-282, and *De Officio Hominis et Civis Juxta Legem Naturalem*, pp. 128-132.

24. Pufendorf, *Of the Law of Nature and Nations*, p. 670.

cil, or a single person: thus, a democracy, an aristocracy, or a
monarchy. Each of these three forms is, of course, capable of
corruption, but the "vicious, distempered, or corrupt" use of
these forms (e.g., anarchy, oligarchy, and tyranny) do not constitute a new "species" of government.

To this point, Pufendorf simply walks in the recognizable
taxonomic shoes of Aristotle and Hobbes. His interest to us,
however, begins with his exposition of the *irregular* form of
government. And he begins by first dismissing the value of
referring to the unusual forms of government as *"mixt
States."*

> . . . when we meet with such a Government, as we can neither
> bring under any of those Forms which are found and regular,
> nor yet explain how it differs from them, by the bare Notion of a
> Disease or Deviation, then the learned are put upon a more
> laborious Enquiry. Most Authors judge it the shortest way of
> getting over this Difficulty, to call such Governments mixt
> States; as if they were the Result of the more regular Forms,
> allayed and blended together.[25]

Likewise, he attacks the practice of some "moderns," his own
contemporaries, who have invented "many kinds of mixt
States," rejected the "greatest part of them as inconvenient,"
and praised "two ways, as especially proper and useful."

> The first is, when the parts of the Sovereignty reside separately
> and independently in different Persons, or Bodies of the same
> Commonwealth, so that each Person or Body hold their respec-
> tive Parts by their own proper Right, and administer it accord-
> ing to their own Judgment, whilst in respect of the other parts
> they are altogether in the Nature of Subjects.
>
> The other way which they propose is, when the Sovereign
> Authority inheres indivisibly in many together, yet so as that
> neither the most considerable Majority, without some few dis-
> senting Members, nor indeed all the rest, when any one of the
> Number stands out, can act to any purpose, or exercise any part
> of the supreme Power. And this again is subdivided into two

25. *Ibid.*, p. 677.

Models, either that all the Members shall have equal Power; or
that someone or two of the Number shall be invested with
certain extraordinary Rights and Prerogatives, which they may
use without the assistance of their Brethren.[26]

However, Pufendorf argues, most of the examples which these
writers give of *mixed* Commonwealths do "not in the least
belong to the Division of the Sovereign Power amongst several
Persons or Council." They simply illustrate the *manner* of
administering the Sovereign Power, no more.

What then is the nature of the *irregular* form of government? As he conceives it, it is essentially a negation of the
regular state; that is, the *irregular* form of government is to be
found wherever sovereignty is fragmented, wherever the "supreme authority" is not exercised through all the parts of the
state by one will. In greater particular:

> [We shall] call those Governments *irregular*, in which we can
> neither discover any one of the three regular Forms [i.e., democ-
> racy, aristocracy, or monarchy], nor yet any proper Disease or
> Deviation; and which at the same time cannot, with due Exact-
> ness, be ranked amongst the *systematical* Models.[27]

How does the irregular State come into being? Through a
variety of causes. For example:

> . . . some Irregularities appeared upon the first settlement of a
> State, others crept in by silent Steps, and in long Progress of
> Time. For it might so happen, that the Authors or the Re-
> formers and new Modellers of a Commonwealth might not be
> able to introduce a regular Frame, either on account of Igno-
> rance, or because the present Posture and Exigence of Affairs
> would not suffer them to consider of a more accurate Consti-
> tution. Sometimes too, Persons, who have been the chief Leaders
> and Assistants in winning a Kingdom, have beforehand con-
> tracted for such Lordships, or such Privileges in it, as that they
> cannot be ranked in the Number of true and proper Subjects.
> Again, many times, either through Neglect of the Governours,

26. *Ibid.*, p. 678.
27. *Ibid.*

or upon some other occasion, a distemper seizeth a State, and
having taken so deep root, that it cannot be removed without the
Destruction of the public Frame, there remains no Cure for it,
but this; to divest it . . . of its Faultiness. . . .

The variations of the *irregular form* are indeed infinite.

[They] can neither be brought within any certain Number, nor
divided into proper Kinds, by reason of that great Variety, which
either really occurs in Fact, or at least may be framed in our
Imagination.[28]

And the two "illustrious" examples of such *irregular* forms are
the Roman Commonwealth and the German Empire.

Pufendorf's entire taxonomy—it may be noted—rests on two
simple normative equations:

the regular state   = undivided   = strength/perfection/
                      sovereignty   moral polity

the irregular state = divided or compro- = weakness/imper-
                      mised sovereignty   fection/shameful
                                           polity

Hence his condemnation of the German "monster," "the like of
which is not to be met within any Kingdom of Europe."

Though it is certain that Germany within itself is so potent, that
it might be formidable to all its Neighbors, if its strength was
well united and rightly employed; nevertheless this strong body
has also its infirmities, which weaken its strength and slacken its
vigour. Its irregular constitution of Government is one of the
chief causes of its infirmity; it being neither one entire Kingdom,
neither properly a confederacy, but participating of both kinds:
For the Emperour has not the entire soveraignty over the whole
Empire, nor each prince in particular over his Territories; and
though the former is more than a bare administrator, yet the
latter have a greater share in the soveraignty than can be attri-
buted to any subjects or citizens. . . .[29]

28. *Ibid.*, p. 679.
29. Pufendorf, *Introduction to the History of the Principal Kingdoms*, p. 280.

But if sovereignty is the bedrock of Pufendorf's analytical schema, what place is there for such "alliance" systems of government as the Swiss or Netherlands confederacies? If the German Empire is an irregularity, what of the various species of "alliance" arrangements? Are they regular or irregular systems, normal or aberrant? The quest for identity had already begun to concentrate on the Althusian idea of a state *composed* (compounded) of other states. And Pufendorf had already foreshadowed his interpretation of "alliance" systems when he distinguished the *irregular* state from "those States composed of several perfect States in Conjunction, which with unskilful Judges pass for single States." His view of "alliance" arrangements therefore flowed directly from his intractable belief in the virtue of one Supreme Authority. For him, the Swiss and the Netherlands confederacies were examples of the *systemata civitatum* (variously translated as *systems of states, composite state, états composés*), a regular form of government brought into being when

> ... several States are, by some special Band, so closely united, as that they seem to compose one Body, and yet retain each of them the sovereign Command in their respective Dominions; these we term *systems of States*.[30]

So defined, however, there were in Pufendorf's view only two known species of the *systema civitatum regulare*; other states, such as "States composed of several *subordinate* bodies," or "States which had vastly increased their Dominions by swallowing up their little Neighbours," were patently excluded. The two species of *systema civitatum*, or alliance-State properly so-called, were, first, when two or more states are subject to the one and the same King; second, "when two or more States are linked together in one Body by virtue of some League or Alliance." The first of these is of little interest to us; it is characteristically the product of the "marriage of Princes" and the "Right of Inheritance." The second, however, is a classic formulation of (what is still regarded as) the conventional idea of a

30. Pufendorf, *Of the Law of Nature and Nations*, p. 681.

confederation, and the way it is to be distinguished from the
commonplace military alliance (*foedus simplex*):

> The other kind of *System* is, when several States are joined to
> each other by a perpetual League or Alliance; the chief Occasion
> of which seems to have been, that each particular People loved to
> be their own Masters, and yet each was not strong enough to
> make Head against a common Enemy. The Purport of such an
> Agreement usually is, that they shall not exercise some part of
> the Sovereignty there specified, without the general Consent of
> each other. For the Leagues to which these Systems owe their
> rise, seem distinguished from others [so frequent amongst dif-
> ferent states] chiefly by this Consideration; that in the latter each
> confederate People determine themselves by their own Judg-
> ment to certain mutual performances, yet so as that, in all other
> respects, they design not in the least to make the exercise of that
> part of the Sovereignty, whence those Performances proceed, de-
> pendent on the Consent of their Allies, or to retrench anything
> from their full and unlimited Power of governing their own
> states. Thus we see that ordinary Treaties propose, for the most
> part, as their Aim, only some particular Advantage of the States
> thus transacting; their interests happening at present to fall in
> with each other. But do not produce any lasting Union, as to the
> chief Management of Affairs. Whereas, in those Leagues we are
> now speaking of, the contrary is observable; they being carried
> on with this Design, that the several States shall for ever link
> their Safety one within the other, and in order to this mutual
> Defence, shall engage themselves not to exercise certain parts of
> their Sovereign Power, otherwise than by a common agreement
> and Approbation.[31]

The apparent paradox of a state which submits a part of its
sovereignty to the judgment of all the confederates, and yet
retains the sovereignty of a regular state (i.e., a complete mastery of its affairs) does not escape nor distress Pufendorf's
schema. Immediately after he has sketched the particular

31. *Ibid.*, p. 682. It is valuable to follow the translation in English, Latin, and
French to get some sense of the different terminology in use at the time.
For example, "L'autre sorte d'Etats Composés, ceux qui se forment par la
Confederation perpetuelle de plusieurs Etats. . . . " Or, "Altera species sys-
tematum provenit, quando plures civitates vicinae perpetuo Foedere. . . . "

"branches" or "parts" of sovereignty which were the appropriate business of the whole confederation (viz., those "parts"
which relate to defense, taxes, subsidies, and foreign affairs as
distinct from those "parts" which can have little or no influence—at least directly—on the affairs of the rest), and after he
has dwelled on the nature of the deliberative ("ambassadorial")
council which should attend those matters of general concern,
he turns to the seeming paradox, and answers:

> A Union or Concurrence of Wills, grounded on bare Compact,
> doth not in the least destroy . . . Liberty.[32]

In other words, unanimity and not a plurality of voices is the
test of the pure confederation. For "if the Votes were to take
place according to the Proportion of Force, or Treasure sup-
plied to the common Cause; then the more powerful State
would actually obtain a Sovereignty over all. . . ." And in that
case, "the regular Form of Systems or Confederacies [*systema
civitatum regulare*] is deserted, and the Members either break
into an irregular Body [*systema civitatum irregulare*] or close
together in one undivided State [*unum imperium*]."

Pufendorf's dichotomous resolution of all *regular* alliance-
or treaty-states into personal unions and pure confederations
illegitimized all possible median positions.[33] Some of his contemporaries, however, and certainly most of the succeeding
generation of scholars, were less persuaded of the logic or the
virtue of indivisible sovereignty—or if persuaded of its logic
and virtue, were not disposed, at least publicly, to praise a
theory which caricatured the Empire as a bastardized mutant.
Plainly, the Empire was not a *foedus simplex*, nor was it

32. *Ibid.*, p. 684.
33. It is interesting to observe that whereas Pufendorf distinguished the *regular*
   and the *irregular* forms of government, he wrote a specific dissertation on
   the irregular form (*De Republica Irregulari*). Contrast this with the contemporary tendency, where texts on "federal government," having distinguished the "federal" form by a process of positive and negative differentiation, proceed to gather all "the rest," whether *proxime accessit* or not,
   into an undifferentiated pile—confederal, devolutionary, unitary, federal
   unitary, etc. Obviously there is a treatise to be written on "the non-federal
   system of government."

wholly like the Swiss Confederation (*confoederatio systema regulare*), nor indeed like any other known system in the world. But if the test of a theory is its correspondence to the facts, then they preferred to read the political facts without either resorting to Pufendorf's morbific scheme or fictionalizing the realities of power in the language of sovereignty. Hence they argued that the Empire was no civic freak ("nothing is foreign to the nature of human affairs"), but a normal and legitimate form of polity, a nontreaty composite state which occupied the middle ground between the simple alliance and the pure confederation of the Swiss type. In this *nova respublica* (as Leibniz called it), sovereignty or the supreme authority (*ius majestatis*) reposed solely in the Empire, the superstate as it were; the imperial orders, the princely territories, for their part exercised by right a "full and independent" power *analogous* to sovereignty (*analogum majestatis*) in all those matters which concerned their territories alone, but vis-à-vis the Emperor they were "dependent," "subaltern," "lesser," "subordinate" substates lacking real sovereignty, and hence real statehood. This focus on the corporate personality, unity, and normality of the Empire, the division of jurisdictions between the Empire and the princely orders within the overarching "supreme authority" of the Empire, is characteristic of the contrasting body of thought which Ludolph Hugo's *De Statu Regionum Germaniae* (1661) largely represents.[34]

34. I am deeply indebted to Patrick Riley of the University of Wisconsin for leave to use his translation of the Introduction and Chap. 2 of Ludolph Hugo's *De Statu Regionum Germaniae* (1661), and Chapters 10 and 11 of Leibniz's *De Suprematu Principum Germaniae* (1678). These works were not available to me in Australia.

It is interesting to note Leibniz's comments on those "learned men" who deemed a "division of the supreme power" to be an inconvenient curse. "I would not deny that, when the supreme power is divided, many dissensions can arise. . . . But experience has shown that men usually hold to some middle road, so as not to commit everything to hazard through their obstinacy. Prominent examples are Poland and Belgium: among the Poles, one territorial representative can dissolve the assembly by his obstinacy; in Holland, when something of great importance is being considered, as peace, war, or treaties, the disagreement of one town upsets everything. And yet, due to the prudence and moderation of those who preside over the

In a prefatory note explaining the purpose of his work, Hugo observes that the Germanic Empire

> . . . is run by a *double rule*. For the entire Empire is ruled by some common government, and the individual regions of which it consists have certain princes of their own, or magistrates, courts, and advisory bodies, and even a certain government of their own, subjoined to the higher one. It is, therefore, our purpose to examine the cause and manner of this distinction; then briefly to explain what of the total power pertains to the administration of the Empire, what to the administration of the lesser regions. For it is not sufficiently clear what sort of power is *he autokrateia* [Greek: the absolute rule, full power] of the Empire's princes and upper orders, by which they have their strength and authority. It seems, if in some things rather free, and almost a law unto itself, yet in others more subject to the Empire which is over it.

And the rationale for "double rule" is this: Since large masses of territory cannot be given order by one government, there must be a division of rule, first at one level, then further subdivision at another, and so on till effective government obtains throughout the land.

> For just as the municipality of one city is composed of homes, so a fairly large empire is composed of subordinate regions. That government, therefore, is the higher which has the highest of all power in the empire, whether it be in one man's hand or in a council of a few men or a multitude, brought from one city or province or from the whole nation, or in a mixed manner. But to this government are subordinate the lesser governments which are established in the parts of the kingdom or empire.

---

whole, most matters are finished according to their wishes. In the German assemblies, too, not everything is transacted by majority vote, but some matters require unanimity, all of which cases would seem anarchy to Hobbes. *Some others, who have expressed themselves a bit freely concerning our state, think them monstrous;* but if this is true, I would venture to say that the same monsters are being maintained by the Dutch and the Poles and the English, even by the Spanish and the French. . . . Therefore Hobbesian Empires, I think, exist neither among civilized peoples nor among barbarians, and I consider them neither possible nor desirable— unless those who must have supreme power are gifted with angelic virtues." (From Patrick Riley's translation of Leibniz; my italics.)

At first it may appear that Hugo is simply describing a political
system which, in the linguistic currency of the twentieth century, could be called a "decentralized unitary state." And were
this so, he would lay only small claim on our attention. But, it
is his discourse on the special nature of the princely power
within their territories that is arresting to contemporary eyes.
For the puzzle he needs to resolve is: *How is it possible for the
princes to be subject to the supreme authority of the Empire,
and yet, in some things, act as if they were free and almost a law
unto themselves?* If subjection seems to conflict with the nature
of a state (*respublica*), what then is the nature of the princely
domain? He answers:

> *We must note that, just as there are various differences in power,
> so too in kinds of subjection.* [My italics.] For power is either
> lordly or civil, and of each there are various varieties. In just as
> many ways, therefore, must differ cities and regions subject to
> some empire. And this may be deduced from the fact that great
> empires are composed of subject states/cities in the way that
> middling cities are composed of citizens. Citizens, however, dif-
> fer according to the diversity of the city they belong to. So we can
> say about states/cities subject to a higher law just what Aristotle
> says about citizens. Here are his words: "No one should find it
> unclear," in things whose underlying principles differ in kind,
> "that one of them must be first, another second, and so forth.
> Things of this nature have in common either nothing what-
> soever, or something extremely tenuous and narrow. Now we see
> that governments differ in kind, and that some of them are prior,
> while others follow. . . ." Now the same applies to states/cities
> subject to another. For *some are so in power over all things that,
> although they may seem subordinate to some government, they
> in truth are not, but are free and independent.* [My italics.]
> Others, on the contrary, are so without power that it is hard to
> find in them a slight resemblance to some real government.
> Others lie in between. It would be difficult to pursue all these
> gradations and varieties, nor would it befit our proposed task.
> Therefore we will survey only some of the principal sorts. . . .

Hugo then lists three principal kinds. The *first* kind is typified by the Achaean, Swiss, and Belgian federations:

> [This] occurs when several states have instituted among them-
> selves a union so close, and concerning so many conventions and
> objects of agreement, that their association exceeds the bounds of
> the usual treaty and seems to take on something of civil union.
> Such as one time was the Achaean League. . . . In our age we
> have examples of the same thing in the Belgian [Netherlands]
> Federation and Switzerland.

But the appearance of civil union and the juridical reality of
civil union are not to be confused. And Hugo agrees with the
prevailing view that since the Swiss and Belgian federations are
the creatures of a treaty, neither is a true civil union; the
individual provinces have not merged into one state, and hence
remain free and independent.

> For the union contracted by treaty does not become the master of
> the states, but the states themselves are the masters of the treaty.
> So that although such a treaty has the look of a superior gov-
> ernment, it is in fact a different sort of administration—true
> subordination of governments does not arise from it.

The *second* kind is the very *opposite* of the first and is
exampled by the Roman Empire:

> It occurs when the power of the magistrates who are in charge of
> a city or some region clearly depends in all things on a king or
> higher government. This was of old the status of the Roman
> provinces. For the magistrates in charge of them were nothing
> but servants of the emperor, who through them ruled the pro-
> vinces with what was obviously a master's authority. . . . Just as
> in the preceding case a true superior government is not to be
> found, so also here the lower special administration cannot be
> considered a state.

The *third* kind, the Germanic Empire, lies between the first
and the second:

> It comes about when the civil power is somehow divided be-
> tween the highest and the lower governments, so that the higher
> manages those matters pertaining to the common welfare, the
> lower those things pertaining to the welfare of the individual
> regions. *It is this model which the administration of our Empire*

fits. There is no other example, or none so perfect. [Quoting
Thuanus: "I do not see what in all of antiquity can be compared
to it." Thuanus adds, the Amphictyonic Assembly and the
Achaean Council, "compared to Germany, are as a fly to an
elephant."] So, in such administration of a *double government*
—the higher in the whole Empire, the lower in the individual
regions—we see considerable propriety. For the Emperor, together with the Senate, has subject to himself the noble orders of
the Empire, while the orders have subject to themselves the
individual private persons. Whence the common distinction
between *mediate* citizens of the Empire . . . and *immediate.*

In a word, the Emperor rules the states, and the states rule the
citizens. But what precisely is the power of those who have the
immediate or direct rule over the citizens? And over what
things? The first he answers:

Although the Imperial Orders [princes] . . . clearly lack free and
complete power in the governing of their realms, their power is
still universal and wide enough to seem to take something from
the Highest Power. It is, therefore, an analogous kind of the
Highest Power. [This is conveyed in the well-worn axiom, "Any
prince has in his territory as much power as the Emperor has in
the whole Empire."] Since, therefore, the power of princes and
of the imperial orders, by which they govern their territories,
corresponds by some analogy to the Highest Civil Power, it follows that the nature of this governing must by the same token be
considered a state/government.

To the second, the question of what "rights of territorial supe-
riority" (or "rights of Majesty," or the "Highest Civil Power,"
as it is variously called) are to be divided, Hugo's criteria of
apportionment are broadly similar to Pufendorf's, and yield
much the same result. The safety of the allies (Pufendorf) or the
empire (Hugo) is the basic principle in both cases, but this
principle receives a more elaborate formulation in Hugo's
hands. "What way each thing is divided—what goes to the
princes and other orders, what is left for the emperor and the
empire . . . is without doubt not random, but proceeds from
definite causes." Cities come together in a wider union to serve

specific ends: to reduce the endless strife among themselves, to strengthen their internal stability, to promote commerce and to resist attack. And it is from the "ends," goals, or purposes of a proper and genuine state (by contrast with a union created by a "fragile" treaty) that "we tell what belongs to its power."

> The remaining things are conveniently left to the lesser states. . . . The things required by the needs of the citizens' life cannot be attended to properly through some universal authority, but should be handled by some lesser civil bodies.

It is not enough, however, to compose a principle of division without relating it to the particular case. Hence Hugo draws attention to the parlous situation of the German Empire:

> . . . although the ends we have stated are those set for our Empire, it still lacks many things, and is thus hindered from achieving these ends. . . . Because . . . the government of the Empire is not so constituted that it can perform its own tasks and accomplish that for which it was established, much must be handled in the individual regions which might more rightly be administered through the Empire. For whatever is neglected by the Empire must be handled by the nobles on their own, whatever way they can.

In fine, Hugo's answer to the puzzle of princely subjection and princely independence was an ingenious attempt to reconcile two seemingly irreconcilable cases: the consolidated rule of a single sovereign monarch (*unio*), and the partial alliance of a number of single states (*foedus*). But it was an uneasy and ambivalent theory, fitting the incoherent body of the Empire only where it touched. He construed the Empire as a median system distinguished on the one hand from *unio* by the quasi-sovereignty (*analogum majestatis*) of the princes within their own territories, and from the Swiss Confederation by the subjection of the princes to the Emperor on the other hand. But if he was correct in the first case, the distinction in the second case was more doubtful. It is dubious, for instance, whether subjection rather than voluntary deference expresses the true relationship of the powerful princes and the imperial nobles to the

Emperor, whether the power of even the least principality was
qualitatively different from the strongest Swiss canton, and
indeed whether the Imperial Diet was much more than an
ambassadorial council operating by a plurality of voices held
together by the hegemony of two kingdoms—Austria and
Brandenburg. However, whether Hugo's theory corresponded
to the facts or not, it is, at the very least, true that the "mutant,"
"monster," "bastard" German Empire was, both historically
and structurally, a unique phenomenon—scarcely comparable
to the Swiss Confederation or any other system. As a practicing
political system, it rested on no single constitutional principle
which could be replicated. If it could be described as a "median" class of government, reposing somewhere between the
"consolidated" (*unio*) and "confederated" (*foedus*) systems,
then it was, as Hugo recognized, a class of one member only,
and the nature of this "median" class could only be revealed by
a complete account of no other system but the Empire itself.

Such was the predominant response of the sixteenth- and
seventeenth-century taxonomists to the political phenomena
born of treaty and empire. But taxonomy is schematization, and
schema are best suited to rocks, less suited to animals and plant
life, and least suited of all to human institutions. And doubtless these early Linnaeans were troubled by the ambivalence of
all political Linnaeans, the drive to bring order to things, and
the awareness of the immense variety and malleability of
things. Certainly Pufendorf, Hugo, and possibly Bodin were
alive to the problem of boxing political systems within tight
categories; moreover, they needed no "vulgar" reminder that
form and practice might differ. How otherwise, when in some
three to four hundred years Europe had experienced such profound change, when in the midst of change political systems
had proliferated, when simple war alliances had developed into
broader civic concerns, when populist claims and representative institutions had laid challenge to monistic sovereignty, and
when change encouraged the consciousness and the possibility
of different kinds of political arrangements. Indeed, is it any
wonder that Pufendorf could remark that "All men don't build

their House just according to that Model which the Rules of Architecture prescribe"?

Also, as in our time, so then, political schema, like all political phenomena, took shape in the eyes of the beholder. All were scholars, some were scholar-advocates, and a few, like Pufendorf, composed their schema with the moral fervor of the American "Federalists" who one hundred years later urged their electors to accept the work of the 1787 Convention. And also, as in our time, so then too the problems of political taxonomy were revealed not merely in the disagreements between the "doctors of civil knowledge," but more strikingly in the vacillations of the individual scholars. Thus, for example, Bodin in *Methodus* distinguishes the Aetolian from the Achaean League, but in the *De Republica*, written some ten years later, brings both under the same head as states which have established one "Aristocratical Commonwealth." And indeed Bodin recounts that he had once taken the German princes and cities as sovereign, and thus interpreted their relations merely as *"jure foederis ac societatis inter se obligati,"* but later, in view of the *jura majestatis* openly exercised by the Imperial Diet, he had to admit that the Empire was an aristocratic unitary state.

If one were to pause at the turn of the eighteenth century to survey the course of the movements and the theories of state that fed into the gene-pool of all political institutions, it appears that the corpus of federal ideas had been fed by two main streams of experience: the covenantal postulates and practice of alliance theory, or *foedus*; and the covenantal customs that underpinned the particular feudal relations and practices of the Germanic Empire. As the simplest and most direct form of commitment to the twin goals of security and autonomy, the stream of alliance was, and is destined to remain, the seminal vehicle wherever and whenever distinct group entities, be they territorial or not, reach out for closer relations. And in this stream, the notion of bonding territorial societies in such a way that they can combine the power of large territories and the virtues of local institutions, which can act as single political systems for some purposes and not others, developed into a sophisticated theory of confederation that still retains some hold upon contemporary usage. The second served in a different way. As the force that dominated European politics for many centuries, it generated, as do most imperial phenomena, two opposing tendencies: at its periphery, the rationalizations of rebellion and territorial independence; and at its center, the rationalizations of unity and coherence. Nowhere did the tension between these two tendencies challenge the ingenuity of the "doctors" more than in the receding body of the Empire itself. The need to explain its incongruous mix of fiction and feudalism, to find a formula which might reconcile emperor and princes, yielded precisely the ambivalent theories that could span *unio* and *foedus*.

Indeed, were constitutional alchemy possible, one could have compounded, if not the perfect replica or clone of the 1787 United States federal model, something that, by its close similarity, would have agonized the latter-day federal taxonomists sorely. It simply needed the fusion of the following ingredients to transform alliance metal into federal gold: the prevailing idea of the composite state, Hugo's notion of double rule, the division of "the rights of Majesty," the feudal obligation of princes to enact the will of the Empire in matters of common concern, the principle of majority rule in the affairs of the common council, the commitment of all to an "everlasting" treaty, and Althusius' catalyst of the sovereign people's will.

But in the age of enlightenment, there was no alchemist to suggest how these elements could be fused, or by what catalyst. And as deeply as the eighteenth-century men Montesquieu and Rousseau inseminated the years preceding the American federation with thoughts upon the nature of community, society, civic fulfilment, and the principle of separating power to restrain tyranny, they did not advance the body of federal theory one whit beyond the point which Pufendorf and Hugo in the seventeenth century, or indeed the later German students (e.g., Pütter) in the eighteenth century, had brought it. Indeed, they stopped far short of it. Montesquieu's four brief pages in

L'Esprit des Lois (Book IX) on how small republics can best protect themselves against larger and predatory neighbours are little more than simple praise for the aggregative value of the classical confederacy. It is certainly not to be compared with Pufendorf's account of it. Montesquieu's concluding remarks immediately after he had commented on the imperfections of the German, Dutch, and Swiss confederations, for example, give the clearest indication of his thoughts:

> Were I to give a model of an excellent confederate republic I should pitch upon that of Lycia.[35]

Shades of Freeman's comparison of the United States of America with the Achaean League!

And Rousseau, an alternately exciting and infuriating enigma, is little different. Enamoured as he is with the small state (*"le petit État"*) as the ideal crucible of individual and civic fulfilment, the question he comes to briefly in several works (e.g., *Contrat Social, Le Gouvernment de Pologne*, and *Emile*) is: By what means can small free states exist beside the great powers? The answer he planned to give, but never brought into full light, was essentially the same as Montesquieu's: in an international society of threat and war, security for the small states lies in a body that combines the strength of a great nation towards the external world with the "free discipline, and the healthy order, of a small one." And the body he had in mind? Simply, the examples of the German Empire, the Helvetic League, or the General Estates of France.[36]

35. Taken from *The Complete Works of M. de Montesquieu*, p. 168. The first three chapter heads of Book IX disclose both his concern and the limited relevance of Montesquieu to a pursuit of federal theory: "(1) In what manner republics provide for their safety; (2) That a confederate government ought to be composed of States of the same nature, especially of the republican kind; (3) Other requisites in a confederate republic." In all, four pages!

36. C. V. Vaughan (ed.), *The Political Writings of Jean-Jacques Rousseau*, Vol. I, pp. 95-102. According to Vaughan, federation for Rousseau "has a double aim. It seeks to do for the whole community, and for all communities concerned, that which the Social Contract has already done for the individual himself; to complete the work of drawing man from the state of

It was a commonplace answer for the times. And from this typical eighteenth-century outlook, Rousseau and Montesquieu would have doubtless praised the American Articles of Confederation and later condemned the United States Constitution. However, the malleability of ideas in the service of political causes is one of the wonders of creation. For only a few decades later, the American federalists were to revile the Articles that Montesquieu would have praised, and praise Montesquieu's arguments to bolster the small republic by advocating a mode of union that Montesquieu would have condemned.[37]

Alchemistry, however, is not the way of things. And what is therefore remarkable is not the dominance of German taxonomy prior to 1787, but how close the expositors of the Empire came to composing the formal properties of contemporary federalism. That they stopped short was not due to the lack of ingenuity, but simply the absence of circumstance and necessity. They had explored the idea of "double sovereignty" and

---

nature. . . . " And, Vaughan adds, far from being a mere offshoot, "the doctrine of Federation springs from the very root of Rousseau's political ideal. . . . " (Pp. 97 and 100.) In other words, confederacy (for this is what Rousseau meant, according to Vaughan) is the answer to the endangered small state, in the same way that the single civil society is the answer for the endangered individual in the condition of nature.

But if this is what Rousseau had in mind, then the idea of confederacy and his idea of civil society do not fit together. On my reading of Book I, Chap. 6, on the social contract, the idea of the social contract cannot be translated into federal terms because, while the individual is *free*, as Rousseau defines freedom—that is, because he "renders obedience to his own will"—he is not *independent*—because he is an indivisible part of the whole! Thus, if we were to project Rousseau's social contract "state" as a model for an international association (i.e., an organization which required every individual state to surrender "all of its rights" to the international body), it would hardly be an association contemplated in the mainstream of federal ideas. On the other hand, if we compose a contract between states (large and small) which left them "in possession of certain rights" as against the larger "sovereign" community (e.g., in the fashion of Althusius' contract between *corporations* as distinct from Rousseau's social contract between individuals), then such a contract would be a violation of the first principles of Rousseau's social contract. (Vaughan, *Rousseau*, Vol. II, p. 8.)

37. See Benjamin F. Wright's introduction to *The Federalist*, pp. 4-5. For Montesquieu's influence on the American federalists, especially on the question of "separating" powers, see, in general, G. Dietze, *The Federalist*.

correctly rejected it; how else, if minds are immured in the logic of indivisible sovereignty and eyes are accustomed to the presence of an Emperor whom history has vested with the *ius majestatis*? The idea of "dual government" was obviously more acceptable, but only within the notion of "subordination" to the one sovereign. For them, indeed, there was no escape from the dilemma of sovereignty, so long as the idea of sovereignty conditioned political jurisprudence, so long as sovereignty was personalized in the body of the Emperor, and so long as any particle of sovereign power was immune from constitutional definition and electoral sanction.

The reconditioning of a civic culture from the experience of sovereignty personalized in a monarch to the depersonalized sovereignty of a constitution, and from an indivisible to a divisible sovereignty, however, cannot be effected before time, circumstance, and necessity; and time, circumstance, and necessity cannot be replicated in any test tube known to man. When the transformation took place in the American Constitution of 1787, it involved the fusion of treaty into a written constitution and the submergence of a personalized sovereignty into popular representative institutions. This translation, however, never destroyed the monumental force of the covenantal legacy of *foedus*, nor the expectations of sovereignty, even when divided in two. The voice of covenant, of promise, of treaty, and of compact, has never been stilled in the conversation and polemics of federalism; and when joined to the language of territorial sovereignty, whether "independence" or "freedom," it compacted into a force which has been felt in every corner of federal history to this day.

4

The United States Model, 1787

Or, what was born in Philadelphia: "amphibious animal," "many-headed monster," or Federalism Mk. I?*

That the original thirteen American colonies should first ally themselves by the Articles of Confederation in a "perpetual union" was wholly in keeping with some two thousand years of European experience. And none but a myopic patriot could claim more than trivial novelty for either the form or the content of the association writ into these articles. For Article III, which pronounced the aims of the association, spoke the essential language of all historic treaties of sworn friendship:

> The said states hereby severally enter into a firm league of friendship with each other, for their common defence, the security of their Liberties, and their mutual and general welfare, binding themselves to assist each other, against all force offered to, or attacks made upon them, or any of them, on account of religion, sovereignty, trade, or any other pretence whatever.

And if Article III did not identify this association, then the completely dependent nature of the power vested in the Congress of state-appointed delegates established its character beyond doubt. Thus while the states vested Congress with "the sole and exclusive right" to manage a number of designated matters of common interest (Article IX) by majority decision (and in some cases the assent of at least nine states), they also made it the complete servant of their will.

* Mk. is a technical symbol denoting design, pattern, or model; hence Mk. I is used here to indicate the first design, pattern, or model of federalism.

> Congress could make treaties with powers great and small but
> could not persuade the state legislatures to honor them; it could
> authorize foreign trade but could neither regulate nor tax it; it
> could call for money but not collect it, borrow money but not
> repay it, print money but not support it. Above all it could
> resolve and recommend but could not command and coerce.[1]

Not merely was this "perpetual alliance" of states the classic
foedus writ in the political metaphors of the eighteenth century, but it is also worthy of note that this association entrusted
Congress and its executive "committee of the States" with far
less force than the Achaean League gave to its *strategos*. Certainly no previous taxonomist would have been greatly troubled to find a name for this arrangement. To Polybios, it would
be an example of *sympoliteia*; to Bodin, *foedus aequum*; to
Althusius, *confoederatio non plena*; to Pufendorf, *systema civitatum irregulare*; to Hugo, it would be of the same genre as the
Achaean, Swiss, and Netherlands leagues, a union "so close as
to exceed the bounds of the usual treaty"; to Montesquieu, it
would be a confederate republic; and to Rousseau, a Helvetic or
Germanic type of confederacy, kin to but more highly developed than the Greek leagues. Indeed, one may well speculate on
the likely course of federal theory if the Articles of Confederation had sustained the American "league of friendship" for as
long as the Second Athenian League, or the Hanseatic or
Netherlands leagues, or indeed any of the great spans of the
Helvetic League, instead of barely eight years.

Fanciful speculation, however, is unnecessary. For there can
be no question at all that the recommendations of the "Grand
Convention" which wrote an end to the Articles of Confederation in Philadelphia in 1787, and introduced the Constitution
of the United States to the world, changed the course of federal
ideas as profoundly as Rome and the Germanic Empire had
affected the political thought and the political institutions of
their world and thereafter. The question, however, is: What
precise changes were brought about in Philadelphia? What did

1. Clinton Rossiter, *1787—The Grand Convention*, p. 52.

the "Founding Fathers" believe, or want others to believe, they had conceived? Had they truly wrought a political system out of "principles which had never before been attempted on earth," a "thing so new that it wanted a name"? Or was this the vale-dictory extravagance of those triumphant fathers whose seed had borne fruit? Such is, and will doubtless remain, the dispute on these questions, that a careful recapitulation of the now familiar positions, argued first in the Convention, then later by the victors in the Federalist Papers, and again by the principal sides in the ratification debates, is unavoidable.[2]

The delegates who assembled in Philadelphia in May 1787 were committed to one simple, though remarkably open, brief: to revise the Articles of Confederation in a way that would "render the federal constitution adequate to the exigencies of government and the preservation of the Union." Possibly this was the one cause they shared in common, for anything less general and less vague than this brief may have failed to bring so many diverse views to a common assembly. Not only were the delegates to the convention disagreed on the precise nature of the "weakness and inefficiency" of the Articles or the seri-ousness of the prevailing ills of the confederation, but they were even more profoundly divided on what was to be done to

2. For the prime sources of interpretation, I took heed of the greater part of James Madison's advice to Andrew Stevenson in a letter of 1827, that the "key to the sense of the Constitution, where alone the true one can be found . . . [is] . . . in the proceedings of the Convention, the contemporary expo-sitions, and above all in the ratifying Conventions of the States." (Farrand (see below), Vol. III, p. 474.) For the proceedings of the Convention, I relied on James Madison's *Notes of Debates in the Federal Convention of 1787*, hereafter referred to as Madison; and Max Farrand (ed.), *The Records of the Federal Convention of 1787*, hereafter to be referred to as Farrand. For the Federalist Papers, I used principally Benjamin F. Wright's edition, here-after referred to as The Federalist. And for the ratification proceedings, Jonathan Elliot (ed.), *The Debates in the Several State Conventions on the Adoption of the Federal Constitution as Recommended by the General Convention at Philadelphia in 1787*, hereafter referred to as Elliot. My in-debtedness to select secondary sources will be apparent in later footnotes to this chapter. But of the many dramatistic chronicles of the Convention and the ratification debates, I have mainly relied on Charles Warren, *The Mak-ing of the Constitution* (hereafter Warren); Carl Van Doren, *The Great Rehearsal*; and Catherine Drinker Bowen, *Miracle at Philadelphia*.

remedy what Madison called the "vices of the political system of the United States."[3]

On the face of it, it seems hardly possible that such a diversity of interests could be aligned, let alone divided on any simple basis, and especially so where the number of potential solutions to the ills of the confederation were so many. Yet from almost the very outset of the Convention it became clear that the great debate would mainly polarize around a single question—whether the cure would be fundamental or cosmetic surgery. The Virginia Plan, embodied in the fifteen resolutions introduced by Governor Randolph on the third day of the Convention and on the first day of its substantive business, outlined the extensive nature of the radical cure, and the New Jersey Plan, introduced fourteen days later, defined the milder course of treatment. The Virginia Plan proposed the full panoply of a national government, electorally obligated and technically equipped as a government to impose its will on its electors; the New Jersey Plan proposed some adjustments to the existing Articles of Confederation, but left the central "deformity," Congressional dependence on the states, largely intact. The Virginia Plan took the stage first, occupied the center, and in the four months of the Convention rarely yielded its position; the New Jersey Plan failed on the fourth day of its debut, but played a continuing obligato almost to the last day of the convention. It is the spirit of the Virginia Plan that is embodied in the United States Constitution. It was mainly the supporters of the New Jersey Plan who compelled the fervent protagonists of a "compleat national government" to give some ground, to elaborate, tighten, amend, and refine the nucleus of what was to emerge as the Constitution of the United States.

Let us look at the Virginia Plan a little more closely now. If we reduce the fifteen resolutions to all but the essentials, it proposed that:

---

3. Madison, p. 16. "Such were the defects, the deformities, the diseases and the ominous prospects, for which the Convention were to provide a remedy. . . ." Cf. Pufendorf's morbific reference to the German Empire.

1. the Articles of Confederation should be corrected and enlarged so as to accomplish the objects proposed by their institution: namely, common defense, security of liberty and general
welfare;

2. a national legislature consisting of two branches should be
established;

3. the members of the first branch of the national legislature
should be elected by the people of the several states;

4. the members of the second branch of the national legislature should be elected by those of the first, from persons nominated by the individual legislatures;

5. each branch should possess the right of originating acts;

6. the national legislature should be empowered to enjoy the
legislative rights vested in Congress by the Confederation, and
moreover *to legislate in all cases to which the separate states are
incompetent, or in which the harmony of the United States may
be interrupted by the exercise of individual legislation; to negative all laws passed by the several states, contravening in the
opinion of the national legislature the articles of Union; and to
call forth the force of the Union against any member of the
Union failing to fulfil its duty under the articles;*

7. a national executive to be established, chosen by the national legislature;

8. a national judiciary to be established;

9. republican government to be guaranteed by the United
States to each state;

10. provision for the amendment of the Articles of Union to
be made.

It is scarcely possible that anyone could be led to think that
the preliminary reference to the "Articles of Confederation"
meant that the remedy proposed in the succeeding clauses were
intended to preserve the existing principle of union.[4] For the

---

4. Note that, about midway in the Convention, when the principle of the
Virginia Plan had been substantially ceded, Dr. Hugh Williamson wrote
to James Iredell: "After much labor the Convention have nearly agreed on
the principle and outlines of a *system which we hope may be fairly called
an amendment of the Federal Government.*" (Quoted in Warren, p. 343; my
italics.) Either this reveals a puckish sense of humor, a disposition to understatement, or both. For taken at its face value, it would be tantamount to
saying that a revision of the U.S. Constitution, to substitute a parliamen-

entire thrust of the plan was to cure "the one great and radical vice of the Articles" by reversing the "principle of legislation for States in their corporate or collective capacity . . . as contradistinguished from the individuals of whom they consist." And if such an illusion was at all possible, then the effect of vesting a general power in Congress, together with a power to supplement and veto state legislation, put the central point of the plan beyond doubt. At this stage, in short, the Virginia Plan sought no less than to exchange the role of master and servant.

No single name was given to the "new" principle which inspired the Plan, for those who composed it were not greatly concerned with the business of lexicography. But in the early stages of the debate, the name that commended itself to the delegates more easily than any other was "national" or "general" government. And in this choice they were simply faithful to the verbal usages of the time; indeed, how else, when the terms "confederal" and "federal" were treated synonymously, and both represented the very "radical vice" of impotence they wished to exorcise?

Thus Gouverneur Morris, for example:

> explained the distinction between a *federal* and *national, supreme,* Government; the former being a mere compact resting on the good faith of the parties; the latter having a compleat and *compulsive* operation. He contended that in all Communities there must be one supreme power, and one only.[5]

---

tary for a presidential system of government, could also be fairly called an amendment!

5. Madison, p. 35. Note also Madison's subsequent explanation of the term "national" in a letter to Andrew Stevenson, 1826: "Will you pardon me for pointing out an error of fact into which you have fallen, as others have done, by supposing that the term *national* applied to the contemplated Government, in the early stage of the Convention . . . was equivalent to unlimited or consolidated. This was not the case. The term was used, not in contradistinction to a limited, but to a *federal* government. . . . There being no technical or appropriate denomination applicable to the new and unique System, the term national was used, with a confidence that it would not be taken in the wrong sense. . . ." (Farrand, Vol. III, p. 473.) On June 20th, in Convention, it was proposed and carried that the word "national" be dropped wherever used, and the words "of the United States" be substituted. On this change of name, also see Warren, pp. 147-148.

Or Mr. Read, who

> was against patching up the old federal System: he hoped the
> idea would be dismissed. It would be like putting new cloth on
> an old garment. The confederation was founded on temporary
> principles. It cannot last: it cannot be amended. If we do not
> establish a good government on new principles, we must either
> go to ruin, or have the work to do over again.[6]

Or Mr. Randolph:

> The true question is whether we shall adhere to the federal plan,
> or introduce the national plan. The insufficiency of the former
> has been fully displayed by the trial already made.[7]

Or Mr. Hamilton, "fully convinced, that no amendment of the
Confederation, leaving the States in possession of their Sovereignty could possibly answer the purpose,"[8] explained that

> A *federal* Government he conceived to mean an association of
> independent Communities into one. Different Confederacies
> have different powers, and exercise them in different ways. In
> some instances the powers are exercised over collective bodies; in
> others over individuals, as in the German Diet. . . . Great latitude
> therefore must be given to the signification of the term. The plan
> last proposed [the New Jersey Plan] departs itself from the
> *federal* idea, as understood by some, since it is to operate even-
> tually on individuals.[9]

In itself the concept of a national or general government
presented no difficulties. As men of politics, those who cham-
pioned the Virginia Plan as well as those who opposed it were,
at the very least, bound in a common understanding of the
language, the institutions, the practice, and the implications
of "government": law-making in a representative legislature,

6. Madison, p. 78.
7. *Ibid.*, p. 128.
8. *Ibid.*, p. 129.
9. *Ibid.*, p. 130. One of the proposals of the New Jersey Plan was that in the
   event that a state refused to comply with any Congressional tax requisition,
   Congress would be empowered to pass acts directing and authorizing the
   collection of the monies.

leadership and administration by the executive, the processes
of courts to rule on disputed issues of private and public
law, and direct contact with electorates. They were familiar
with these elementary symbols[10] of "real and regular" *government*, as they knew of the want of power in Congress to act, to
enforce, to coerce, and to manipulate electorates directly under
the Articles of Confederation. One was simply the obverse of
the other.

The great question where no known experience could guide
them, the classic question which never ceased to depress and
vex the opponents of the Virginia Plan, and indeed many more
after the Convention debate ended, was: How can two complete
governments live side by side without the greater dominating or
consuming the lesser? How indeed can there be two equal masters? Surely, "if the rod of Aaron do not swallow the rods of the
Magicians, the rods of the Magicians will swallow the rod of
Aaron." Committed as they were so early in the debate to the
gamble of a national government, but confronted by the unknown, they groped for analogues from public and private law,
from ancient and contemporary history, from the constitutional practice of other states—Britain, the continent, the colonies
—and from abstract principles; and some attempted to give precise answers where only speculative answers could be given. "If
it could be shown," said Dr. William Johnson, "that the States
would not suffer, their objections to the Virginia Plan would be
allayed." But how could anyone demonstrate this? How could
anyone quiet these apprehensions, especially when those who
tried to do so spoke in so many different voices? "The controversy must be endless," complained the same Dr. Johnson,
"whilst gentlemen differ in the grounds of their arguments."
Indeed, it was as if twenty or more real estate agents combined

10. Cecelia M. Kenyon (ed.), *The Antifederalists* (hereafter Kenyon), pp. xxiv-
    xxix, describing the principles of government which Americans, both Fed-
    eralists and Antifederalists, were agreed on. Also see the letter of William
    Steele to his son, Jonathan Steele, 1825. (Farrand, Vol. III, pp. 467-468).
    For a comparison of the U.S. Constitution, as it emerged from the Conven-
    tion, and the state constitutions, see the comments of Mr. Bowdoin in the
    Massachusetts ratification debates. (Elliot, Vol. II, pp. 127-128.)

to sell the one house, but extolled different virtues, and gave totally contradictory answers to the anxious questions of the prospective buyer.

Madison's Notes are illuminating, and nowhere more so than in the early stages of the debate on the question of "what would become of the States" in the Virginia Plan. Here is a sample of some revealing comments:

> Mr. Wilson observed that by a National Government he did not mean one that would swallow up the State Governments as seemed to be wished by some gentlemen. He was tenacious of the idea of preserving the latter. He thought, contrary to the opinion of Col. Hamilton, that they might not only subsist but subsist on friendly terms with the former. They were absolutely necessary for certain purposes which the former could not reach. All large governments must be subdivided into lesser jurisdiction. As examples he mentioned Persia, Rome, and particularly the divisions and subdivisions of England by Alfred.[11]
>
> Col. Hamilton. . . . He had not been understood yesterday. By an abolition of the States he meant that no boundary could be drawn between the National and State Legislatures; that the former must therefore have indefinite authority. If it were limited at all, the rivalship of the States would gradually subvert it. Even as Corporations the extent of some of them as Virginia, Massachusetts, etc., would be formidable. As *States*, he thought they ought to be abolished. But he admitted the necessity of leaving in them, subordinate jurisdictions. The examples of Persia and the Roman Empire, cited by Mr. Wilson, were he thought in favor of his doctrine: the great powers delegated to the Satraps and proconsuls, having frequently produced revolts, and schemes of independence.[12]

11. Madison, pp. 151-152. Cf. Ludolph Hugo's division of the supreme power.
12. Madison, p. 152. For some indication of the strength of feeling against the states, note the letter written by General Henry Knox (an advocate of a general consolidation of the states into one government) to Rufus King, a delegate from Massachusetts. "The State systems are the accursed things which will prevent our being a Nation . . . the vile State Governments are sources of pollution which will contaminate the American name, perhaps for ages —machines that must produce ill, but cannot produce good. Smite them, in the name of God and the people." (Quoted in Warren, p. 308.)

Dr. Johnson. On a comparison of the two plans which had been proposed from Virginia and New Jersey, it appeared that the peculiarity which characterized the latter was its being calculated to preserve the individuality of the States. The plan from Virginia did not profess to destroy this individuality altogether, but was charged with such a tendency. One gentleman alone (Col. Hamilton), in his animadversions on the plan of New Jersey, boldly and decisively contended for an abolition of the State Governments. Mr. Wilson and the gentlemen from Virginia, who also were adversaries of the plan of New Jersey, held a different language. They wished to leave the States in possession of a considerable, tho' a subordinate jurisdiction. They had not yet however shewn how this could consist with, or be secured against, the general sovereignty and jurisdiction, which they proposed to give to the national Government. If this could be shewn in such a manner as to satisfy the patrons of the New Jersey propositions, that the individuality of the States would not be endangered, many of their objections would no doubt be removed. If this could not be shewn their objections would have their full force. He wished it therefore to be well considered whether in case the States, as was proposed, should retain some portion of sovereignty at least. . . .[13]

Mr. Lansing. . . . The system was too novel and complex. No man could foresee what its operation will be either with respect to the General Government or the State Governments. One or other it had been surmised must absorb the whole.[14]

Mr. Wilson's respect for Dr. Johnson, added to the importance of the subject, led him to attempt, unprepared as he was, to solve the difficulty which had been started. It was asked how the General Government and the individuality of the particular States could be reconciled to each other; and how the latter could be secured against the former? Might it not, on the other side, be asked how the former was to be secured against the latter? It was generally admitted that a jealousy and rivalship would be felt between the General and particular Governments. . . . But taking the matter in a more general view, he saw no danger to the States from the General Government. . . . The General Government

13. Madison, p. 163.
14. *Ibid.*, pp. 156-157.

will be as ready to preserve the rights of the States as the latter are to preserve the rights of individuals. . . .[15]

Mr. Williamson thought that if any political truth could be grounded on mathematical demonstration, it was that if the States were equally sovereign now, and parted with equal proportions of sovereignty, that they would remain equally sovereign. He could not comprehend how the smaller States would be injured in the case, and wished some Gentleman would vouchsafe a solution of it.[16]

Mr. Madison (having scorned the weakness, and pointed to the failures of ancient and modern confederacies). . . . In a word; the two extremes before us are a perfect separation and a perfect incorporation, of the 13 States. In the first case they would be independent nations subject to no law, but the law of nations. In the last, they would be mere counties of one entire republic, subject to one common law. In the first case the smaller States would have everything to fear from the larger. In the last they would have nothing to fear. The true policy of the small States therefore lies in promoting those principles and that form of Government which will most approximate the States to the condition of counties.[17]

Mr. Madison agreed with Dr. Johnson, that the mixed nature of the Government ought to be kept in view; but thought too much stress was laid on the rank of the States as political societies. There was a gradation, he observed, from the smallest corporation, with the most limited powers, to the largest empire with the most perfect sovereignty.[18]

Mr. Gouverneur Morris. . . . "We must have an efficient Government and if there be an efficiency in the local Governments the former is impossible. Germany alone proves it. Notwithstanding their common diet, notwithstanding the great prerogatives of the Emperor as head of the Empire, and his vast resources as sovereign of his particular dominions, no union is maintained: foreign influence disturbs every internal operation, and there is no energy whatever in the general Government. Whence does this proceed? From the energy of the local authori-

15. *Ibid.*, pp. 163-164.
16. *Ibid.*, p. 204.
17. *Ibid.*, pp. 207-208.
18. *Ibid.*, p. 213.

ties; from its being considered of more consequence to support
the Prince of Hesse, than the Happiness of the people of Germany. Do Gentlemen wish this to be the case here? Good God,
Sir, is it possible they can so delude themselves?"[19]

How different the circumstances of these Founding Fathers
from all other federal Founding Fathers to come! From the very
outset, and almost to the very end of the Convention, the
attempt to explain the relationship of the national government
to the states, even by those most ready to compromise on almost
everything but the idea of a national government, was translated in the language and analogies of hierarchy: primacy/sub-
ordinacy, supremacy/inferiority, independence/dependence,
general power/limited power; the states in the union were to be
like "towns," "corporations," "counties," "local governments," "subordinate areas of jurisdiction" in the existing
states, or like "the divisions and subdivisions of England by
Alfred," or like the subdivisions of Persia and Rome. Rarely, if
at all, were they spoken of as "co-ordinate," or "co-equal," or
"co-sovereign" in status or authority. Indeed, the more erudite
champions of national government, like Madison and Hamilton, read the political history of the ancients and the moderns

---

19. *Ibid.*, pp. 255-256. It is interesting to note Gouverneur Morris' vindication
of his stand some 28 years later in a letter to a Mr. W. H. Wells, in 1815:
"Shortly after the Convention met, there was a serious discussion on the importance of arranging a national system of sufficient strength to operate, in
despite of State opposition, and yet not strong enough to break down State
authority. I delivered on that occasion this short speech. 'Mr. President; if
the rod of Aaron do not swallow the rods of the Magicians, the rods of the
Magicians will swallow the rod of Aaron.'
    "You will ask, perhaps, how, under such impressions, I could be an ad-
vocate of the Federal Constitution. To this I answer, first, that I was warmly
pressed by Hamilton to assist in writing the Federalist, which I declined.
Secondly, that nothing human can be perfect. Thirdly, that the obstacles to
a less imperfect system were insurmountable. Fourthly, that the Old Confederation was worse. And, fifthly, that there was no reason, at that time, to
suppose our public morals would be so soon and so entirely corrupted. . . .
[Morris was referring to the "overwhelming flood of Democracy"] . . . Sur-
rounded by difficulties, we did the best we could; leaving it with those who
should come after us to take counsel from experience, and exercise prudent-
ly the power of amendment, which we had provided." (Farrand, Vol. III,
p. 421.)

in much the same way as Bodin, Pufendorf, and Hugo. For them, historical wisdom supported a simple thesis: effective, strong, and coherent rule for a nation requires a national government; a national government is inconsistent with claims to equality by any other government within the nation; if equality is conceded, there can be no effective, strong, and coherent rule for the nation!

The course of the debate is in every way as revealing as the point of departure and the point of arrival, if we are seeking clues to the kind of "federalism" or the "principle" that was fathered in Philadelphia. It is evident from Madison's Notes that when the preliminary fanfares had been sounded, the major areas of agreement and disagreement had crystallized fairly plainly. The division of power, that is, the things Congress was to do, had been settled in principle if not in detail.[20] Except for the Virginia proposal to invest Congress with the unqualified power to negative or supplement state legislation, little divided the two plans on this front.[21] The existing areas of jurisdiction itemized in the Articles of Confederation provided the nucleus for both plans. Indeed, it would have been remarkably perverse, given the brief that brought the Convention together, if anyone had argued that the functions of the national government should be fewer in scope and number than those of the existing Congress.

What a government is given to do, however, is only as significant as its means to act effectively as a government. This the delegates were well aware of; for after all, the whole point of the invitation to Philadelphia was not to cure the want of jurisdiction, but the want of power to act within any jurisdiction. For example:

20. See Warren, pp. 388-389, for a derivation of the "powers" vested in Congress in the first draft of the Constitution as it was prepared by the Committee of Detail.

21. Madison to Van Buren, May 13, 1828: "The *threatening contest*, in the Convention of 1787, did not, as you supposed, turn on the degree of power to be granted to the Federal Government: but on the rule by which the States should be represented and vote in the Government. . . . The contests and compromises, turning on the grants of power, tho' very important in some instances, were Knots of a less 'Gordian' character."

Mr. Gerry thought it would be proper to proceed to enumerate and define the powers to be vested in the General Government before a question . . . should be taken, as to the rule of representation in the second branch.[22]

Mr. Madison observed that it would be impossible to say what powers could be safely and properly vested in the Government before it was known, in what manner the States were to be represented in it. He was apprehensive that if a just representation were not the basis of the Government it would happen, as it did when the Articles of Confederation were depending, that every effectual prerogative would be withdrawn or withheld, and the New Government would be rendered as impotent and as short-lived as the old.[23]

Mr. Gouverneur Morris moved to reconsider the whole Resolution agreed to yesterday concerning the constitution of the two branches of the Legislature. His object was to bring the House to a consideration in the abstract of the powers necessary to be vested in the general Government. It had been said, "Let us know how the Government is to be modelled, and then we can determine what powers can be properly given to it." He thought the most eligible course was, first to determine on the necessary powers, and then so to modify the Government as that it might be justly and properly enabled to administer them. He feared if we proceeded to a consideration of the powers, whilst the vote of yesterday including an equality of the States in the second branch, remained in force, a reference to it, either mental or expressed, would mix itself with the merits of every question concerning the powers.[24]

In a word, the integral relationship between structure, power, and action was always before their eyes.[25] And, expectedly,

22. Madison, p. 254.
23. *Ibid.*
24. *Ibid.*, p. 302.
25. Madison to Sedgwick, 1831: "The two subjects, the structure of the Government and the question of power entrusted to it, were more or less inseparable in the minds of all as depending a good deal, the one on the other, after the compromise which gave the small States an equality in one branch of the Legislature, and the large States an inequality in the other branch. . . ." (Farrand, Vol. III, p. 496.) On the same question, see Madison's comments in the Virginia ratification debate. (Elliot, Vol. III, pp. 259-260.)

therefore, the struggle centered on the design and the organization of the national government: on the principles of representation in the two branches of Congress, a persistent and critical issue; on the power, tenure, and relations of the two branches; on the nature and manner of composing the executive; on the power of the executive; on the control of elections; on the nature and appointment of the judiciary; and so on. And as the various interests—the interests of trade and of agriculture, of large states, small states, Northern states, Southern states—generally took their direction from the orientation of the two plans, so there were two dominant stratagems. For the champions of the Virginia Plan: to establish direct links with a national electorate; to minimize the presence of the states qua states in the framework of the national government; to retain some general supervisory power over the states (e.g., veto); and to express the powers of Congress in the broadest possible way. For the other: to maximize the presence of the states in every corner of the structure, composition, and election of the national government; to deny the national government any supervisory rights; and to limit and specify the heads of Congressional power in the tightest possible terms.

At least three-quarters, if not more, of the time in Philadelphia was preoccupied with the design of the national government, and less than a quarter of the time with what the national government was to do. A brief selection of the motions proposed in the sequence of the debate gives some insight into the course of "federal" constitution-making in Philadelphia.[26] From Madison's Notes:

May 31st, 1787: "that the National Legislature should be elected by the State Legislatures, not by the people."

Lost.

"that the first branch of the National Legislature be elected by the people."

26. For easy reference to the voting record on the various motions proposed in the Convention, see A. T. Prescott, *Drafting the Federal Constitution.*

Won. (6 in favor; 2 "no"; 2 divided.)

"that the second branch ought to be chosen by the first branch out of persons nominated by the State Legislatures."

(The clause was disagreed to and a chasm left in this part of the plan.)

"that the National Legislature should have power in all cases to which the State Legislatures were individually incompetent, or in which the harmony of the United States may be interrupted by the exercise of individual Legislation; to negative all laws passed by the several States, contravening in the opinion of the National Legislature the articles of Union. . . ."

Won. (9/1 on the first part; *nem. con.* on the power to negative.)

June 2nd: "that the Executive should be removable by the National Legislature at the request of a majority of the State Legislatures."

Lost. (9/1.)

"that the first branch be elected by the State Legislatures."

Lost. (8/3.)

June 7th: "that the Senate should be appointed by the State Legislatures."

Won. (*nem. con.*)

June 8th: On a reconsideration of the clause giving the National Legislature a negative on such laws of the States as might be contrary to the Articles of Union . . . Mr. Pinkney moved, "that the National Legislature should have authority to negative all laws which they should judge to be improper."

       Lost. (7/3; one divided.)[27]

     "that the National Executive should be elected
by the Executives of the States by the same proportion of votes as allowed to the States in the
election of the Senate."

       Lost. (9 "no"; one divid-
ed.)

June 21st: (Resubmitted) "that the first branch should be
elected in such manner as each State Legislature directs instead of being elected by the
people."

       Lost. (6/4.)

June 22nd: "that the State representatives in the first
branch be paid by the States, not out of the National Treasury."

       Lost. (5 "yes," 4 "no," 2
divided.)

     "that payment of members of the Senate be left
to the States."

       Lost. (5/6.)

July 2nd: "that each State to be allowed one vote in the
second branch."

       Lost. (by equal division of
votes.)

July 16th: (Resubmitted by a committee elected to find a
compromise) "that in the second branch of the
Legislature of the U.S., each State shall have
an equal vote."

       Won. (5 "yes," 4 "no,"
one divided.)

     "that the National Legislature ought to pos-
sess the Legislative Rights vested in Congress
by the Confederation."

       Won. (*nem. con.*)

27. For an explanation of the *unanimous* vote early in the Convention to em-
power the "National Legislature" to veto state laws, and its reversal a
month later, see Warren, pp. 165-171 and 317-324.

(Immediately after equal State representation in the Senate had been affirmed by a slender majority) "that Congress should be able to legislate in all cases for the general interests of the Union, and also in those to which the States are separately incompetent, or in which the harmony of the United States may be interrupted by the exercise of individual Legislation.

> *Won.* (6/4. The power to legislate in those cases where the States are "separately incompetent" was dropped at a later stage.)

"that the National Legislature be given the power to negative all laws passed by the States which in its opinion contravene the articles of Union, or any treaty subsisting under the authority of the Union."

> *Lost.* (7/3, reversing the previous vote.)

"that the National Executive be chosen by the National Legislature."

> *Won.* (*nem. con.*)

(This was resubmitted and amended on several subsequent occasions.)

July 18th: "that the judges of the National Judiciary should be appointed by the second branch of the National Legislature."

> Not voted on, motion changed to:

"that the judges of the National Judiciary be appointed by the Executive instead of the second branch."

> *Lost.* (5/2; one absent.)

"that judges be nominated and appointed by the Executive by and with the advice and consent of the second branch."

                                    Lost. (4/4; one absent. La-
                                    ter submitted and won.)

August 6th: (Resubmitted) "that members of each House
               shall receive a compensation for their services
               to be ascertained and paid by the State, in
               which they shall be chosen."

                                    Lost. (9/2.)

August 9th: "that the time and place and manner of hold-
               ing the elections of the members of each House
               shall be prescribed by the Legislature of each
               State, but their provisions concerning them
               may at any time be altered by the Legislature of
               the United States."

               Motion put to strike out the overriding power
               of Congress:

                                    Lost.

Sept. 12th: "that a Committee be appointed to prepare a
               Bill of Rights."

                                    Lost. (10/0; one absent.)[28]

It was a process of advocacy, rebuttal, concession, trucking,
bargaining, wheedling, and threatening, and it continued for
almost four months, when, on the last day but one, the order
was given to engross the Constitution. Words, phrases, sentences, figures, and fractions were subjected to an unremitting
scrutiny. Time and again issues won by one side on one day
were resubmitted for a second, third, fourth, and indeed a fifth
round of debate on another day. "Every article," wrote one delegate, "is again argued over, with as much earnestness and obstinacy as before it was committed." Indeed, at a moment of
impasse, when the Convention came close to disaster on the
issue of equal state representation in the Senate, and the chairman almost despaired "of seeing a favorable issue to the proceedings," he called on prayer to guide the delegates. But more

28. For an explanation of this surprising, albeit *unanimous* rejection and the
    reinstatement of the debate on a Bill of Rights by the Antifederalists as a
    major cause in the ratification debates, see A. T. Mason, *The States Rights
    Debate* (hereafter Mason), pp. 74-86; also Warren, pp. 507-510.

decisive than the bravura of scholarship and the appeals to providence were the intimations of hard political practice. "Experience," said Mr. Dickenson, "must be our only guide. Reason may mislead us."[29] And at every point of the Convention, experience made it plain that without mutual concessions, without give and take, there would be no national government of any kind, and just conceivably, no Union.

The engrossed Constitution read on the last day of the Convention, September 17th, 1787, was in every sense, therefore, a "bundle of compromises," "a mosaic of second choices"[30] on almost everything except the establishment of a national/ general government. It was less than some had wished, and more than others had wanted to yield. To one view or another, there were both desirable and "odious" features.[31] But how else, remarked Dr. Franklin, at the close of the Convention:

> For when you assemble a number of men to have the advantage of their joint wisdom, you inevitably assemble with those men, all their prejudices, their passions, their errors of opinion, their local interests, and their selfish views.[32]

Indeed, the Constitution could be no other than the product of necessity, circumstance, and the imperatives of compromise. As Madison wrote later:

> Would it be wonderful if, under the pressure of all these difficulties, the convention should have been forced into some deviations from that artificial structure and regular symmetry which an abstract view of the subject might lead an ingenious theorist

29. Madison, p. 447.
30. Charles and Mary Beard, *Rise of American Civilization*, quoted in Warren, p. 733.
31. John Jay, "Address to the People of the State of New York, On the Subject of the Proposed Federal Constitution," 1788: "Let it be admitted that this plan, like everything else devised by man, has its imperfections. That it does not please everybody, is certain; and there is little reason to expect one that will. . . . They tell us, very honestly, that this plan is the result of accommodation. They do not hold it up as the best of all possible ones, but only as the best which they could unite in and agree to. . . ." (Elliot, Vol. I, pp.498-499.) Note also Mason, p. 52.
32. Madison, p. 653.

to bestow on a Constitution planned in his closet or in his imagination?[33]

The key question, however, is: Precisely what sort of compromise, what sort of principles, were writ into this Constitutional mix? Clinton Rossiter, for example, spoke of the agreement to compose the House of Representatives on the principle of state population and the Senate on the basis of equal state representation as the "grand" 50-50 compromise between the confederate principles of the Articles of Confederation and the nationalist principles of the Virginia Plan.[34] If so, what arithmetic metaphors should one employ to describe the long list of other compromises concluded by the bargainers? Indeed, what precise mix of "confederal" and "nationalist" principles would have resulted if, for example, the states had been divided into three classes, and representation in the Senate (as it was suggested at one stage) were scaled between one to three members? Or what if they had agreed on a Senate to be chosen by the House of Representatives from a list of persons nominated by the state legislatures, or indeed, a Senate composed partly by states and partly proportional representation? Or what if the Executive had been made removable by Congress at the request of a majority of the state legislatures? Or what if Congress had been left with the power to negative state legislation? Or, instead of a general power of veto, what if Congress had been given a power to legislate in all cases where, in its view, the states were "individually incompetent" to act? Or what if a supreme national judiciary, elected from a panel of state chief justices, had been associated with the Executive in exercising revisionary power over Congressional legislation? Or what, indeed, if the matter of the judicial arbitrament of national/state conflict had been specifically raised and rejected in favor of some political form of reconciliation? Presumably by assigning specific arithmetic proportions of "confederality" and "nationality" to each and every item of the final constitution, one could

33. The Federalist, No. 37.
34. Rossiter, 1787—The Grand Convention, p. 191.

persuade an artistically gifted computer to draw a profile of the first-born "federal" constitution of the United States.

What the Founding Fathers in 1787 had wrought, however, was both obvious and not obvious, unambiguous and ambiguous.[35] Obviously, they had created a national government which, like any ordinary government, would operate on individuals; they had equipped it with a bicameral legislature on the parallel principles of popular and state representation, a single presidential executive, and a judiciary; they had "separated" these governing powers on the principle that "separation" would restrain the tyranny latent in all human government; they had empowered the national government to act in a broadly defined jurisdiction, declared the supremacy of its laws, and explicitly denied certain powers to the states; they had confirmed the political role of the states not by any positive or general declaration but simply by interposing their presence throughout the machinery of the national government; they had obligated the national government to protect the states against invasion and domestic violence; they had guaranteed them republican government; and they had embodied all this in a Constitution which was to be fundamental law, binding on all and alterable only by a procedure which partnered the national government with the states.

However, if much of what the Founding Fathers achieved in Philadelphia was obvious, there was also much that was not obvious. It was far from obvious, for example, how in this dual system of government, and in the knowledge of their interdependence, the two governments, national and state, were to relate to each other; it was not obvious what principles of conduct were to govern their actions; it was not obvious what was the precise reach of the Congressional powers; it was not obvious how far the states would be allowed to pursue the accustomed tenor of their ways; it was not obvious what would transpire if the two governments came into conflict; and it was not obvious what monies the states could rely on if national claims on public resources took priority over state claims. In-

35. Mason, p. 55.

deed, in the light of these and a host of other uncertainties in a constitution built of shorthand abstractions, well might the three authors of the Federalist Papers (Hamilton, Madison, and Jay) feel that a "Case for Ratification" was imperative. And this precisely was their aim—to pacify the mounting fears of experimentation (fears which were not wholly implausible),[36] to dispel uncertainty wherever it could be dispelled, and if it could not be dispelled by reason or experience, to justify it in the name of a more perfect union.

Thus, on the question of "what was to be the fate of the States," Hamilton was at a loss to know how people could reasonably fear the designs of a national government. "All apprehensions on the score of usurpation ought to be discarded." If anything, the national government was more threatened than the states. The general powers of the new government were limited; commerce, finance, negotiation, and war seemed to comprehend all the objects necessary for the "national depositary," and those matters left to the states could "never be desirable cases of a general jurisdiction." (*O mores, O tempora!*) The original constitutions of the states had invested them with complete sovereignty, and "in all the unenumerated cases the States would be left in the enjoyment of their *inviolable sovereignty* and independent jurisdiction." As for those areas where the sovereign power was divided, the states would continue to enjoy coordinate authority with the national government. And to those who argued that the *co-ordinate* or *co-equal* authority was an impossible chimera, Hamilton gave the answer that "the fact and reality of history," particularly the dual operation of the *Comitia Centuriata* and *Comitia Tributa* in Rome, offered ample example of coordinate authority.[37]

36. In the light of history, the anxieties voiced in the Convention and the ratification debates were not all "phantoms" of paranoic minds. Note in Kenyon, pp. lxii-lxxiv, "Abuses of Power Predicted Under Various Clauses in the Constitution." Also see Warren, p. 760; and Elliot, Vol. III, pp. 441-442, where Mr. Mason, in the Virginia ratification debate, discusses the generality of the welfare and the tax powers.

37. The Federalist, No. 34. Hamilton was referring to the co-existence of the two legislatures in the Roman Republic, the *Comitia Tributa* and the *Co-*

To those who questioned the possibility of "marking the proper lines of partition between the authority of the general and that of the State government," Madison gave the answer by explaining the normality of this difficulty in all human affairs.

> Every man will be sensible of this difficulty, in proportion as he has been accustomed to contemplate and discriminate objects extensive and complicated in their nature. The faculties of the mind itself have never yet been distinguished and defined, with satisfactory precision, by all the efforts of the most acute and metaphysical philosophers. . . . The most sagacious and laborious naturalists have never yet succeeded in tracing with certainty the line which separates the district of vegetable life from the neighbouring region of unorganized matter, or which marks the termination of the former and the commencement of the animal empire. . . . When we pass from the works of nature . . . to the institutions of man . . . we must perceive the necessity of moderating still further our expectations and hopes from the efforts of human sagacity. Experience has instructed us that no skill in the science of government has yet been able to discriminate and define, with sufficient certainty, its three great provinces—the legislative, executive, and judiciary. . . . Questions daily occur in the course of practice, which prove the obscurity which reigns in these subjects, and which puzzle the greatest adepts in political science.[38]

And as to the fragility of words—"the medium through which the conceptions of men are conveyed to each other"—and the uncertainty they must engender in those who commit their political hopes to paper, Madison went on to say:

> . . . no language is so copious as to supply words and phrases for every complex idea, or so correct as not to include many equivocally denoting different ideas. Hence it must happen that

---

mitia Centuriata, which had the power to annul each other's acts. The plebeian interest was dominant in the first, the patrician in the second. It is interesting to note Calhoun's later use of precisely this illustration of coordinate power, though for a very different purpose. See William H. Bennett, *American Theories of Federalism*, p. 143.

38. The Federalist, No. 37.

however accurately objects may be discriminated in themselves, and however accurately the discrimination may be considered, the definition of them may be rendered inaccurate by the inaccuracy of the terms in which it is delivered. And this unavoidable inaccuracy must be greater or less, according to the complexity and novelty of the objects defined.

. . . Here, then, are three sources of vague and incorrect definitions: indistinctness of the object, imperfection of the organ of conception, inadequateness of the vehicle of ideas. . . . The convention, in delineating the boundary between the Federal and State jurisdictions, must have experienced the full effect of them all.[39]

As for the "most important of the authorities proposed to be conferred upon the Union," the unabridged power to tax, a power that like several others (e.g., the supremacy clause) had become the target of "virulent invective and petulant declamation," Hamilton composed the rebuttal. He first acknowledged the "justness of the reasoning which requires that the individual States should possess an independent and uncontrollable authority to raise their own revenues for the supply of their own wants."

And making this concession, I affirm that (with the sole exception of duties on imports and exports) they would, under the plan of the Convention, retain that authority in the most absolute and unqualified sense; and that an attempt on the part of the national government to abridge them in the exercise of it, would be a violent assumption of power, unwarranted by any article or clause of its Constitution.[40]

Then, having affirmed what he could scarcely avoid without disaster to his cause, he turned to the core of the problem that no federal system to come has been able to avoid or cure: Who shall command the purse? If the power to tax is "manifestly a concurrent and co-equal authority in the United States and in the individual States," what of conflict? If the supremacy clause gave the national government the first bite of the loaf, what

39. *Ibid.*
40. *Ibid.*, No. 32.

assurance could be given to the states that there would be more than crumbs left over for their needs? Again without compromising the cause of strong national government, or making light of the supremacy clause, Hamilton gave the only possible diplomatic reply. He confessed that the "particular policy of the national and of the State systems of finance might now and then not exactly coincide, and might require reciprocal forbearance. . . ." For example, in the event that "an improper accumulation of taxes on the same object rendered the collection difficult or precarious," the mutual interest of the two governments would obviously dictate a concert of action. In all cases, however, the answer lay in restraint, and faith in the people of the United States. It was hard to predict the future; the nature and the extent of powers were set out in the constitution, and beyond this

> Everything . . . must be left to the prudence and firmness of the people; who, as they will hold the scales in their own hands, it is to be hoped, will always take care to preserve the *constitutional equilibrium* between the general and the State governments.[41]

Undeniably superb polemicists! Brilliant constitutional advocates! But their work of eighty-five papers is not an academic disquisition so much as a remarkably orchestrated *livre de circonstance*, an unmistakable tract of ex parte advocacy. And, of course, tracts are not expected to speak in the voice of impartial commissions of inquiry, to give full weight to all views, or to subdue the author's bias.[42] The medium was indeed the message. And the message of the first twenty-two papers was crystal clear: If you wish to restore the public faith and credit; revive commerce, agriculture, industry, and the arts; if you wish to escape the fate that befell the Grecian leagues, and all the European confederacies which sought union but distrusted strong union; if you wish to do away with the same manifest weaknesses of your own system, vote YES for ratification. "A

41. *Ibid.*, No. 31. (My italics.)
42. A. T. Mason and R. H. Leach, *In Quest of Freedom*, p. 145. See also W. W. Crosskey, *Politics and the Constitution*, Vol. I, pp. 8-9.

nation without a national government," wrote Hamilton in the
last paragraph of the last paper, "is, in my view, an awful
spectacle." And if the Federalists had composed an election pla-
card to bear their message throughout the cities and towns of
America, it could have been:

A vote for ratification is a vote for a free people's national
government.

A vote for national government is a vote for security, pros-
perity, and liberty.

Almost all of the remaining sixty-three papers are explanation,
justification, rationalization, reassurance, and exhortation.

As campaign pamphleteers and propagandists, however, they
were given to most of the sins of partisan advocates—exaggera-
tion of virtues, understatement of problems, inconsistency, ambiguity, obfuscation, illogicality, and misquotation. Why
indeed should one believe that their concern was anything
other than to sell the first and basic idea of the Virginia Plan, a
supreme national government, and the rest but a masterful mix
of constitutional reality, gloss, and fantasy. Certainly the conversion of the two most formidable exponents of the Virginia
Plan to the language of *co-ordinate*, *co-equal*, and *co-sovereign*
in the Federalist Papers was suspect, when only several months
earlier, both before and during the Convention, they had spoken of the States as "subordinate" bodies, compared them to
counties and local authorities, and even more significantly
continued to speak of them in the very same papers as "municipal establishments" and "subordinate governments."[43] Their
contempt for the "sovereign" pretensions of these "municipal
establishments" was barely concealed.

43. For example, The Federalist, Nos. 14 and 46. See also Madison's letter to
   Washington (he wrote a similar letter to Randolph) prior to the Convention, in which he set out his views on the question of drawing a line between the nation and the states. Referred to as Madison's "middle ground,"
   its nature is apparent in the following: "Conceiving that an individual independence of the states is utterly irreconcilable with their aggregate
   sovereignty, and that a consolidation of the whole into one simple republic
   would be as inexpedient as it is unattainable, I have sought for a *middle
   ground*, which may at once support a due supremacy of the national autho-
   ity, and not exclude the *local authorities whenever they can be subordi-
   nately useful.*" (Quoted in Rossiter, *1787*, p. 126; my italics.)

Was, then, the American Revolution effected, was the American Confederacy formed, was the precious blood of thousands spilt, and the hard-earned substance of millions lavished, not that the people of America should enjoy peace, liberty, and safety, but that the government of the individual States, that particular municipal establishments, might enjoy a certain extent of power and be arrayed with certain dignities and attributes of sovereignty?[44]

Were these slips of the tongue, or their true understanding of what the compromise at Philadelphia was about?

Indeed, why should anyone want to put complete trust in their learning when they chose to illustrate the possibility of coordinate authority between governments by the false analogy of the veto relations between the two Roman legislatures, the *Comitia Centuriata* and *Comitia Tributa*? Why should their reading and repeated deprecation of Greek, Roman, German, Dutch, and Swiss experience of association be taken seriously, when there was enough reason to think that they read and quoted history not only to suit their cause, but at times to demonstrate diametrically opposite lessons? Witness, for example, Hamilton's call on the Abbé de Mably's authority to support his own view of what one must do to cure conflicts between neighbouring states:

An intelligent writer expresses himself on this subject to this effect: "NEIGHBOURING NATIONS [says he] are naturally enemies of each other, unless their common weakness forces them to league in a CONFEDERATIVE REPUBLIC, and their constitution prevents the differences that neighbourhood occasions, extinguishing that secret jealousy which disposes all states to aggrandize themselves at the expense of their neighbours."

From this statement by the Abbé, Hamilton had concluded that

This passage, at the same time, points out the EVIL and suggests the REMEDY.[45]

44. The Federalist, No. 45. (My italics.)
45. The Federalist, No. 6; the extract is taken from the Abbé de Mably's *Principes des Negociations*.

However, while the Abbé de Mably had certainly spoken of the great evil of neighbours in conflict, the remedy he had proposed was not the remedy of national government, but the remedy of confederacy, the like of which Hamilton and Madison had scorned throughout the Convention and the Papers.

Even more strikingly, witness Hamilton's manipulation of Montesquieu's *The Spirit of the Laws*. In an early paper (No. 9), immediately after he had accused his opponents of adapting and perverting Montesquieu for their own ends, Hamilton, in order to correct their views, cited a lengthy passage from that work with the justification that

> I have thought it proper to quote at length these interesting passages, because they contain a luminous abridgment of the principal arguments in favor of the Union, and must effectually remove the false impressions which a misapplication of other parts of the world was calculated to produce. They have, at the same time, an intimate connection with the more immediate design of this paper, which is to illustrate the tendency of the Union to repress domestic faction and insurrection.

Yet in rebutting his opponents, Hamilton found it pardonable to resort to the polemicist's crudest dodge of omitting three paragraphs from the passage in *The Spirit of the Laws* where Montesquieu, like the Abbé de Mably, praised the very examples of association (Greece, Rome, Holland, Germany, and the Swiss cantons) which Hamilton and Madison used to illustrate the "evils" of the Articles of Confederation. Thus, in speaking of the manner whereby "Republics provide for their safety," Montesquieu had written of the confederate republic as

> . . . a kind of constitution that has all the internal advantages of a republican, together with the external force of a monarchical government. I mean a confederate republic, [a form of government] by which several petty states agree to become members of a larger one . . . a kind of assemblage of societies, that constitute a new one, capable of increasing by means of farther associations, till they arrive to such a degree of power, as to be able to provide for the security of the whole body.

This Hamilton had quoted faithfully, but he omitted the important illustrative passage which followed. For what Montesquieu had immediately gone on to say was:

> It was these associations that so long contributed to the prosperity of Greece. By these the Romans attacked the whole globe; and by these alone the whole globe withstood them. For, when Rome was arrived to her highest pitch of grandeur, it was the associations beyond the Danube and the Rhine, associations formed by the terror of her arms, that enabled the barbarians to resist her. From hence it proceeds that Holland [the State of the United-Provinces composed of about fifty different republics], Germany, and the Swiss Cantons, are considered in Europe as perpetual republics.[46]

So one may go on to evidence the mind and style of partisan, albeit highly enlightened, advocates. But if we set aside the propaganda, the special pleading, the dialectical license and elaborate conjectures, to ask "What system, what model, or what principle of government was born in Philadelphia in 1787?" the answer will doubtless vary with the time perspective of the beholder. The simplest answer two hundred years later, in the terms of twentieth-century linguistic usage, is "federal" system, "federal" model, and "federal" principle. And if currently asked to define the term "federal," one may pull out almost any and every one of the going definitions, calling on such concepts as "the division of power," "coordinate and independent" status, or any of the more finely tuned contemporary embellishments of "coordinate and interdependent" or "coordinate and cooperative." But the answer in 1787, or indeed at almost any time prior to the American Civil War, was even less clear, and certainly more controversial, than it is now.

What precisely was "federal"? The entire scheme and content of the United States Constitution, every principle which informed every clause, every article, every procedure, and every device? Obviously not; certainly not the principle of a constitution limiting and superintending the activity of government;

46. Montesquieu, *The Spirit of the Laws*, Chap. 1, pp. 165-167.

certainly not the principle, structure, and powers of the presidential form of executive; nor indeed the principle of separating the powers of the three organs of state action, the legislature, the executive, and the judiciary; certainly not the principle of direct and representative democracy; certainly not the principle of national legislative supremacy; and certainly not the principle of reposing the liberties of the citizen in a Bill of Rights.[47] But what of the "Great Compromise" giving all states, large and small, *equal representation in the Senate*? Or what of the considerable powers given to the Senate, or indeed of a second chamber at all? Plainly, without agreement on the principle of representation, the convention would have been aborted, as most likely it would have been aborted if the fervid nationalists had insisted on a supervisory legislative power (veto, etc.) for the national government. But to point to those institutions, powers, procedures, and devices fashioned by compromise—and which, in the absence of compromise, may have either aborted the Convention or yielded another form of compromise and hence another constitution—is not to identify the indispensable "federal" elements of the United States Constitution. If our practice (as indeed the practice of every nation in the past hundred and fifty years, at least) is to treat the United States Constitution as the very quintessence of federalism, how did the Founding Fathers identify the principle and the form of the Constitution? Did they believe that the principle embodied in the Constitution simply differed from all other previous confederacies by the *mode* in which a national government of "few

47. That the Federalists were concerned with political "liberty" is unquestionable. It is part of what Wright calls "the assumed spirit of '76." It is not so clear, however, that "liberty," rather than effective national government, was at the forefront of their minds in the course of drafting the Constitution —unless one equates the two. Note, for example, Mr. Wilson's comment in the Pennsylvania ratification debate: "I cannot say, Mr. President, what were the reasons of every member of that Convention for not adding a bill of rights. I believe the truth is, that such an idea never entered the mind of many of them. I do not recollect to have heard the subject mentioned till within about three days of the time of our rising; and even then there was no direct motion offered for any thing of the kind." (Elliot, Vol. II, p. 435.) On this question see also Wright's introduction to The Federalist, pp. 15-25; and G. Dietze, *The Federalist*.

and defined" powers operated on individuals, like any ordinary
government—"not like the power of the old Confederation
operating on States"? Or did they identify the principle more
widely than this?

Conceivably Madison's own description of the Philadelphia
mix is a likely pointer to the profile of the Constitution which
others may have drawn. Thus, if we read "confederal" for
"federal" in the following passage, for example, we obtain a
vision of a constitutional patchwork quilt in which two dominant colours, "national" and "federal," and a third, an indefin-
able and varying mix of these two, are distributed by the
accident of compromise rather than design.

> The proposed Constitution, therefore, is, in strictness, neither
> a national nor a federal Constitution, but a composition of both.
> In its foundation it is federal, not national; in the sources from
> which the ordinary powers of the government are drawn, it is
> partly federal and partly national; in the operation of these
> powers, it is national, not federal; in the extent of them, again, it
> is federal, not national; and, finally, in the authoritative mode of
> introducing amendments, it is neither wholly federal nor wholly
> national.[48]

And of course this scheme "so full of irregularities in its
intricate structure and form" was not Madison's first choice.[49]
The Virginia Plan which was closer to his heart's desire would
have reduced the "federal" (confederal) features of the mix even
more drastically. Likewise the acceptance of any one of the

48. The Federalist, No. 39. Also note Madison to Henry Lee, 1824: "What a
    metamorphosis would be produced in the code of law if all its ancient
    phraseology were to be taken in its modern sense! And that the language of
    our Constitution is already undergoing interpretations unknown to its
    founders will, I believe, appear to all unbiased inquirers into the history of
    its origin and adoption." (Farrand, Vol. III, p. 464.)
49. See his letter to Philip Mazzei, October 1788: "You ask me why I agreed to
    the Constitution proposed by the Convention of Philadelphia. I answer,
    because I thought it safe to the liberties of the people, and the best that
    could be obtained from the jarring interests of States and the miscellaneous
    opinions of politicians; and because experience has proved that the real
    danger to America and to liberty lies in the defect of energy and stability in
    the present establishment of the United States." (Warren, p. 741, n. 1.)

great number of alternative proposals touching the structure and powers of the national government would have altered the design of the whole, delicately or drastically. And unfortunately, we shall probably never know what Madison had in mind when he spoke of that "artificial structure and regular symmetry which an abstract view of the subject might lead an ingenious theorist to bestow on a Constitution planned in his closet or in his imagination." He could hardly be referring to his own or indeed Hamilton's private thoughts on the model of government they would have first chosen if they had been free to choose!

Whatever Madison's own characterization, however, what of the other founders? If they had been asked the question "What form of government, or what new principle do you think you have fathered?" what answer would they have given? Doubtless they would have agreed on the very obvious elements in the Constitution. But if, instead of simply describing the contents of the new document, the delegates were pressed to characterize the principle governing the relations of the national and state governments, or to name the principle they had consented to, or to spell out the implications of the changes they had wrought in the Articles of Confederation, is it at all conceivable that with such an evident diversity of interests and beliefs they would have given the same answer?

It is important to note that there was no agreed language to describe the new situation. Next to the familiar terms of "sovereign, free, and independent," the Federalists and others had begun to speak of the relations of the national and state government in the new terms of "co-ordinate," "co-equal," "co-existing," "co-extensive," and "co-sovereign" within their own domain. And the imagery they projected, intentionally or not, had a formal and persuasive simplicity. To be coordinate was to be of equal standing; the national and the state governments were "co-ordinate" or "co-equal" in status because both were equally subject to the Constitution, not each other; as "co-ordinate" governments neither could command, direct, control, dictate, compel, or regulate the other; the relationship of equal status was different from any previous relationship, different from the Articles of Confederation, and different from the relationship of Westminster to the counties of England. Indeed, what better evidence of the desire to ensure equal status than the denial of a veto power to the national government?

But language operates within a grid of knowledge, a framework of usage, expectations, interest, time, and space. The delegates could easily conjure with the imagery, the facts, and the fictions of parliamentary sovereignty—they had merely to refer to the experience they knew best, their own, or to the constitutional system they knew second best, Westminster. And for some, doubtless these were the idylls of constitutionalism they preferred to cling to. But what in fact did the delegates understand by the new language of "co-ordinate" status,[50] what kind of political relations did it imply? What precise imagery did an "inviolable" but less than omnicompetent "divided sovereignty" convey to them? If Madison was clear about what had been done, or what was to be the operative principle of the new relations, there is nothing in his Notes of the Convention to suggest that either his or Hamilton's understanding or vision

50. See, for example, Mr. Tredwell, in the New York ratification debate: "The idea of two distinct sovereigns in the same country, separately possessed of sovereign and supreme power, in the same matters at the same time, is as supreme an absurdity, as that two distinct separate circles can be bounded exactly by the same circumference." (Elliot, Vol. II, p. 403.) Or Mr. Grayson continuing the Antifederalist arguments in the Virginia ratification debate: "Is it not a political absurdity to suppose that there can be two concurrent legislatures, each possessing the supreme power of direct taxation? If two powers come in contact, must not the one prevail over the other? Must it not strike everyman's mind, that two unlimited, coequal, coordinate authorities, over the same objects, cannot exist together?" (Elliot, Vol. III, p. 284.)

And per contra, note Hamilton again on the taxing power in the New York debate: "The meaning of the maxim, there cannot be two supremes, is simply this—two powers cannot be supreme over each other. This meaning is entirely perverted by the gentleman. But it is said, disputes between collectors are to be referred to the federal courts. This is again wandering in the field of conjecture. But suppose the fact certain; is it not to be presumed that they will express the true meaning of the Constitution and the laws? Will they not be bound to consider the concurrent jurisdiction; to declare that both the taxes shall have equal operation; that both the powers, in that respect, are sovereign and coextensive? If they transgress their duty, we are to hope that they will be punished." (Elliot, Vol. II, p. 356.)

was shared by everyone else, certainly not by those who refused to sign the Constitution, and certainly not by those who led the Antifederalist campaign against its ratification.[51] Indeed, Luther Martin, a Maryland delegate, must have voiced the uncertainty of many more than the committed anti-nationalists when he interjected, "the language of the States being *sovereign* and *independent* was once familiar and understood; though it seemed now so strange and obscure."[52]

The Founders and their heirs, however, were destined to live with the "strange and obscure" for many decades yet. For not only does this sense of uncertainty pervade the Convention, it is evidenced repeatedly in the ratification debate in the state legislatures, and again when the national government took the first steps to act as a government in its own right. Indeed, were it possible to carry out a contents analysis of the questions asked, the doubts expressed, and the answers given during the ratification debate, or if one could compose a systematic inventory of what new institutions, mechanisms, procedures, or powers could be taken as "certain" and "uncertain" (or "unambiguous" and "ambiguous"), one would be entitled to conclude that

---

51. If Madison was persuaded that the Constitution had not created a consolidated system of government (the "unio" of Bodin and Althusius), the Antifederalists were equally clear and persuaded of the opposite. Thus, for example, Tredwell, in the ratification debate in New York: "We are told that this is a federal government . . . it is, in my idea, as complete a consolidation as the government of this state, in which legislative powers, to a certain extent, are exercised by the several towns and corporations." (Elliot, Vol. II, pp. 402-403.) Or Patrick Henry: "We are told that this government, collectively taken, is without an example; that it is national in this part, and federal in that part, etc. We may be amused, if we please, by the treatise of political anatomy. In the brain it is national; the stamina are federal; some limbs are federal, others national. The senators are voted for by the state legislatures; so far it is federal. Individuals choose the members of the first branch; here it is national. It is federal in conferring general powers, but national in retaining them. It is not to be supported by the states; the pockets of individuals are to be searched for its maintenance. What signifies it to me that you have the most curious anatomical description of it in its creation? To all the common purposes of legislation, it is a great consolidation of government." (Elliot, Vol. III, p. 171.) Also see Luther Martin's reply to the Landholder in Farrand, Vol. III, p. 292.

52. Madison, p. 217.

the division between the protagonists of the Constitution (the Federalists) and their opponents (the Antifederalists) was not between those who understood more and those who understood less about the new constitution, or between those who had greater prescience than others, or those who feared for the states and those who did not, but rather, in Cecelia Kenyon's expressive thesis, between those who had "faith" in the unknown, and those with "little faith."[53]

Fundamentally, it was only the hour of decision and the momentum that had changed between the closing of the Convention and the beginning of the debate in the states. Otherwise, the ratification campaign was, in so many ways, a public repeat performance of Philadelphia. The issues were essentially the same as the dominant and minor issues in Philadelphia, except for the late surge of concern for a Bill of Rights. The arguments were essentially the same, neither transfigured by new insights nor enlarged by new information; the ancient and contemporary historic examples were the same; the optimistic and pessimistic auguries were the same; and the leading voices of the Convention either led again, or were heard among the leaders. Only now the whole debate was replayed on a greater stage, in a greater variety of keys, a far greater variety of arrangements, and often in language and tones far more dramatic, more strident, and more choleric than in Philadelphia.[54]

Time had given all participants the opportunity to refresh themselves with the issues and the arguments, and public confrontation provided the compulsive incentive to sharpen their differences. But in the very nature of the problem, neither time nor debate could dispel the logical ambiguities strewn throughout the document, nor could it dispel the puzzles, doubts, fears, and misgivings. Indeed, what decisive "once-and-for-all-time" arguments could the Federalists mount to give Madison's characterization of the Constitution greater conviction than, say,

53. Cecelia M. Kenyon, "Men of Little Faith: The Anti-Federalists on the Nature of Representative Government."
54. For a brief representation of the arguments in the ratification debates, see either Mason, *The States Rights Debate*, or Kenyon (ed.), *The Antifederalists*.

Patrick Henry's anatomic parody of it, especially when its "nature" is still in issue today?[55] Or, by what decisive means could the Federalists have proved that in the presence of an unlimited federal power to tax, and the overriding supremacy of its legislation, the states could always expect to find enough in the taxpayer's larder for their own needs? How could a call for faith in the forbearance of Congress, or faith in the people, or faith in Hamilton's ex parte jurisprudence, dissolve the logical force of the Antifederalist argument? Or again, what "checkmate" arguments could the Federalists use to convince the men of "little faith" that the limited powers vested in Congress were not limitless, when the Constitution was cast in language of almost "studied ambiguity," when its terms expressed collective compromises rather than private intentions, and when almost any national action could be accommodated within its loose folds? Or, in the light of the received constitutional learning and experience, what irresistible arguments could the Federalists, or anyone, use to convince the Antifederalists that the idea of "two coordinate sovereigns" was not a political absurdity, though there had been "nothing quite like it before in the history of man"?

The ratification debate achieved the Federalists' goal—the adoption of the Constitution—and the settlement of the question: Was there to be a national government or not? But it settled little else; certainly not the question how two masters could or should live together; nor the question what their precise powers were to be; nor how the frontier between them was to be drawn. One could hardly infer, for example, that the ratification of the Constitution, substantial though it was,[56] involved the acceptance of any clear operational rule for either the

---

55. See Mason, Chap. 4, "Must We Continue the States Rights Debate?" Also the valuable symposium, The Federal Polity, edited by Daniel J. Elazar.
56. Andrew C. McLaughlin, "Social Compact and Constitutional Construction": "No one who has studied the primary material will be ready to assert that men consistently and invariably acted upon a single principle, that they were altogether conscious of the nature and import of what was being done, and that they constantly spoke with logical accuracy of the process." (Warren, pp. 733-734, n. 2.)

national or state governments, any more than the acceptance of
any complex referendum implies the acceptance of any single
item in it.[57] On the contrary, of those who entertained fears—
that the "states could become tributaries to a consolidated fab-
ric of aristocratic tyranny"—many remained fearful; and of
those who harbored misgivings—that a "consolidated system"
or a "many-headed monster" of undefined and undefinable
powers had been created by a "total alteration" of the confederal form—many were left with their misgivings; the puzzles remained, and the unknown remained unknown.[58] In the circumstances, it could not be otherwise; for the only kind of "proof"
that could be given to either the Federalists or the Antifederalists was the proof of action.

And the early years of action, when the miniscule national
government took its first steps, again speak of the dilemmas of
uncertain powers, uncertain principles, and uncertain relations.[59] Thus, for example, it would have been reasonable to
assume that the acceptance of a constitution which invested the
national government with exclusive powers in a number of specific matters, or the acceptance of a clause giving supreme and
binding effect to the Constitution, had altered the standing of
the states fundamentally.[60] Yet there were some who presumed
that as signatories to the act of constituting a national government, the states had become parties to a compact which gave
each one the right to judge whether its interests (as a state) had
been violated by Congress; to exercise, in consequence, virtually
all the normal prerogatives of a contracting party; to declare
Congressional legislation null and void; and to oppose the will
of the national government in every possible manner short of
open rebellion—though even this limitation was not always
clear and certain, as time was to prove.

57. The voting in favor of ratification was: Pennsylvania, 46-23; Delaware, 30-
    0; New Jersey, 38-0; Georgia, 26-0; Connecticut, 128-40; Massachusetts, 187-
    168; Maryland, 63-11; South Carolina, 149-73; New Hampshire, 57-47;
    Virginia, 89-79; New York, 30-27; North Carolina, 184-84. Rhode Island
    refused to call a Convention, but joined the Union later.
58. Mason and Leach, *In Quest of Freedom*, pp. 137-146.
59. C. B. Swisher, *American Constitutional Development*, p. 86.
60. Mason, p. 52.

Witness, for example, the language of the Virginia and Kentucky resolutions (1798, 1799), prepared in their original drafts by no less than Madison and Jefferson, protesting against the excessive and oppressive use of federal power. The proprietorial tone of the state objections to the controversial national sedition laws is more redolent of the confederal era than the early voices with which Madison and others had urged a strong and independent national government on the electors. Thus, in the Virginian assembly:

> That this Assembly . . . declare, that it views the powers of the federal government as resulting from the compact to which the states are parties . . . and that, in case of a deliberate, palpable, and dangerous exercise of other powers, not granted by the . . . compact, the states . . . have the right, and are in duty bound, to interpose, for arresting the progress of the evil. . . .[61]

The Kentucky resolutions of 1798 and 1799 were an even more forthright assertion of the states' rights to decide the constitutionality of a Congressional action:

> . . . that this [the national] government, created by this compact, was not made the exclusive or final judge of the extent of the powers delegated to itself . . . but that, as in all other cases of compact among parties having no common judge, *each party has an equal right to judge for itself, as well of infractions as of the mode and measure of redress.*

Again, for example, it might have appeared that the judicial arbitration of any conflict between the national and state governments, and particularly the obvious arbitral role of the national judiciary, would be implied in the judiciary clauses of the Constitution. Yet witness the Supreme Court of the State of Pennsylvania in 1798:

> In such a case [petition for transfer from the state Supreme Court to a federal circuit court], the Constitution of the United States is federal; it is a league or treaty, made by the individual states, as

---

61. Elliot, Vol. IV, pp. 528-529 and 540-545; also see Madison's report on the Virginia Resolutions, *ibid.*, pp. 546-580.

one party, and all the states, as another party. When two nations differ about the meaning of any clause, sentence, or word in a treaty, neither has an exclusive right to decide it; they endeavour to adjust the matter by negotiation, but if it cannot be thus accomplished, each has a right to retain its own interpretation, until a reference be had to the mediation of other nations, an arbitration, or the fate of war.[62]

Or again, witness, some ten years later, the resolution of the Massachusetts Legislature in rejecting what it believed to be an illegal tariff imposed by Congress in 1813, though it had declined to support the Virginia Resolution fifteen years earlier.

We spurn the idea that the free, sovereign and independent State of Massachusetts is reduced to a mere municipal corporation, without power to protect its people, and to defend them from oppression, from whatever quarter it comes. Whenever the national compact is violated and the citizens of this state are oppressed by cruel and unauthorized laws, this legislature is bound to interpose its power, and wrest from the oppressor its victim. This is the spirit of our union, and thus has it been explained by the very man [presumably President Madison] who now sets at defiance all the principles of his early political life.[63]

A new power game had clearly begun, only the players had found new ways of gaming. Thus for some it became tactically necessary to argue that "sovereignty" had been divided between the national and the state governments; for others, with different interests, it became equally necessary to argue that the notion of "divided sovereignty" was a conceptual absurdity that must not be used to undermine the authority of the national government. Witness therefore the renewal of the maddening casuistries of "sovereignty" through which the new politics and the new jurisprudence took over from the old. For example: (a) both the national and state governments were sovereign; (b) neither the national nor the state governments was sovereign, for sovereignty reposed in the Constitution and the people of

62. Bennett, *American Theories of Federalism*, p. 104.
63. *Ibid.*, p. 103.

the United States; (c) both the national and state governments were sovereign, but the national government, by virtue of its supreme responsibility to protect the states against invasion and domestic violence, possessed a superior standing to the states; (d) the states had never been sovereign, and did not acquire sovereignty under the Constitution; (e) the states were sovereign prior to the Constitution, and they retained their sovereignty, albeit limited, under the Constitution, etc., etc.

If we now repeat our early question—What did the Founding Fathers believe they had conceived in Philadelphia?—then one may conclude that only the principle of *duality* articulated in a single constitutional system of two distinct governments, national and state, each acting in its own right, each acting directly on individuals, and each qualified master of a limited domain of action, stands out as the clearest fact.[64] And if one can speak of a consensus on first principles, then on this principle alone was there evident consensus and cause for celebration.[65] All else was controversial presumption, inference and supposition. Indeed, there is nothing to indicate that the fifty-five delegates to Philadelphia would have agreed, either during or after the convention, in characterizing, naming or spelling out the aims, ideals or implications of the new relations; and, if they had agreed to name the principle in such terms as "co-ordinate" or "co-sovereign and independent" status, it is doubt-

64. Madison to Thomas Cooper, some forty years after the Convention: "With respect to the term 'national' as contradistinguished from the term 'federal,' it was not meant to express the *extent* of power, *but the mode of its operation,* which was to be not like the power of the old Confederation operating on *States;* but like that of ordinary Governments operating on individuals. . . ." (Farrand, Vol. III, pp. 474-475; the italics are Madison's.) Also see Martin Diamond's important essay, "The Federalist's View of Federalism." Cecelia Kenyon has argued that the Antifederalists failed to grasp the principles of the new federalism, but this is no less true for the bulk of the Federalists, who spoke of the "subordinate" role of the states and yet referred to them from time to time as "coordinate" and "independent." (Kenyon, p. xlii.)

65. See letter published in the *Packet*: "The year 1776 is celebrated . . . for a revolution in favour of liberty. The year 1787, it is expected will be celebrated with equal joy for a revolution in favour of Government." (Warren, pp. 631-632.)

ful whether they would have translated the language in the same way. For whatever the logic of "co-ordinate" status, the jurisprudence of "divided sovereignty", or the "plain sense" of the Constitution, the ingrained habits of speech and behaviour, the familiarity of their "confederal" practices, and the different ways in which the particular interests attuned themselves to the uncertain perspectives dominated their understanding and fed the ambiguity of the new situation.

In truth, the Constitution of the United States had grafted two centers of authority into a union of unfamiliar and unpredictable relations. And like the conciliatory medieval formula of *regnum et sacerdotium* which acknowledged the two distinct but equal powers of Pope and Holy Roman Emperor in their separate realms, the language of "co-ordinate" or "co-equal" status in 1787 was no more than a formal symbol of political accommodation. Indeed, it could only be this. It did not express the true political hopes of everyone in the Convention, or after. It was not familiar in the glossary of constitutional terms; it was not called into service by the constitutional draftsmen in 1787; and no subsequent Constitution has ever chosen to use the term. As a guide to practice, it was of little or no value; it could never house, direct, educate, or arbitrate the infinite variety of relations which develop in a system of dual government. Only a political disquisition, setting out the guidelines of the conduct appropriate to the relations of coordinate governments, could attempt to do this. And the Convention was not in the business of articulating a complete ideology of co-existence. From time to time the Federalist Papers may have counselled the ethic of forbearance, cooperation, and mutual regard; and from disappointment, Calhoun, Gallatin, and many others may have been called by later necessity to propose the kind of relations they believed were implied in the act of union. But the Convention of 1787 and the ratification debates knew only one immediate and practical necessity: to take what steps they could to improve the evident deficiencies of the political system embodied in the Articles of Confederation.

To have attempted to append a manual of political conduct

appropriate to the new Constitution would have involved the
delegates in discoursing and agreeing on many things: how, for
example, the two governments should regard each other in the
exercise of their powers, whether they should act in total isolation from each other, or join together, whenever possible, in
carrying out their activities; on the nature of the duty of care
they owed each other, if any; on the nature of injury, pressure,
coercion, influence, and manipulation; they would have had to
prescribe what political stratagems could be used or not used in
relation to each other; they wo··ld have had to comment on the
use of financial resources, political groups, and powerful individuals to circumvent, extend, amend, reduce, frustrate, deflect,
or diminish the policies of the national government by the
states, the states by the national government, and states by
states; they would have had to propose the kinds of activity
which maintain and those which destroy the "balance" or
"equilibrium" of the Constitution; and much more. But not
only would this enterprise have been a labor of Sisyphus, not
only would such a manual have to be written differently for
each set of political presumptions about the meaning of "co-
ordinate," "co-equal," "independent," and "sovereign" status,
not only would it produce the generalities of ideology which
make poor guides to action, but like Canute it would have attempted the impossible political task of prescribing and pro-
scribing political conduct for a society not given to political
prescription.

And after all, there were no complete political innocents at
the Convention.[66] All of them, the very brightest luminaries of
American public affairs—"those who were capable of giving
ingenious explanations to such as they wished to have adopted," and "those who could assign ingenious reasons for opposite constructions of the same clause"—as well as those less

66. "Americans were as familiar with back-room politics as with the principles
    of natural law. . . . In the course of the ratification debate, one can find
    evidence of reason and riot, patriotism and propaganda, the most exquisite-
    ly sophisticated politics of the cloakroom side by side with the crudest
    politics of the mob in the street." (Kenyon, p. xxiii.)

gifted, must have been aware of the play of politics, and equally aware that the political contests of influential men and powerful interests, as much as law, would breathe meaning into the form they had created, and continue to renew its meaning through time. They must have sensed from their knowledge of men and their nature that no words, however precise, could give them ultimate guarantees or refuge; and that to attempt to draw a line between national and state powers was to wring concessions from the present, not from the future.[67] But as uncertain as the players were about the new principles, or how the new politics and the new system would be played, who would win and who would lose, they knew the ground rules, and doubtless had some confidence in their ability to play a new variation on an old game.

Late in the Convention, a Mr. Mercer remarked:

> It is a great mistake to suppose that the paper we are to propose will govern the United States. It is the men whom it will bring into the government and interest in maintaining it that is to govern them. The paper will only mark out the mode and the form. Men are the substance and must do the business.[68]

The truth is sometimes simple. However, men are their beliefs, and whether these are grounded in fact or fiction, they define the reality of men, and are real in their consequences. The men of 1787 had created an instrument of national government, but in doing so they had opened Pandora's box and released concepts as capable of generating profoundly different beliefs as the historic concepts of liberty and freedom. Not only did the expected conflicts between the national and state governments find an ideological foothold in the phrases of "coordinate and independent," "co-equal and independent," or

---

67. Mason, p. 73. Also Gouverneur Morris, in a letter to Timothy Pickering some twenty-five years later: "But, after all, what does it signify that men should have a written constitution, containing unequivocal provisions and limitations? The legislative lion will not be entangled in the meshes of a logical net. The legislature will always make the power which it wishes to exercise. . . ." (Elliot, Vol. I, p. 507.)

68. Madison, pp. 455-456.

"co-sovereign" status, but these same phrases became the vehicles through which the broadest political values were brought to issue in the guise of contending theories of federalism.

One brief coda to 1787: How novel, how unique was the work of the men of Philadelphia? Did they truly fashion a political system so new that it wanted a name, a social compact set on principles never before attempted on earth?[69] The Federalists themselves are curiously ambivalent, sometimes speaking with the exultant voice of Cortez, and sometimes in subdued tones. At the Convention, and indeed after in one of the very early Federalist Papers, Madison, for example, consistently asserted the novelty of the principle which had brought two proper governments to rule the nation where previously there were many. "The compound government of the United States is without a model, and to be explained by itself, not by similitude or analogies." Yet, whether from the prudential belief that electors were more prone to appeals of continuity than experimentation with the unknown, the advocate's voice changes:

> The truth is, that the great principles of the Constitution proposed by the Convention may be considered less as absolutely new, than as the expansion of principles which are found in the articles of Confederation. The misfortune under the latter system has been, that these principles are so feeble and confined as to justify all the charges of inefficiency which have been urged against it, and to require a degree of enlargement which gives to the new system the aspect of an entire transformation of the old.[70]

If we set their perceptions aside, however, to focus our own eyes on the lens, it is readily apparent that the question of novelty, originality, discovery, and invention in the history of ideas and political systems is an epistemological minefield that we enter at our peril. Of course, various claims have been made at different times on behalf of various inventors of "federal-

69. J. H. Robinson, "The Original and Derived Features of the Constitution"; also Gilbert Chinard, "Polybius and the American Constitution."
70. The Federalist, No. 40; contrast No. 14 and No. 40.

ism"; for example, Brie for Hugo, Mogi for Grotius, Friedrich
for Althusius, and Freeman for the Greeks. And obviously the
matter is tied to *what* we are looking for, *where* we are looking,
how we are looking, and by what means we test the truth of our
discoveries. Thus, for example, if it were possible to strip the
1787 Constitution of all its particular prenatal circumstances,
and all the ex post facto theory projected by the Federalists, we
are left with only the mechanical design of a dual territorial
system of rule under the guarantee of a popularly ratified constitution to present to the Registrar of Patents. And even then
we could only hope to succeed if we could persuade him to
brush aside the prior claims of the Hellenic systems.

The likeliest answer, especially in the light of the preceding
history, is *ex nihilo nihil fit*, nothing can emerge from nothing,
rather than *creatio ex nihilo*. All political systems are derivative, but some are more derivative than others.[71] However, if all
ideas and systems are derivative, if the Federalists can neither
claim originality for the ideas of "dual government," "co-
ordinate" power, "divided sovereignty," or perhaps even the
idea of imbedding a system of dual government in a written
constitution, then the manner in which all these components
were mingled and articled in the U.S. Constitution was quin-
tessentially an American mix—as American indeed as American cherry pie. It was not wholly like nor unlike anything
before, during, or after. Its form was not destined by any genetic
inevitability. It emerged; an evolutionary accident, as it were,
brought into being out of the historical experience of all those
who, from whatever motives, from whatever beliefs, for what-

71. J. N. Figgis, *Political Thought from Gerson to Grotius*, p. 1. Also Martin
Landau, *Political Theory and Political Science*, p. 39; and Sir Karl Popper,
Objective Knowledge: An Evolutionary Approach, pp. 142-150. For two of
many contrasting views regarding the "novelty" of the Constitution, note
Robert L. Schuyler, *The Constitution of the United States* (p. 6): "The
Constitution is not to be regarded as in any true sense an original creative
act of the Convention at Philadelphia, which framed it." And per contra, E.
S. Corwin, "The Progress of Constitutional Theory Between the Declaration of Independence and the Meeting of the Philadelphia Convention," p.
511. See also The Federalist, pp. 41-42.

ever purpose, or in whatever form, had ever sought the benefits of association without surrendering their identity as individuals.

5

Federalism, Mk. II, III, IV, V . . . n

Or, variations, permutations, and combinations
on a theme from Philadelphia

Whatever considerations govern the award of "firsts" in the history of ideas, there are two pragmatic tests that seem to arbitrate the issue for our time—repute and imitation. For the plain fact is that to all those who have been engaged in federal constitution-making since 1787, it is the United States model which enjoys the reputation of being "first"—not the Achaean League, the Germanic Empire, or Switzerland. Whatever other models they have been drawn to later, or whatever innovations they have fabricated themselves, it is the U.S. model which defines the conceptual starting-point of their enterprise.

This model may be read differently from place to place, and from time to time, often according to the contemporary reading of American history, American society, and American practice. The face of the post-Civil War, nineteenth-century-federal-American model that the Canadians (1867), Germans (1871), Swiss (1874), and Australians (1901) looked to for guidance, and the 1976 "crazy-quilt" pattern of intergovernmental relations that a constitutional designer would see before him in America now, could scarcely be the same. But what is *minimally* understood in the trade by the U.S. model is simply this: that the business of state is "divided"[1] between two popularly elected governments, a national government embracing the whole ter-

---

1. See the discussion of what is implied by a "division of power" in my article "The Federal Principle Reconsidered." Part II is reprinted in Aaron Wildavsky, *American Federalism in Perspective*, pp. 3-33.

ritory of the nation and a "regional" government for each of the lesser territories; that each government will possess the basic facilities to make, manage, and enforce its laws "like any ordinary government"; that subject to the provisions of the constitution, each government is "free" to act "independently" of, or in concert with, the other, as it chooses; that jurisdictional disputes between the national government and the governments of the lesser territories will be settled by judicial arbitration; that the principle of national supremacy will prevail where two valid actions, national and regional, are in conflict; that the instruments of national government, but not necessarily the lesser territories, are set forth in a written constitution; that the national legislature is a bicameral system in which one house, the "first branch," is composed according to the size of population in each territory, while each territory has equal representation in the "second branch"; lastly, that the constitution is fundamental law, changeable only by a special plebiscitary process.

But a model is a model, a pattern, a paradigm, a dummy, a mock-up, a formal abstraction, a frame, a conceptual artifact, a nonliving thing, a simplification of complex and elusive reality. To become a living thing it must be invested with a history, a political culture, personality, circumstance, and will. This is the first and most neglected lesson for all would-be students of federalism. And to grasp this lesson is to confront the second and equally neglected lesson: the immense and dynamic variety of these living elements, and the idiosyncratic manner in which they manifest themselves in the structure and changing practice of each "federal" system. Thus, it should surprise no one that if the U.S. Constitution is the Mk. 1 federal model, it is also in many of its features the sole product of the Mk. 1 model. For as "all men don't build their house just according to that model which the rules of architecture prescribe," so no federal constitutional system (acknowledged, purported, or problematically "federal") has been built, or indeed could be built, in the mirror image of the U.S. model. No system, for example, has come to the federating act from precisely the same needs, the same motives, for the same reasons, or in the same circumstances; no system has adopted its precise "division" of legislative power or its language; no system has designed its legislative and executive authority in the same way; no system has woven the states into the structure of the national government in the same way; no system has adopted the schema of its Constitution; no system has incorporated the same set of prohibitions to protect the national government from the states, and the states from the national government; no system has worked in the same way; and not only does each system vary from the Mk. 1 model, but no two later models are exactly alike. In a word, each system has adapted the U.S. model of its time, precisely as the United States composed its constitution—in response to its own imperatives of necessity and circumstance.[2]

All this is easily demonstrable. But how does this affect the matter? After all, if not all are perfectly alike, neither are they wholly unlike, though, to be sure, some are more like the parent model than others. Further, their likeness is more than the simple resemblance that ties the world of all political institutions together. Theirs is the special likeness, it is said, which comes from having adopted the basic 1787 model, albeit with modifications, and the likeness of keeping sufficient faith with its credo of "co-ordinate and independent" political quthority to set them apart from all other political systems. The eternal Linnaean question, however, is: How close or how distant is the consanguineous relationship within the so-called family of

2. See Charles Pinckney's speech in the Convention: "The people of this country are not only very different from the inhabitants of any State we are acquainted with in the modern world; but I assert that their situation is distinct from either the people of Greece or Rome, or of any State we are acquainted with among the ancients. Can the orders introduced by the institution of Solon, can they be found in the United States? Can the military habits and manners of Sparta be resembled to our habits and manners? Are the distinctions of Patrician and Plebeian known among us? Can the Helvetic or Belgic confederacies, or can the unwieldy, unmeaning body called the Germanic Empire, can they be said to possess either the same or a situation like ours? I apprehend not. They are perfectly different, in their distinctions of rank, their Constitutions, their manners and their policy." (Madison, pp. 181-187, esp. 185.) Note also Warren, pp. 239-240.

"federal" systems? How significant is the general and how significant the particular? Is the resemblance significant enough to mount a multistoried descriptive, explanatory, and predictive theory, as some would claim, a one-story theory, or no theory at all, only history? The implications of this for the scope and future of the subject are quite crucial. And we can better illustrate the problems by examining two matters: the reasons for federation, and the "division" and practice of "divided" power.

THE REASONS FOR FEDERATION

On the face of it, it seems scarcely conceivable that all parties that join in federal union (or for that matter in any kind of political association) come together at all times and in all places for the same reasons, wanting the same things, in the same proportions, or indeed that the texture and the intensity of the desires within any one group of people who come together at one time, in the one place, should be the same.[3] And one may well conclude from history that the reasons which move communities to federate are finely woven into the specific historical experience of each community, and the experiences of each community are its reasons. Indeed, to extract universal reasons is, as Tolstoy remarked, to conclude that human life is always guided by reasons.

> Why then did these things happen thus, and not otherwise?
> Simply because they did so happen.

There are other views, however, and I propose to look at two contemporary examples of attempts to answer the question: Why do people choose to unite in the federal form in preference to any other? I will take two works, W. H. Riker's *Federalism: Origin, Operation, Significance*, and R. L. Watts' *New Federations: Experiments in the Commonwealth*. I have chosen these

---

3. Cf. Martin Diamond, "The Ends of Federalism." Diamond argues that federalism can only be understood "by the ends men seek to make it serve. At various times, men have sought varying ends from federalism, and the variety of federal systems has resulted from that variety of ends. . . ."

two not because they represent the "comparative" method, but because they present two different hypotheses and two different styles of analysis. Riker characterizes what may be called the quasi-scientific style of the "behavioural movement," aspiring to transcend the "unique" historical and cultural setting of each federal experience to establish "tested and testable" generalizations; while Watts' study stands in direct succession to the traditional historically oriented comparative study (e.g., Wheare) in quest of some "significant patterns" rather than "testable" scientific conclusions.[4]

Riker's argument is this: Federalism is "a bargain between prospective national leaders and officials of constituent governments for the purpose of aggregating territory, the better to lay taxes and raise armies." And the parties are predisposed to favor this kind of bargain by "the existence of at least two circumstances" which he names: the expansion condition, and the military condition. He describes them in the following way:

1. *The expansion condition*: The politicians who offer the bargain desire to expand their territorial control, usually either to meet an external military or diplomatic threat or to prepare for military or diplomatic aggression and aggrandisement. But, though they desire to expand, they are not able to do so by conquest, because of either military incapacity or ideological distaste. Hence, if they are to satisfy the desire to expand, they must offer concessions to the rulers of constituent units, which is the essence of the federal bargain. The predisposition for those who offer the bargain is, then, that federalism is the only feasible means to accomplish a desired expansion without the use of force.

2. *The military condition*: The politicians who accept the bargain, giving up some independence for the sake of union, are willing to do so because of some external military-diplomatic threat or opportunity. Either they desire protection from an external threat or they desire to participate in the potential aggression of the federation. And furthermore the desire for either protection or participation outweighs any desire they may have

4. W. H. Riker, *Federalism: Origin, Operation, Significance*; and R. L. Watts, *New Federations: Experiments in the Commonwealth*.

for independence. The predisposition is the cognizance of the
pressing need for the military strength or diplomatic maneuver-
ability that comes with a larger and presumably stronger government. (*It is not, of course, necessary that their assessment of
the military-diplomatic circumstances be objectively correct.*)[5]

These two conditions, Riker asserts, "are *always* present in the
federal bargain, and each one is a *necessary* [and he suggests
both are probably sufficient] condition for the creation of a
federalism." As proof of, what he calls, "the more modest hypothesis of necessity":

> ... I have examined *all* the instances of the creation of a federal-
> ism since 1786 [27; 18 in existence and 9 failed], giving most
> detailed attention to the invention of centralized federalism in
> the United States. (More exactly, I have examined all the in-
> stances I have been able to discover. It is quite possible, however,
> that I have overlooked some obscure instances.) For those feder-
> alisms which have survived, I am able to show that the two
> conditions existed at the origin; and, for those which failed, I am
> able to show that either the conditions never existed or they
> existed only momentarily. *Though such evidence does not con-
> stitute absolute proof of the hypothesis, it comes as close to a
> proof as a non-experimental science can offer.*[6]

His concluding sentence at the end of the chapter "The
Origin and Purposes of Federalism" typifies Riker's lab-science
mode of reporting his findings throughout the work. "On the
basis of the evidence here set forth [that is, in his thirty-page
summary of the origins of the twenty-seven federations], we
may conclude that the hypothesis is confirmed that the military
and expansion conditions are *necessary to the occurrence of
federalism.*"[7] And prefacing the brief review of the federal experience in the former British colonial territories of Canada, Australia, India, Pakistan, Malaysia, Nigeria, and the "unsuccess-
ful British federations" ("British colonial officials as a group
never understood federalism") of New Zealand, the British West
Indies, and Rhodesia and Nyasaland, is the comment:

5. Riker, pp. 12-13. (My italics.)
6. *Ibid.*, p. 13.
7. *Ibid.*, p. 48. (My italics.)

As the following survey demonstrates, federalism in former British colonial territories has occurred in *precisely* the fashion set forth in the hypothesis at the beginning of this chapter.[8]

One need only note Riker's dismissal of "two widely asserted fallacies about the origin of federalism," viz.: the "crude ideological fallacy" that federal forms are "adopted as a device to guarantee freedom" and the "more impressive *reductionist* fallacy" (typified in the work of Deutsch and his collaborators, who produced a list of nine "essential conditions for an amalgamated security-community of which class the class of federalisms is a sub-class") that "federalism is a response to certain social conditions that create some sense of a common interest."[9]

We shall return to Riker a little later, but let us first note Watts' view of the originating forces. Watts examines the six new federal experiments (India, Pakistan, Malaya and Malaysia, Nigeria, Rhodesia and Nyasaland, and the West Indies) launched in the post-1945 phase of the British decolonization policy. He observes that the distinguishing characteristic of the new, as indeed with the old federations, was the "existence, at one and the same time, of a desire to be united under a single general government for certain purposes and to be organized under independent regional governments for others." With this difference only—that "the ambivalence between the motives for union and the motives for autonomy" was more complex in these six new societies than in the older federations. Watts then proceeds to a detailed study of the factors involved in the new alchemy.[10] Among the social factors and motives which have

8. *Ibid.*, p. 26. (My italics.)
9. *Ibid.*, pp. 15-16. My italics. Riker cites Deutsch et al., *Political Community and the North Atlantic Area.* His critique of Deutsch's "nine essential conditions" is "that it attempts to reduce the explanation of the political phenomenon of joining together to an explanation of the social and economic condition of the population. In bypassing the political, in bypassing the act of bargaining itself, it leaves out the crucial condition of the predisposition to make the bargain." This is a strange complaint in the light of Riker's own procedure.
10. I have abstracted these "factors" from Watts, *New Federations*, Chap. 3, "Motives for Union," and Chap. 4, "Motives for Regional Autonomy," pp. 41-92.

been relevant in most of the new federations, he claims, have been:

1. the desire for political independence;
2. the hope of economic advantage;
3. the need for administrative efficiency;
4. enhancing the conduct of external relations, both diplomatic and military;
5. a community of outlook based on race, religion, language, or culture;
6. geographical factors;
7. the influence of history;
8. similarities and differences in colonial and indigenous political and social institutions;
9. the character of political leadership;
10. the existence of successful older models of federal union; and
11. the influence of the United Kingdom government in constitution-making.

Each of these factors is potentially centripetal or centrifugal, unifying or separating; in no two cases has their importance been the same, but "most of them have been present to at least some degree in each" of the six new cases. To particularize the formative circumstances in these cases, here is a summary of the major unifying and separating factors culled from Watts' account.

India: *Unifying motives*:
                 The potent forces for unity were:
                 Nehru's dynamic leadership;
                 the force of a common nationalism;
                 the desire for economic planning;
                 historical interdependence;
                 common religion and basic culture;
                 strategic considerations following partition;
                 geographical compulsion in the princely states.
                 Separating motives:
                 vastness of territory and population;
                 the historic and institutional differences of the prince-
                     ly states;
                 the deep roots of linguistic regionalism.

Pakistan: *Unifying motives:*
The most important motives by far were:
the influence of Islam;
the intense fear of a Hindu Raj;
Jinnah's leadership;
and to a lesser degree, common inherited British traditions.
Separating motives:
similar cultural and historical differences at work as
in India; and
the crucial separation of East and West Pakistan.

Malaya: *Unifying motives:*
Unity was primarily due to British insistence, for stra-
tegic, administrative, and economic reasons;
Malayan nationalism and the desire to protect their
communal position;
and later, the demand for "merdeka" (independence)
cemented an intercommunal Alliance.
Separating motives:
fears of racial domination;
religious, linguistic, and economic differences.

Nigeria: *Unifying motives:*
Economic interdependence was the decisive factor in
preserving Nigerian unity in 1953-4;
other influential factors were:
the compromises necessary to achieve independence;
the effect of common British rule;
and the continued British insistence upon unity.
Separating motives:
Overwhelming size of the North, and superior modernization of the South;
the deep cultural and institutional contrasts between
the three dominant national groups.

West Indies: *Unifying motives:*
The forces for unity were relatively weaker, but the
major motives were:
the desire for political independence and the hope of
economic advantage.
Separating motives:
Geographic separation of the islands;

distinct history and traditions of the islands;
contrasts in wealth and development between the
islands.

Rhodesia and
Nyasaland: *Unifying motives*:
White settlers wanted amalgamation but accepted federation:
to gain freedom from British control, and to protect
   their position in the face of rising African consciousness.
The British Government came to accept federation:
for its economic benefits to settlers and Africans as a
   means of establishing an experiment in racial partnership; and
to forestall a seizure of power by white settlers.
Separating motives:
Need to allay African fears of white domination;
the North Rhodesian fear of Southern Rhodesian
   domination.

Watts concludes from all this that varied as the dominant
motives were in each case,

> two features stand out as common to them all. *First,* there was a
> geographical distribution, at least to some degree, of the diversi-
> ties within each of these societies, with the result that demands
> for political autonomy were made on a regional basis. *Secondly,*
> in each of the recent federations, as in the older ones, *there
> existed at one and the same time powerful desires to be united for
> certain purposes,* because of a community of outlook or the
> expectation of common benefits from union, *and deep-rooted
> desires to be organized under autonomous regional governments
> for others,* because of contrasting ways of life or the desire to
> protect divergent interests. The result in each was a *tension*
> between the conflicting demands for territorial integration and
> for balkanization.[11]

If tension is the result of ambivalent desires, however, why
did its resolution in each of these six cases take the federal form

11. *Ibid.,* p. 93. (My italics.)

Federalism, Mk. II, III, IV, V . . . n.   131

and no other? After all, if we are to believe James Bryce's argument that the forces of unification and separation, association and dissociation, integration and disintegration, are
present in all societies, and the tensions between them, if resolved, are resolved in many ways, when therefore will the
federal form be preferred to all others? Watts' theory is:

> An examination of the recent federations suggests that, like the
> older federations, what was distinctive about the social situa-
> tions which produced them was not merely the duality of de-
> mands for union and regional autonomy, but *the relative
> balance or equilibrium in each between the conflicting forces for
> unity and diversity.*[12]

How should we regard Riker's and Watts' theories? We have
been long advised by Aristotle in the Nicomachean Ethics that
"it is the mark of an educated man to look for precision in each
class of things just so far as the nature of the subject admits.
. . ." But the question, of course, is: What precision does the
nature of *this* subject admit? It is a devilishly difficult matter,
and Aristotle's only hint is that "each man judges well the
things he knows, and of these he is a good judge." If we skirt
the epistemological issues, it is plain that many generalizations
distort the particular, and some generalizations distort the particular more than others. What, however, is the order of Riker's
and Watts' generalizations? Do they go to the outermost limits
of the subject and illuminate all that can be known, do they
go beyond the limits and reduce what is worth knowing by
straining for a hyperambitious political science, or do they fall
short of the limits?

As a quick comment on both Riker's and Watts' theories, it is
tempting to give Bishop Butler's judgment on all reductionist
theories: "Everything is what it is, and not another thing." But
let us eschew this counsel and look at each more carefully. As
an absolute minimum, one can make the trite observation that
those who join in a federal union in preference to any other
form of union have a *desire* to do so. Though of course even

12. *Ibid.* (My italics.)

this assumption is dubious, for, as is well known, individuals and states may enter contractual bonds without love or desire, just as marriage and international treaties may be soleminized at the end of a gun. However, if we could say no more than this—that people enter a federal union because they desire this form of union before all others—the value of our information is nearly zero. Obviously, to be of significant explanatory value, the reasons which move societies to enter a federal form of union must be not merely distinctive and applicable to all cases but must also yield a useful level of information. Do Riker and Watts satisfy this test?

To Riker first: To begin with, Riker's idea of what constitutes a "proof" of his hypothesis is highly argumentative. For even if his twenty-seven (living and dead) federations were to constitute a homogeneous group, and even if it were true that the two factors he names, the expansion condition and the military condition, are invariably and significantly present in each of the eighteen extant cases, it does not necessarily constitute a *proof* of his hypothesis. Not if one accepts, that is, the view that induction is a dubious mode of establishing the truth, and certainly not when he structures his hypothesis in such a way that it is impossible to disprove.[13] His hypothesis or conjecture may be plausible, even highly plausible; but it is not proof! But let us put his mode of proof aside, and take one of Riker's two tandem conditions, the factor of military security or defense, for it appears throughout the history of all alliances from time immemorial.

In a sense, *all* unions or associations of any kind are formed with the desire or hope of promoting the well-being of their members. And insofar as considerations of internal/external security are fundamental to the commonweal of individuals and states (*salus populi suprema lex*), and insofar as it is commonly presumed that security, defense, or offense is enhanced by numbers, it is a mere truism that in all but say eco-

13. See, for example, Popper, *Objective Knowledge*, Chap. 2, "The Two Faces of Commonsense," esp. pp. 78-89 where he discusses Hume's critique of induction.

nomic or religious associations (e.g., customs unions or the Grecian amphictyonies), security motives are present in the calculations of all communities which seek greater strength through association, whether simple or complex, temporary or permanent. And of course the possible variations in the ways in which security or threat situations may present themselves are endless. It may be the only factor, as in the case of the simple Hellenic military alliance, the *symmachia*; it may be one of a small number of factors, as in the case of the *sympoliteia*; or one of a great number of factors, as in the case of, say, the Indian Federation. Where it is one of a compound of factors, it may be dominant, conspicuous, and constant, or it may be secondary, negligible, remote, vague, and inconstant. Again, what is perceived or what is believed to be a security or threat situation, and the levels of apprehension or the intensity of the belief, may vary profoundly in the calculations of each party contemplating some form of security association.[14]

All this is obvious, as it is obvious that the belief in the security of numbers has expressed itself in innumerable instances in the past through different types of protective association. And it is to be expected, therefore, that every writer would note the presence of this factor in the list of motives for federal union. However, while this is so, not every writer is as bold as Riker in assigning a significant and constant responsibility to the military condition. Wheare, for example, though he has written of "a sense of military insecurity and . . . the consequent need for common defense" among the *seven* factors which "seem always to have been present" at the birth of federation, nevertheless concludes:

> It is not possible to pick on any one of them or any one combination of them and say that unless this or these are present, the

14. See John C. Ranney, "The Bases of American Federalism," esp. pp. 14-18; this gives a more complex role to the military factor in the American experience. Note also in Australia the different reactions of the states of Victoria and New South Wales to the threat of a French annexation of the New Hebrides for the purpose of settling its convicts; see Geoffrey Serle, "The Victorian Government's Campaign for Federation, 1883-1889."

desire for federal union will not arise. That desire may be produced by any one of them.[15]

And Watts similarly; only Riker alone has argued that "the
military condition" must be one of the two (and probably sufficient) conditions for the birth of a healthy federal system.
Here, for example, is an abbreviation of his own summary of
four cases—U.S.A., Australia, India, and Nigeria—to illustrate
his reading of history.

> *U.S.A.*: . . . Consider the objective international situation they
> [the thirteen colonies] found themselves in [1783] . . . an uneasy
> peace with the British imperial power . . . The British occupied
> forts in the Northwest Territory . . . The English threat in the
> Northwest was matched by the Spanish threat in the Southwest
> . . . The States had neither fleet to forestall invasion nor army to
> repel it. . . . In such circumstances wise politicians could seldom
> be free of the fear of war and in fact they were not. The chief
> criticisms . . . of the peripheralized federalism of the Articles was
> that the system . . . was inadequate for war and the prospect of
> war. . . . Washington . . . throughout 1785 to 1787 emphasized
> the military weakness of government under the Articles. . . .
> Madison [in a manuscript criticism of the Articles circulated on
> the eve of the Philadelphia convention, devoted] the first, the
> longest and the most passionately argued items in the list of
> weaknesses of the Articles . . . to the military or diplomatic
> inadequacies of Congress. . . . [Similarly] the structure of *The
> Federalist* and the content of its first papers suggests the primacy
> of military considerations in the process of centralization. . . .
>
> *Australia*: Although Australian federation has often been in-
> terpreted as a bargain made for strictly economic reasons (i.e.,
> intercolonial free trade) and although there was no immediate
> threat of war when the union was consummated, only a slight
> survey of the circumstances of union indicates the omnipresence
> of the military-diplomatic concerns. . . . The federation move-
> ment [which dates roughly from 1850] really gained momentum
> in the early 1880's coincident with the French expansion in the
> New Hebrides. The first convention on federation in 1890,
> which was called because of a British military investigation that

15. K. C. Wheare, *Federal Government*, p. 42.

had recommended the unification of the colonial defense forces, also coincided with a frustrated Australian imperialism toward Oceania that had failed to maintain Queensland's annexation of New Guinea. But the most important event of all was the swift Japanese victory in the Sino-Japanese War of 1894. . . . With substantial imperial ambitions of their own and faced with a proven imperial naval power close by, the Australian colonials who could not agree on a federation in 1890-91 found it possible to do so in 1897-1900. . . . *Thus, although the recognized military need is not so obvious in the case of Australia as in most others, military concerns were the ostensible reason for the federation movement* and were probably crucial to its consummation.

India: Nowhere have the British more elaborately and consciously prepared their ex-colonies for federalism than in India. Throughout the entire period of British occupation of India, in fact, the British operated a kind of federal system. . . . When forced to concede some degree of self-government, the form in which the British naturally chose to grant it [in the Government of India Act of 1935] was federal. . . . When Indian independence was granted in 1947, it came in the form of a partition . . . into India and Pakistan . . . [occasioning] great rioting, vast transfers of people, and an undeclared war between the two new nations over the possession of the princely states of Kashmir and Jammu. From the very beginning, therefore, the Indian nation has faced the prospect of immediate foreign war. *As in the instances already mentioned, therefore, Indian federalism, though foreshadowed by the Government of India Act of 1935, was actually entered into in a time of real threat of foreign war.*

Nigeria: . . . For most of its history under British rule, Nigeria had a unitary government. It was only as withdrawal became an immediate prospect that the British split Nigeria into three parts in anticipation of a future federalism. The justification for doing so was . . . the existence of three geographically distinct and politically hostile cultures within the colony. . . . The only clearcut reason—aside from the fact that the British prepared the way for it—that one can give for the continued existence of this federation during its first few years is the presence of Ghana and the pan-African (read: "imperial") propositions uttered by its leader, Nkrumah. . . . No Nigerian leader could fail to be aware of the proximity of the western (and depressed and minority) re-

gion of Nigeria to Ghana. Nkrumah's personal pan-Africanism
. . . seems to have diminished in the last few years, and with this
diminution the rationale of a federal Nigeria has diminished
also. Only the future can tell whether this initial threat was sufficient to create a viable Nigeria federation or whether the peri-
pheralization will culminate in dissolution. Because of the peri-
pheralization, Nigeria is a marginal instance; nevertheless, the
two conditions are verified for it: the second because of the
Ghanaian threat and the first because of the unwillingness of
Nigerian leaders to upset the bargain the British had made for
them.[16]

And so on, in a similar vein, for the origin of the other living
federations—European, African, Southeast Asian, and Latin
American. His portraiture throughout, however, consists of
only two primary colours, no shades. Nothing else, neither
political culture, geography, demography, charismatic leadership, history, nor any factor listed by Wheare or Watts can give
birth to the federal organism *unless* there is a conjunction of
two factors, an "expansionist" and a "military" condition.

As one reads these accounts, it is difficult to resist the impres-
sion that Riker translates history with the reductionist zeal of a
salvationist, an apocalyptic or materialist historian. And needless to say, modified or totally contrary accounts may be and
have been given of every instance he discusses. Observe, for
example, Birch's quite different account of the founding circumstances in Nigeria and Malaysia.[17] Or note Watts' own view
that "the necessity of common defense has been significant *only*
in the Asian federations"—not in Nigeria, where Riker asserts
that the two conditions have been verified! Indeed, Nigerian
political history could be read in a way that denies any influence whatever to Nkrumah's pan-Africanist postures in the
decision to federate; or, the evidence could suggest, with at least
equal plausibility, that aside from influential British pressure,

16. Riker, pp. 16-48. (My italics.)
17. A. H. Birch, "Approaches to the Study of Federalism." Birch found that
    neither Riker's nor Deutsch's conditions favoring the creation of a feder-
    ation held true for the founding of either the Nigerian or the Malaysian
    federations.

and the cultural differences between the three regions, the main rationale for the existence of Nigerian federalism was the ability of the central government to get hold of, and distribute, spoils to the regions. Again, (as La Nauze points out[18]) recent work on the history of the Australian federation suggests that the explanation for the movement that was consummated in 1901 must comprise more than a reference to Australian apprehensions about the appearance, and the intentions, of major European powers in the Pacific; and it is evident that the "more" cannot be simply straitjacketed into either of Riker's two conditions. Or again, what is one to make of the repeated assertions of Indian historians that cultural diversity alone made unitary government in India unthinkable? And so on, and on.

Wars of historians, however, will not settle this matter. The central question, even if we accept Riker's own reading of history, is: What is the explanatory value of his hypothesis? Riker's two conditions of the federal "bargain" may be translated in many ways; one may speak of the "expansion condition" in terms of an imperialist, or aggrandizing, or hegemonic drive for gain, glory, security, etc., and the accompanying "military condition" as classic Hobbesian fear (objective, reasonably believed, paranoic) or protective self-interest (enlightened or greedy). But however translated, to propose that these two conditions are invariably present (as it were, an expansionist sperm and a protective ovum) at the birth of each federation is to state a commonplace that is hardly worth noting. It would be remarkable indeed if one could point to any of the multiforms of territorial political association throughout history and suggest that neither of these two factors were present, or indeed that the sole rationale for their origin and existence was brotherly love. It would have given some credence to his hypothesis if he had explained *why* the presence of these two factors should result in the birth of a federal child, or indeed what measure or ration of these two factors produced a viable federal

18. J. A. LaNauze, *The Making of the Australian Constitution*, pp. 1-5.

child instead of a sickly confederal or quasi-federal offspring, or indeed a benign or monstrous mutant. But Riker's hypothesis does not tell us this, nor does it even tell us whether the invariable presence of these two factors invariably results in a federal offspring—or if not, when and under what conditions does parturition take place? In a word, the counterpart of Riker's thesis would be the observation that, except for parthenogenesis, a man and a woman are invariably involved in the act of creation.[19]

And Watts? Watts, as we have noted, calls upon a theory of "relative *balance*" or "approximate *equilibrium*" to explain the process of federal parturition. In effect: Whatever the number or the relative importance of the factors working for union or regional autonomy in each case, parturition takes place in all cases only if the desire for union and the desire for regional autonomy are nearly balanced.

> It has *only* been where there was an *approximate equilibrium* between the wider and narrower nationalism that federal political institutions have been adopted. [My italics.]

It is a pretty, tidy, symmetrical, mechanistic, and simple theory.[20] But it also calls upon a multi-meaning and awesomely confusing concept that has appeared and performed in many roles on many stages.[21] It probably found its way onto the federal stage through the imagery of co-equal status as constitutional equilibrium (e.g., Hamilton: "It is to be hoped that

19. For a critique of two other Riker hypotheses—"Is federalism worth keeping?" and "Does federalism make any difference in the way that people are governed?"—see Vincent Ostrom's "Can Federalism Make a Difference?"
20. On the mechanistic fallacy, note R. E. Dowling, "Pressure Group Theory: Its Methodological Range," *American Political Science Review*, Vol. 54 (1960), pp. 944-954. Also Martin Landau, "On the Use of Metaphor in Political Science," *Social Research*, Autumn 1961; and "Baker v. Carr and the Ghost of Federalism," esp. pp. 241-242.
21. I know of no better critical analysis of this concept, albeit in the context of international relations theory, than in the two following references: Ernst B. Haas, "The Balance of Power, Prescription, Concept, or Propaganda?" in *World Politics*, Vol. V (1952), pp. 442-477; and Martin Wight, "The Balance of Power," in Herbert Butterfield and Martin Wight, *Diplomatic Investigations* (London: Allen & Unwin, 1966), pp. 149-175.

they [the people] will always take care to preserve the *constitutional equilibrium* between the general and State governments''); the same imagery is projected through a great deal of federal polemics (e.g., "the central government has progressively destroyed the *balance* between . . .''); it was repeatedly used in early stock-taking studies of federal systems (e.g., "war, welfare, and judicial interpretation have been responsible for shifting the *balance* between . . .''); and it is occasionally used, as Watts has done, to explain the origin of federal systems.

Its difficulties, however, are patent. For example, the very least we can presume, as I have argued earlier (and then only with some reservations), is that wherever there is a federal system, there has been something called a "desire" to enter this type of union, even if lukewarm. But how can we possibly establish or infer a *balance* of desire (if only approximate) for union and regional autonomy? To be sure, one could construe a syllogism resting on the premise that a balance of these twin, though ambivalent, desires is necessary to the creation of a federal system, and then complete the remaining two steps of the syllogism: This is a federal system; ergo, there must have been such a balance! But what evidence is there for such a premise, and indeed what would such a "balance" look like? In what way, for example, can one handle the variable valency of the near-dozen common ingredients that Watts extracts from the six "new" federations? What kind of external insecurity plus what expectations of economic gain, for instance, are roughly balanced by what measure of interregional fears of political hegemony plus what attachment to a specific cultural identity? Or in the same terms, what does "imbalance" look like? Is one to infer, for example, that if the desire for unity is far greater than the desire for regional autonomy, or vice versa, that a federal system will not be adopted—or if adopted, that a settlement reflecting these disproportionate or unbalanced preferences will not be "federal," or "federal" in name only? Doubtless Watts does not contemplate some Heath-Robinson type of device to give the notion of "balance" the kind of operational precision that goes with statistical techniques of weighting and correlation. But neither does he give us any means of identifying the presence or absence of balance or imbalance.

The gravest fault of his theory, however, is that it presumes that the question "Shall we unite in accordance with federal rites or shall we unite in some other fashion?" is an issue in every case, that it presents itself in the same way, is understood in the same way, and generates the same kind of tensions. But the federal form of association may not be at issue at all; for whether or not there is a "balance of desire" between union and separation, the constellation of facts may make all other options unthinkable—e.g., India. Or the question may be at issue in the gestating phases of a movement for closer union and be settled in principle before the parties sit down to constitution-making (e.g., India, Australia). Or the matter may be at issue from the beginning to the very end, even though the parties are driven on to constitution-making because "federalism" is the master's price of independence (e.g., Central African Federation). And indeed, the question of "federalism" or not may not even be understood by all.[22]

What is common to all cases, whether "federalism" is at issue or not, or whether "federalism" is understood or not, is the question "What will the total system of government look like?" and, in particular, "What version of 'federalism' is it to be?" —the U.S. model, the Canadian, the Australian, the Swiss, the German, or a piece of this model and a piece of that, or a piece of something entirely different from any other existing combination of pieces, because no known system quite fits the

22. Referring to the Round Table Conference in London, 1931, S. P. Aiyar writes: "Regarding the federal idea itself, as revealed in the discussions, one notes that the members approached it purely as a political solution to the Indian problem. They had no sociological interest in federalism. They made no attempt to examine the suitability of federalism to Indian society. . . . Moreover, even the classical theory of federalism was probably not well understood by the Indian delegates, for it could not have figured much in their own studies. Indeed . . . a story went round St. James's Palace in 1930 that a distinguished delegate from India had proposed at one of the sub-committee meetings that eminent professors of political science should be invited to lecture to the delegates on federalism." (Aiyar, "The Federal Idea in India," pp. 12-13.)

local needs?[23] It is here in the short or long (but always exhausting) process of hammering out an agreement (call it "bargain," "consensus," or "compromise"), in accommodating interests, needs, problems and circumstances, that each society arrives at its own distinctive translation of the "federal" model —how the legislative power will be "divided," how it will be protected, and how it will blend into the total constitutional system. A theory of federal parturition relying on a "balance of ambivalent desires" cannot possibly express the range of tangled desires, different understandings, conflicts, and tensions generated in the process of settling the mass of principles and details. Indeed, Watts' theory is alien to his own data, and is no more helpful or corrigible than if he had proposed the completely opposite thesis: "federal systems have only been adopted where the desire for union is significantly greater than the desire for regional autonomy; for wherever the two desires are approximately balanced, federal political institutions are aborted."

THE DIVISION AND PRACTICE OF DIVIDED POWER

It is possible to hypothesize that each federal system is more like itself than it is like any other federal system; and that what it has in common with others by virtue of being a system of "divided" power is less significant than the political culture in which the "division" is set, the way power is divided, and the way the "division" is practiced. How sound is such a view? Let us look at this in the context of one of the laws of the world: change and metamorphosis.

We may begin by first noting that constitutions purporting to be federal share many features with every other kind of constitutional system. For example, all modern constitutions, federal or otherwise, genuine or ceremonial, contain some reference to the organs that will make, execute, and adjudicate the law, or, as it is sometimes called, "the will of the people"; and

23. See Watts, pp. 128-137, for the influence of earlier federal models on the six new Commonwealth federations proposed in the post-1945 decolonization era.

in most constitutions there are, in varying degrees of generality, provisions relating to the structure, composition, tenure, powers, and interrelations of these organs. Needless to say, there is a great variety of forms, and a great difference in their substance, according to indigenous preferences for one kind of political expression or another. But in the main, these are the matters which all constitutions are about, and in many respects (e.g., the basis of representation, or the relations of the two branches of a bicameral legislature), there is little which is specifically exclusive to federal systems. Indeed, if we take some of these provisions, item by item, there is often more in common between some federal and nonfederal constitutions than between two or more federal constitutions: for example, in the choice between presidential and parliamentary executive systems, or between elected and appointed second chambers, or between proportional and nonproportional systems of representation, or between systems incorporating a Bill of Rights or systems relying on uncodified common-law liberties.

The exclusive hallmark of every constitutional system which purports to be federal, however, is the presence of an explicit "division" of legislative power in the constitution. This is the first instruction in any federal engineering manual, and the first checkpoint for any inspector of federal constitutions. Of course each "division of power" ("distribution of authority," as some have named it) varies in manner, content, and scale; and this is so because each division originates in particular calculations about what is advisable, expedient, relevant, or compromisable in each political setting at a particular moment in time. But however the division is effected (and there are scores of ways), a division there must be. Hence find the clause or clauses which list what the central government can do, or what the regional governments can do, or what both can do, or neither one nor the other or both can't do, and the first checkpoint is cleared. If there are no such clauses, then whatever decentralist practices animate the political system, the public face of U.S.-model federalism is missing.

A "division of power," however, is an artificial, an imperfect, a generalized, a linguistic, a skeletal thing. Political life simply cannot be perfectly or permanently compartmentalized. Players, resources, beliefs, issues, the language of politics, the name and the dimension of things, the ways of persuasion and coercion all change, sometimes dramatically, but more often as imperceptibly as the changing voice of address and communication between aging parents and growing children. However ingenious constitutional draftsmen may be in composing a "division of power" that will work for and beyond their time, their words can rarely be more than approximate, crude, and temporary guides to the ongoing or permissible political activity in any federal system. They cannot anticipate what meanings will be given, or what limits set, to their words (e.g., interstate commerce, general welfare), or to what uses their words will be put (e.g., power to tax); they cannot anticipate new political demands (e.g., "quality of life" issues), or whether these demands will be dressed in a new language (e.g., "ecological and environmental" policy), or whether new combinations of powers will be called for to cope with new demands (e.g., power to tax plus power to make grants-in-aid).

This being so, adaptation—the survival imperative of all political systems—poses a particular problem for those systems where legislative power is divided in the federal form: how to work, manipulate, improvise, bridge, adjust, extend, bend, and accommodate the "division" to cope with the new, the unforeseen, and the unintended; in a word, how to minimize the uncertainties of divided power, and how to overcome the accident of power failure. The nature of the problem varies profoundly from system to system, both with the precise "division of power" in each system and the adaptability of all the factors that signify the distinctive shape, content, tempo, and temperament of each. Compare, for example, the content of the "division of power" between the older nineteenth-century and the newer twentieth-century federal systems. It would suggest that the new federations, born into a new era of expansive political expectations, and doubtless guided by some of the difficulties of the older versions, took care to "divide power" in such a way

that the central government would have better constitutional
means to manage a modern society. Yet, true though this is, it
would be wrong to infer that a division of power conceived in a
Mills-ian era of minimalistic state responsibility was thereby
incapable of coping with the contemporary brands of economic
and social ills. As wrong, indeed, as it would be to equate constitutional capacity with the political ability or the political
will to act. For the adaptive capacity or incapacity of any system
where power is divided in the federal form is not related to
either constitutional ability or political disposition alone. System A, for example, may be faced with both problems, system B
with one or neither, and system C with any one of a countless
number of variations on both these themes. Illustrated dia-
grammatically—albeit simplistically, as with all political dia-
grams—we have the following possible situations:

Constitutionally able ←————————→ Politically able
Constitutionally unable ←————————→ Politically unable

This given, how have living federal systems adapted themselves to change? Like all other political systems, federations
have had to cope with both old and new social afflictions; war,
want, growth, and speed. It is highly doubtful, however, whether a comparative analysis of the prophylactic or remedial
measures taken, in at least the Western-style industrialized societies, over the period from say 1930 to 1974, would reveal any
consistent two-camp categorization of federal/nonfederal
modes of adaptation.[24] And it is even more doubtful whether
any two federal systems (or systems purporting to be federal)
have perceived the problems in the same way, have responded
to them in the same way, or have coped with them in the same
way. Again, a comparative analysis of policies and actions
would doubtless reveal a gallery of different approaches, styles,
techniques, and results.[25]

24. For instance, see Soia Mentschikoff, "Federalism and Economic Growth,"
    p. 199.
25. See G. F. Sawer, *Modern Federalism*, Chaps. 5 and 6, pp. 64-105; also A. H.
    Birch, *Federalism, Finance and Social Legislation*.

The examples are endless, and a few will suffice. Thus, in one place, a federal government supported by Congress in a policy of national economic relief but frustrated by judicial rejection of its "New Deal" legislation, cajoles, threatens, and finally stacks the Supreme Court to validate its policies; elsewhere, a central government constitutionally powerless to introduce interstate marketing controls to assist the recovery of primary industry from a decline of world commodity prices, and unable to win sufficient popular support for an amendment to the constitution, devises, in cooperation with the affected states and primary industry, a circuitous route to achieve a home-price stabilization scheme. In another, a central government on the plea of a wartime need to rationalize federal and state income tax policies, and failing to secure the agreement of the states to a temporary centralization plan, acts unilaterally through its concurrent tax power to monopolize the field of income taxation and devise a reimbursement formula for the states; elsewhere, a central government in quest of the same object—viz., a uniform scheme to eliminate the inequities of the differential tax rates in the different provinces—concludes a tax rental agreement with eight of the ten provinces whereby each of them can choose one of two ways of minimum reimbursement, while the two other provinces, the most affluent and politically powerful, are left to continue their own way. In one place, a central government with limited constitutional power in specific fields of social welfare (e.g., health, education, and housing) but extensive fiscal resources, though preferring to act independently, induces the states to cooperate in a national development program by brandishing generous grants before them: in another, a central government with unquestioned constitutional power to act on its own, but preferring to work through the states, employs carrot money for the poorer states, plus unofficial party pressure and public propaganda to persuade the reluctant "affluent" states to cooperate. And so on, and on.

In a word, no federal system lives, or has lived, by its "division of power" alone, though some live by it more than others;

no two federal systems live by their "division of power" in the same way, at the same time; and no two federal systems have used the same battery of techniques to accommodate change. But more than this, however, as no two federal systems began with the same relationship between the central government and the states, so no two federal systems developed their internal relations with the states (singly or collectively)[26] in the same way, or exhibit the same relationship now.

This can be best illustrated if we consider their experience of growth, and its twin concomitants, integration and centralization. These phenomena are, of course, known to all developed and developing industrial societies. In federal systems, however, growth, especially exponential growth, has altered fundamentally the historic conditions in which the U.S. model evolved, and it has expressed itself in two ways: first, the central and state governments have been driven at an ever-increasing pace to a realization and an acceptance (pleasant or unpleasant) that they inhabit a single system[27] in which they are inescapably dependent upon each other for welfare and survival; second, the acceleration in the volume and speed of interaction has thrust the central government into a more emphatic hegemonic role in all federal systems. Let us take each of these in the broad.

The reality of every political system is interdependence and interaction. For imminent in every form of union, elementary or complex, is an acknowledgment that a bond of mutuality, however limited in purpose or fragile in texture, exists and transcends the random communality of man in the world. However power is divided in a political system, therefore, or for whatever ends, whether to form an association of equals or any other relationship, the fact of association inevitably generates both intended and unintended relations. And this is so because it is no more possible to insulate such a verbal artifact as a

26. Charles D. Tarlton, "Symmetry and Assymetry as Elements of Federalism: A Theoretical Speculation."
27. Morton Grodzins, *The American System*. Chap. 1 is headed "The American System as a Single Mechanism." Grodzins and Elazar's sharing hypothesis is discussed below in Chap. VI, "The Twentieth-Century 'Doctors'."

"division of power" against unintended interactions than it is to insulate heat in a hot body! No theory of political association can ignore this without becoming fictitious. And a division of power which attempted to deny the natural flow of relations generated through association, or to prohibit specific forms of interaction, would be destined to fail, unless the parties to it were willing to employ draconian methods to achieve their aim.

Thus, if the early nineteenth-century federalist rhetoric of dual worlds where two political streams flowed in parallel and splendid isolation from each other, serving only those who had need of their waters, bore any resemblance to reality in their own time, only a stubborn man could ignore the fact that no citizen could enjoy his rights to a dwelling without security against a foreign enemy, or protection from foreign plague without inspection in the ports. And though it was not a McLuhanesque supersonic world which attended the adolescent years of American federalism, the implications of interdependence were not wholly ignored.[28] The tentative, albeit modest efforts of the federal and state governments to concert their action in a number of ways already signalled the changes to come. And by the mid-twentieth century, the two conditions which characterized their first political setting, the insulated remoteness of agricultural communities and the minimalism of government intervention in the affairs of the community, were dead.

The tale has been told many times, in many different ways. But however one explains this change, whether by the clichés of the "global village," the "rise of the welfare state," "total war," "the impact of science and technology," or "modernization," the fact is that the nineteenth- and early twentieth-century worlds which gave birth and sustained the constitutional doctrines of dual federalism (e.g., the immunity of instrumentalities or the doctrine of implied prohibitions) were dead also. No longer could one divide the field of political action so confi-

28. See Daniel J. Elazar, *The American Partnership*; also *American Federalism: A View from the States*, esp. Chap. 3.

dently into "national/local" or "external/internal" affairs. The concern of the township became the concern of the nation, and the concern of the nation the talk of the township. Increasingly the traditional eighteenth- and nineteenth-century areas of unquestionable local attention—land use, health, education, civil and criminal justice, transport, the governance of townships, etc.—became unquestionable no longer. Where in 1787 Hamilton could hardly imagine that the national government would have need to extend its domain beyond what it was given to do[29] (or was he merely comforting the doubters?), some hundred years later in Australia, Deakin, its second Prime Minister (1903), prophesied the tangled intergovernmental relations in the world to come. Almost every activity—whether the cleansing of air or of a local creek, the conservation of forests, the improvement of kindergartens, city transport, local sewerage, crime and urban development, town libraries, or town art, whether on the borders or in the heart of the country—has become the subject of national concern and federal-state politics. And because of this, because federal-state interaction and interpenetration have developed on such a scale and with such speed, so the scope of independent action by any single member, and particularly individual states, has altered dramatically. Indeed, what does "independent" action mean when two governments, whether from love or necessity, become so wedded to each other in the common bed of nationalized politics that neither can turn, talk, or breathe without immediately affecting the other?[30]

Related to the factor of closer integration is the second factor, the increasing centralization or the hegemony of the federal government: the emergence of the central government in every federal system as leader, financier, director, promoter, coordinator, guide, stimulator, pacifier, aggressor, pace-setter, equalizer, and standardizer; the most prestigious, the most influential, the

29. The Federalist, No. 45.
30. A. H. Birch, "Opportunities and Problems of Federation," p. 6; Ivo Duchacek, *Comparative Federalism*, esp. Chaps. 7-10; and Michael D. Reagan, *The New Federalism*, pp. 77-81.

political superior and most effective manipulator of all the parts, singly or collectively. The tendency manifests itself in each case almost from the day of the first national action.[31] The indicators, as they developed, were everywhere—the relative status of the national leader, the preoccupation of the media with the affairs of the capital, the civic knowledge of the electorate, and so on.[32] Looking backwards, it all seems obvious that it should happen thus. After all, it is probably a historic commonplace of all societies at all times that he who protects a community against its foes becomes the nerve center of their lives. In addition, a central government that is given, at the very least, the unlimited power (because of the unlimited fears of a community) to preempt the total resources of a community for war or peace, the power to dispense its monies among the states, the power to manage the national currency, the power to control the postal services, and the power to determine the composition of its citizens by controlling the ports of entry and exit, is invested with an incomparable advantage to lead and impose its values on a nation. While the potential was always there— otherwise why Madison and Hamilton's strenuous efforts to assuage the fears of the Antifederalists?—there is no longer any doubt now that the way a central government chooses to use its power is more decisive of the character of a federal system than the division of power could possibly suggest.

The combined effect of this highly generalized representation of these several factors—growth, integration, and centralization —would lead, of course, to the conclusion that one can no longer describe the *realpolitik* relationship in any federal system by the traditional terms of either "coordinate" or "independent," except in a purely formal or constitutional sense (viz.: "They can paralyze you by stripping you of income, they can deride your constitutional dignity by bullying and coercion, but they cannot deprive you of your badges of office"). There is, to be

31. For the beginning of the American experience, see Kenrick C. Babcock, *The Rise of American Nationality, 1811-1819*; and Lloyd M. Short, *The Development of National Administrative Organization in the United States.*
32. Note Reagan, p. 146.

sure, a good deal of truth in such a view. But like many of the generalities in federal theory, it suppresses the specificity, the plasticity, and the complexity of the differences in each system. For whether we employ the traditional terms of "coordinate" and "independent" to denote the quintessential properties of a federal system or not, it is hardly contestable that the power relationship within each federal system varies constantly and markedly. And it is as important to take hold of this truism as it is to understand that the relationship between the center and the parts, in every federal system, has never consisted of one kind of interaction or one kind of interdependence. By choice or by necessity, federal-state relations have spawned a vast criss-cross of formal and informal transactions, traversing both the areas demarcated within the "division of power" and areas untouched by and unknown to the original division.[33]

Thus, even if an old-time inspector of federal systems prefers to use the traditional terms of identification, it is plain that in some transactions (e.g., the attempt to achieve uniform drug control or company regulation in Australia) the relationship may be more/less "co-ordinate" or more/less "independent" than in other transactions (e.g., the decision of a federal government to grant flood relief to a politically hostile state or not); and indeed, the federal inspector may find that in the very same transaction there is a more/less "co-ordinate" or "independent" relationship between the federal government and some states than with others.[34] The same will apply whether he wishes to use this language or operate with other dichotomous categories such as "co-ordinate/subordinate," "independent/dependent," or indeed "master/servant." Consider briefly the complexity of this in the key instance of federal-state fiscal relations.

The problem of dividing fiscal resources between different levels of government is, of course, not unique to federal sys-

33. "Untouched by and unknown to"—that is, except to the fiction of "divided sovereignty" which implies that all the possible activities of man have been attended to by the act of division.
34. Reagan, p. 8.

tems. Every system of territorial delegation or decentralization involves the distribution of monies, and the criteria of apportionment vary considerably according to the ends, purposes, or values of each system. What is particular to the federal system is the notion that every division of tax resources should keep faith with two ideals: to assure each government sufficient monies to do what it is (or what it is believed to be) constitutionally responsible for, and to assure each government "independence" (i.e., the independence befitting its "co-ordinate" status) in deciding how and in what order to spend its monies. These are probably irreconcilable expectations, but whether they are or not, the fact is that no federal system has found a permanent and mutually satisfying way to relieve the chronic tension between them. Instead, every division of the ways of raising monies has given (intentionally or unintentionally, by accident or necessity) the central government almost unlimited means of mobilizing the wealth of a community, whereas the states (cantons, provinces, or länder) have been given less privileged fiscal means. The result is that, periodically, every federal system has been put to the Robin Hood task of relieving the scarcity of state treasuries by tapping the relative plenty of the central government. And in this process of adjusting means to responsibility, the central government has assumed everywhere a commanding role.[35] The remedies fluctuate and vary extensively within and between federal systems. But what must be noticed is that each different remedy may and often does affect quite critically the political and administrative relations between the central government and the states. Thus, for example, some may invest the central government with overlordship in all crucial fiscal operations, while some confer only a partial and conditional overlordship in a limited range of operations; or some may safeguard the interests of the states by incorporating elaborate participatory machinery in the constitution, while some invest them with a simple consultative role only, and so

35. The literature on federal finance is voluminous, but one of the most useful references is the symposium by W. K. Hicks et al., *Federalism and Economic Growth.*

on and on. Observe the following selection of arrangements that have been or are being practiced in one federal system or another:[36]

1. The level of taxation, the level of borrowing, and the standards of service are mainly determined by the central government, though only after extensive consultation with the states collectively.
2. The level of taxation and the standards of service are determined by each government, but the level of public borrowing is mainly determined by the central government.
3. All tax sources, with the exception of customs, and all avenues of borrowing are equally open to every government, but the claims of the central government take precedence over the states.
4. Tax sources are divided, but the major sources are monopolized by the central government, transfers to the states by the central government constitute the bulk of their revenue (e.g., over 50%); the amount is determined by an impartial tribunal appointed by the central government or the "states" chamber of the central legislature.
5. Tax sources are divided, but the poorer states need periodic assistance from the central government, which determines the scale of assistance solely by itself.
6. Tax resources are divided, but the poorer states need continual assistance from the central government, which settles the scale on the recommendation of a centrally appointed "impartial" tribunal.
7. Tax sources are divided, but all transfers to the states are by conditional grants which constitute less than half of the state revenue (e.g., 10% to 30%), and the states are only ritually consulted.
8. Tax sources are divided; conditional grants are extensively used to achieve broad national objectives; states are closely consulted, are given a significant measure of discretion in administration, and the auditing control is very relaxed.
9. Tax sources are divided; conditional grants are extensively used for both national and state objectives, but each program is carefully specified, and the states are given little discretion other than "to dot the i's and cross the t's."[37]

36. Taken from R. J. May, *Federalism and Fiscal Adjustment*; G. F. Break, *Intergovernmental Relations in the United States*; R. L. Mathews (ed.), *Fiscal Federalism: Retrospect and Prospect*.
37. For example, one Australian state minister, commenting on state govern-

10. Tax sources are divided; conditional grants are extensively used by the central government for state objectives, but the states are given Hobson's choice: "accept the conditions or lose the grant."
11. Tax sources are divided; conditional grants are used extensively for both national and state objectives, but no state is financially penalized if it refuses to accept the grant.
12. Tax sources are divided; conditional grants are used; the terms are uniform for all states except one, where the conditions are changed by the central government for reasons of political pacification.

These are but a few examples from an endless pharmacoepia of variations. It is also important to note that not only do these different solutions affect the texture of federal-state relations in each case, but each one reflects the strength and alignment of forces in each system at the precise moment of choice. In each case, the projection of a remedial formula and its adoption, modification, or rejection will depend on a changing constellation of factors. Listed, though not in any particular order, some of the more obvious ingredients are: first, and crucial, is the party system; the nature of the party in power at the center, its beliefs about what federalism is about, its organization, its territorial and social bases of power (e.g., in all the states, or some only), its programs, its duration in office, and the nature of the opposition party(s); the nature and state of the economy, the distribution of wealth among the states (how many rich, how many poor), what remedies they favor; the electoral popularity of national or local objectives, initiative, and action (awareness, concern, indifference); the area of negotiation, if negotiation is available; the bargaining skill, knowhow, and political leverage of the negotiators; the changing understanding and conflict between the central government and the states about who should be doing what at any given moment, and so on and on. In brief, the name of the money-apportionment game in each

_____

ment plans to build new primary school libraries with federal funds at a standard below those set by the Commonwealth Primary School Libraries Committee, complained: "They [Canberra] will be telling us next the size we are allowed for our cubicles and lavatories, and what students will be taught at 11 a.m. on Thursdays."

federal system, as everywhere, is politics; and as no two games of politics are the same, so no two games of *divided* power politics are the same, either.[38]

38. See Reagan, pp. 6, 51, and 148.

6

The Twentieth-Century "Doctors"
Or, as many men, so many theories

The questions now are these: How do we capture all this teeming and changing variety in any generality that would serve federal theory, let alone any theory at all? Can we continue to compress this multicellular and idiosyncratic experience into the simplistic dichotomies of "co-ordinate/sub-ordinate," "independent/dependent," or for that matter into almost any known analogue, whether it is the relationship of master/servant, Westminster to Scotland, Wales and Cornwall, king to feudal baron, Holy Roman Emperor to his territorial monarchs, Roman Emperor to his proconsuls, or the hegemonic Greek state to its vassal city-states? How can we discipline history, as Riker would have us do, without brutalizing it? And above all, how can we avoid eunuch theories that stand guard over a federal harem of a thousand different variations, impotent to explain or mate with a single variation?

The claims to a significant federal theory since 1787 have been of many kinds, ranging from the modest to the immodest. As each new federal model has been put on the market, it has faced the federal inspectors with the dilemma of either keeping faith with the 1787 model as they understood its assumptions, or of recasting federal theory to accommodate the new situations. In almost all cases, however, the legacy of a formalized politico-constitutional language grid sits like an ox on their shoulders. It envelops and impregnates every nook and crevice, every proposition in federal theory and every argument in federal polemics. And it is no easier to break free of it than for Laocoon and his sons to escape from the coils of the serpents sent across the sea from the island of Tenedos to destroy them. Despite the numerous attempts to reconstitute the subject in the image of the thousand and one faces of politics rather than the dichotomous fixism of constitutional theory, the legacy of the past and the experience of the present have not been, and probably will never be, brought into harmony.

Various routes of escape have been explored by various expeditions. But their approaches to the subject correspond to no single school of thought ("historical," "sociological," etc.), nor any single doctrine to justify a single name. It is mostly the work of individuals bombarding the matter from different directions. If they have anything in common, it may be their civilized acceptance that, in life, not all is black and white; that political theory never squares with reality; that the power relations of two or more individuals, groups, tribes, cities, regions, or states cannot be put together in tidy heaps in the way that our predecessors boxed "sovereign" and "non-sovereign" legislatures; that always there are loose strands, untidiness, paradoxes, inconsistencies; that there are no pure cases of "federal" states, only mixtures, hybrids, and occasionally aberrant "monsters" defying all efforts to trap human institutions in iron-clad Linnaean categories. Hence their resort to the language of approximation, and the metaphors of arithmetic, measurement, balance, degree, spectrum, segment, and continuum. For example, Arthur W. MacMahon:

> . . . there is virtue in making such a word [as federal] do service in varied applications, provided it carries an essence or logic that is remembered and respected.
> The test on the borders of usage is likely to be *one of degree.*
> . . . A further characteristic of federal systems is that the matters entrusted to the constituent units . . . must be substantial and not merely trivial; *this, too, is a problem of degree.*
> . . . Through all these prime characteristics of federalism runs a discernible logic, but *the definition is a question of degree.*.

Or W. H. Morris-Jones:

> If it is fair to describe India's present Constitution as federal but with important unitary features, it may not be wrong to say that

the constitution she inherited in 1947 was unitary but with strong federal features. *Federalism, like democracy, is a matter of degree.* . . .

Or R. L. Watts:

. . . Livingston's image of a *spectrum* of societies, ranged in *degree* of territorial integration, may still be useful. If federal societies are conceived as a *segment* of this *spectrum*, it may help us to recognize that within the "colour" representing federal societies, where the pressures for unity and diversity are fairly closely balanced, there could be a range of "shades" or variations, and that the borders of this range are not distinct but shade on one side into societies in which homogeneity, *in varying degrees*, predominates, and on the other side into societies in which heterogeneity, *in varying degrees*, predominates.

Or C. J. Friedrich:

The extension of the range of vision that federalism in theory and practice has called for means, as we have shown, the inclusion of international federalism; that is to say, the recognition that there is a *continuum* linking the federal state with loose leagues on one side, with decentralized systems of government on the other.

Or G. F. Sawer:

Finally, the world community of nations and particular continental groupings of nations also present something of a federal situation, and world government along federal lines has long been advocated by the internationally minded. Here we are in the *"alliance to confederation" spectrum* which extends beyond the *end of the federal spectrum*. In this *spectrum*, a body like the United Nations occupies a *middle* position; it has a good deal more institutional structure and normative and executive power than was possessed by the League of Nations, and very much more than the [British] Commonwealth of Nations has possessed in its last stages, and is more than a mere alliance like the NATO, ANZUS, and SEATO pacts. But the systems contemplated by Common Market Treaties are a good deal more "confederate" still, and one of them, the European Economic Community or Common Market, . . . is *right at the point joining the federal spectrum with the confederal*.[1]

But if the metaphysics of calibration is their common trait, they differ in many other, often fundamental, respects: in the elements composing the spectrum or continuum in each case; in the manner in which they combine the language of "spectrum," "segments," and indeed multiple "spectra" to sharpen their notions of "federalism"; in their "*tests*" of federalism; in the way they practice art or science in arranging their specimens along the spectrum or continuum of federalism;[2] in what they see to be the "structure," "pattern," or "design" of federalism; in their scanning ambit for comparative material; in their readiness to employ alternative concepts; and in their results. Let me try to capture something of this variety by examining four different approaches to the subject. The *first* is what I want to call the "federalism is a matter of degree" approach; *second*, "federalism as a quality of society"; *third*, "federalism as a process"; and *fourth*, "federalism as sharing," or the "new" American federalism.

"FEDERALISM IS A MATTER OF DEGREE": WHEARE ET AL.

The general tenor of this approach is that there is no great uncertainty as to what the subject is about. It has a fairly precise model of "federalness" in mind, and while it readily admits that it may be slightly "fuzzy at the edges," its core is sound and clear. It knows what is at one end of the spectrum and what at the other; what is to the immediate right and to the immediate left of each single case,[3] and its analytic style is accordingly confident. It is best typified in K. C. Wheare's *Federal Govern-*

---

1. Arthur W. MacMahon, "The Problems of Federalism: A Survey," in *Federalism: Mature and Emergent*, p. 4; W. H. Morris-Jones, *The Government and Politics of India*, p. 17; R. L. Watts, *New Federations*, p. 95; C. J. Friedrich, *Trends of Federalism*, p. 177; G. F. Sawer, *Modern Federalism*, pp. 60-61. (My italics.)
2. For example, Riker, "The Measurement of Federalism," in *Federalism*, pp. 125-133.
3. See, for example, Sawer, *Modern Federalism*.

ment,[4] a text which enjoyed considerable popularity with post-1945 federation-makers.

Like Dicey and virtually all other late-nineteenth-century constitutionalists, Wheare begins with the acknowledgment of the United States as the popular archetype of the modern federal state.

> . . . since the United States is universally regarded as an example of federal government, it justifies us in describing the principle, which distinguishes it so markedly and so significantly, as the *federal principle.*

And more succinctly:

> . . . the federal principle has come to mean what it does because the United States has come to be what it is.[5]

With this model as his basic referant, he sets out to identify its "fundamental characteristic . . . as an association of states." He finds, by reference to its constitutional provisions, that the distinctive feature of the arrangements is the establishment of an "association of states so organised that powers are divided between a general government which in certain matters . . . is *independent* of the government of the associated states, and, on the other hand, state governments which in certain matters are, in their turn, *independent* of the general government."[6]

With this identification of the United States model, Wheare then proceeds to illustrate this particular principle of association by comparing and contrasting the form of the American Constitution with a number of other associations of states, "which have described themselves or been described as federal": viz., the American union under the Articles of Confederation, the Constitution of the Austro-Hungarian Empire, the German Empire of 1871-1918, and the Union of South Africa. These four examples of political association, he argues, illustrate two

4. For comments on Wheare's procedure, I have mainly relied on my article, "The Federal Principle Reconsidered," pp. 60-67.
5. K. C. Wheare, *Federal Government,* pp. 1 and 11-12.
6. *Ibid.,* p. 2. My italics.

different kinds of intergovernmental *dependence* or *subordination*; either the "subordination" of the general government to the provincial governments; or conversely, the "subordination" of the regional governments to the general government. In the first case, the principle of association is *"confederal,"* and in the second case, the principle of association is, for want of a better term, *"devolutionary."* Whichever of these two principles of association is operative, however, both types are clearly distinguishable from an association of states in which the regional and central governments are mutually *independent* and *coordinate*.

In passing, we may quickly note two things. *First,* that "federalism," as Wheare conceives it, is exclusively a relationship between two levels of government—the federal government and the states. Unlike the "new" American federalism, it does not entail any additional autonomous relationship, whether between the federal government and local governments in the states, for example, or between the federal government and state corporations (public or semi-public), or the state governments and federal corporations (public or semi-public), unless the relationship is established with the consent of the relevant constitutional superior in each case. *Second,* we may note that Wheare, unlike Ludolph Hugo, does not address himself to different kinds of subordination, which typify different confederal and devolutionary associations of states. For his purpose, the difference between the subordination of the general government under the American Articles of Confederation and in the German Empire is as irrelevant as is the difference, for Dicey, between the constitutional power of an English school board and that of the U.S. Congress for the purpose of classifying nonsovereign legislatures! In the manner of Dicey, it is simply enough for Wheare that in each of the four instances there was "none of that independence of general from regional [or regional from general] governments which is the characteristic of the Constitution of the United States."[7]

7. *Ibid.,* p. 7.

Given the principle as Wheare defines it, however, how do we test its presence or absence? To begin with, Wheare proposes two important operational conditions. *First*, he advises us to distinguish between the formal constitution and the actual system of government. "A country," he writes, "may have a federal constitution [e.g., Brazil], but in practice it may work that constitution in such a way that its government is not federal." Or, "a country with a nonfederal constitution [e.g., Canada] may work it in such a way that it provides an example of federal government."[8] *Secondly*, he recommends, albeit tentatively, that to operate the federal "test," it "*seems essential to define the federal principle rigidly, but to apply the term 'federal constitution' more widely.*"[9] Why? Because otherwise it would be possible to deny a "federal" classification to a constitution or system of government that satisfied the requirements of the federal principle in all but minor respects. The "sensible" or "reasonable" question in each case, he argues, is not to ask does this system of government satisfy the federal principle *absolutely*, or completely and without exception?, but "Does a system of government embody *predominantly* a division of powers between general and regional authorities, each of which, in its own sphere, is coordinate with the others and independent of them?"[10]

Now, whether the constitution of a country is one thing (viz., its practice), two things (viz., its formal provisions and its practice), or many things (viz., its appearance and reality, form and practice, beliefs and fantasies), the entire point of the analysis, whatever we choose to inspect, centers on the one big elusive question: What kind, what measure of "independence" is enjoyed by the general and regional governments? This is the question which is targeted on the federal principle, as Wheare defines it, which guides us to the search-areas where we can expect to find it, and which dictates at all times the inventory of check-questions we must ask in each case.

8. *Ibid.*, pp. 21-22.
9. *Ibid.*, p. 16. (My italics.)
10. *Ibid.*, p. 32.

Thus, if it is a question of where we mainly concentrate our search, then from a reading of Wheare it appears that our inquiry is concentrated in five broad areas; the first two form almost the whole of the traditional juridical litmus-test of a federal system, and the next three are the ingredients by which Wheare attempts to bring nineteenth-century federal jurisprudence into line with twentieth-century political realism. The five search-areas are: (1) the immutability of the division of power at the will of either the federal or state legislatures; (2) the self-sufficiency of federal and state governmental machinery; (3) the fiscal autonomy (or the fiscally "co-ordinate" status) of the federal and state governments; (4) a distribution of functions of such a kind that neither the federal nor state governments, if they choose to exercise their powers to the "full," can nullify the activity of the other; and (5) a "good" party system.

Again, if these are the dominant search-areas, then the kind of questions we must ask are also fairly clear. Thus, for example, if we are to check the first criterion, our concern must be with every possible way in which the federal "will" may have overridden or displaced state policy; whether by direct veto provisions, whether by stacking the tribunals which arbitrate the constitution, whether by the manipulation of the amendment procedures, etc. And if, say, we trace the source of interference to the use of the federal veto, then we must deal with the question of frequency: How often has the veto been used?—heavily, moderately, infrequently, on minor or major matters, capriciously or only after negotiation, etc. Or if we are probing the third criterion, the requirement that the federal and state governments must be "financially co-ordinate with the other," we are called on to examine an extensive variation of fiscal arrangements[11] to determine, who gets money from whom, in what proportions, when, how, under what conditions, involving what relations, through what machinery, etc. Or if we are

11. See my article, "The Federal Principle Reconsidered," Part I, in Wildavsky, *American Federalism in Perspective*, pp. 15-23.

concerned with the fifth criterion,[12] we are required to examine every possible way in which party ideology, structure, organization, and behaviour may have assisted or inhibited the federal manipulation of state policy-makers, and vice versa; for example, whether by threats of expulsion of state political leaders, or threats of withdrawing party endorsement at forthcoming elections, or by threats of federal (or state) intervention into state party machinery, etc.

On the face of it, it may appear that Wheare's analytical kit is fairly straightforward; and with reasonable patience any skilled inspector of federal systems might be expected to reveal the one and true identity of any political association. What he is simply called on to do is to take hold of a federal or purportedly federal system, subject its constitution and its politico-constitutional practice to a battery of test questions, satisfy himself to what extent the five criteria are satisfied, strike a balance between the total pattern of conformity and the total pattern of deviation, and locate the given system on the spectrum of federalism and nonfederalism.

However, the appearance is deceptive. The formidable difficulties of the task become readily apparent in the kind of questions that cluster around each of the five criteria, and the kind of considerations we must bring together in order to enter a final judgment. To begin with, the questions vary greatly in their susceptibility or resistance to objectivity and precision. For example, we can easily talk about the proportion of federal grants received by the states under tight operating conditions as opposed to the proportion of unconditional block grants; and just as easily, we can chart the number of times the federal government has used the veto against state legislation, as opposed to the number of times it has been persuaded to hold its hand. But it is plainly a more difficult matter to determine what anticipations are created by what use of the veto power, and what decisions are inhibited by what anticipations. Equally, it is a far more personalized geiger-counter that will discover the

12. *Ibid.*, pp. 23-29.

differences of "feel," "mood," "tone," and "morale" between
one state bureaucracy which has steadily succumbed to fiscal
servitude and another which continues to hope for the day of
fiscal independence. And in either case, we can hardly expect
that the judgment will be the same, or if the same, then for the
same reasons. But even if the judgment is the same, and for the
same reasons, then it is again unlikely that the system will be
located on precisely the same point of the spectrum of federalism and nonfederalism by all inspectors.

If we can illustrate this mode of spectrum analysis, a sce-
nario may run something like this:

> Let us take two political systems, X and Y, and compare them.
> System X is styled federal, and it has the outward look of a
> federal system. There is a division of power and provision for a
> dual system of governmental machinery, except that the central
> government is empowered, if it chooses, to use the apparatus of
> the states to carry out its administrative and judicial work in a
> number of designated areas; the central government has a power
> to disallow state legislation if, on the petition of one percent of
> its electors, it decides that the legislation is prejudicial to the
> national interest; provision is made for the central government
> to raise all the major taxes (e.g., customs and excise, income tax,
> etc.) but the distribution among the states is to be made by an
> impartial finance commission appointed by the central govern-
> ment; and the constitution can be amended by a two-thirds ma-
> jority of the total number of members in the bicameral central
> legislature and the approval of the majority of the state legis-
> latures.
>
> *Question: What is it?* Federal or not? Plainly it is not like the
> U.S. model, and judged by its structure alone, one would hesi-
> tate to call it "federal," for there are a number of transgressions
> from the model. But how serious are the deviations? The power
> of veto in the hands of the central government, even if it must
> wait for the initiative of one percent of the electors, is important;
> and so too is the ability of the central government to amend the
> constitution if it has overwhelming strength in the central legis-
> lature, and furthermore, the party in control of the government
> can control enough of its party allies in office in the state legisla-
> tures through the national party machinery. As for the depen-

dence of the central government on the states to give effect to its legislation, this is not really serious, because if any state refuses to act in accordance with central policy, the central government can compel it to do so by law, or failing this it can create administrative machinery of its own, either for the period of emergency or permanently. And in any event, given the further fact that the public service commission of the central government controls the recruitment and appointment of senior officers in these delegated federal services, it is hardly likely that they will refuse, even if so ordered by the states, to carry out the will of the central government.

[From a speculative exploration of the formal possibilities, the analysis then considers the system as it is practiced.]

To answer the question properly, however, it is necessary to examine the system at work. To begin with, the veto power has not been used many times; only fourteen times in the first sixty years of the system, and in the last twenty years, covering the great depression and World War II, barely five or six times; and with the possible exception of two or three occasions, it has only been used in matters palpably offensive to the national interest. Of course, there have been several occasions, perhaps six or seven times, when the threat of initiating the veto procedure has prevented the states from introducing a piece of legislation, and the states have claimed at odd times that the knowledge of this possibility has inhibited their initiative. It is difficult, however, to establish the truth of this. But on the whole, the veto does not appear to have been a major element in defining the relations of the central and state governments.

As for the allocation of resources, the states occasionally complain that the national finance commission is stacked by the nominees of the central government, and they always complain that they receive less than their rightful share of the total revenues raised by the central government. The truth of the matter, however, is that while the central government appoints the members of the finance commission, there is no reason to question the impartiality of most of the members; and as to the fairness of the distribution of revenue, the fact is that while the rich states have not fared as well as if they had imposed their own taxes, the poor states have done much better; and it must be further remembered that all the states receive extra monies from the central government, though to be sure by way of conditional grants-in-aid for purposes nominated and closely defined by the central government.

And so on for the other "oddities"—the use of the amending procedure, and the use of the state administrative services by the central government. Finally the analysis is brought to a close.

If you add all these considerations together, you will find that on the whole, system X, though not like the U.S. model, is in attitude and spirit near enough to it to be called "federal." True, the constitution gives the central government considerable powers of interference. In practice, however, the states enjoy a large degree of independence. And if one hesitates to call it "federal," then, at the very least, it is a "quasi-federal" system.

[Then system Y is submitted to a similar analysis.]

In form, Y conforms more closely to the U.S. model, and has none of the oddities of X. There is a division of power, a complete set of separate governmental machinery for the central and state governments, concurrent taxing powers in all fields except customs, and the U.S. type of constitutional amending procedure. However, in relation to the states, the division of power in the case of Y confers a far more extensive body of powers on the central government than in X, and this has different consequences, according to the party in office at the center, and according to the way it uses its powers. When party A (a strongly centralist-oriented social democratic party) is in office, it loses no opportunity to expand central action, and its manner is directive and coercive. It pushes national standards, national guidelines, and national welfare programs on a scale, at a pace, and in a "no beg your pardon to the states" style that continually strains its relations with the states. It doesn't hesitate to use its superior financial strength and the state-based party organization to bully the states to fall in line with its policies, and it constantly aims at tightly drawn, tightly controlled, conditional-grant programs that leave the states little room to maneuver. However, the situation is different when party B is in command of the center. Though in speech it is nominally opposed to the "economic planning" state, controlled social-welfare policies of

its opponents, it does not greatly differ from them in deeds. With
this exception: that in the exercise of its powers it is less oriented
to expansionist centrally directed action programs, it is more
sympathetic to initiative by the states, and is temperamentally
more disposed to negotiate its relations with the states as equals.
If party A were in power all or most of the time, one could hardly
describe this system as "federal" or even "quasi-federal" in anything but form. But this is not the case: in the seventy-year
history of this system, party B has been in office for thirty years
and party A for forty, twenty of which were in the postwar
period.

And so on, and on. Ultimately, the question is: *What is it?*

Note that throughout this kind of analysis, weights are at-
tached (explicitly or implicitly) and degrees of deviation from
some standard of "independence" are estimated—"small," "minor," "major," "fundamental," "predominantly"—by the federal inspector. When this metaphysical arithmetic is concluded,
each system is then arranged along either a notional or arith-
metized spectrum of federalism. Expectedly, since "each man
judges well the things he knows," each one will call his wares
in the Linnaean marketplace according to his own subjective
mode of calibration. Thus while there is common agreement on
vesting pure "federalness" on four systems (U.S.A., Canada,
Australia, Switzerland), there is disagreement on others; to one
federal inspector there are only four systems properly entitled
"federal," to another eight, to another fourteen, another eighteen, and another twenty-seven! The denial of full-blooded
"federalness," however, does not wholly exclude a system. It
depends on how the deviance is judged. If, for example, the
deviance is "significant" but not fundamental, it may still find
a place on one spectrum or another, and be designated "quasi-
federal" or "uncertain quasi-federal." But if the deviance is
judged fundamental, it will be cast off the spectrum, and left
nameless; for as Pufendorf might have remarked, today there
are too many of these mutants "to be brought within any
certain number, or divided into proper kinds." Like the bastard
unchristened child, we are left with an unnamed political association.

"FEDERALISM AS A QUALITY OF SOCIETY": LIVINGSTON ET AL.

This "sociological" approach is linked with William Livingston's influential *A Note on the Nature of Federalism*.[13] His
argument, in summary, is this: The legal/formal or jurisprudential approach to the understanding of federalism is one
approach only, and functioning as it does through the language grid of law it can only cope with legal questions. There
are other questions, however, for which the language and the
interpretative procedures of law are quite unsuited. These are
questions related to the social configuration of a society—i.e.,
the type of interests which compose it, their diversity, their
geographic distribution, their scale, their significance, etc. It is
these elements which constitute the infrastructure of its political system, and it is these elements which define and guide the
effective (as distinct from the formal) system. To the degree that
these social diversities are distributed on a territorial (i.e., geographic) basis they constitute the "federal" qualities of a society, and to the extent that territorially dispersed social
diversities are given "instrumental" recognition (e.g., the
Scottish Committee of the House of Commons), to that extent
the political system is federal.

Now observe some of the telling passages from his *Note*.

> The essence of federalism lies not in the institutional or consti-
> tutional structure but in the society itself. *Federal government is
> a device by which the federal qualities of the society are articu-
> lated and protected.*[14]

The sentence in italics is the scanning eye of Livingston's approach, and he explains it as follows:

> Every society, every nation if you will, is more or less closely in-
> tegrated in accordance with its own peculiar historical, cultural,
> economic, political and other determinants. Each is composed of
> elements that feel themselves to be different from the other ele-

13. See Livingston, "A Note on the Nature of Federalism," in Wildavsky's
American Federalism in Perspective, pp. 33-47.
14. *Ibid.*, p. 37. (My italics.)

ments in varying degrees and that demand in varying degrees a
means of self-expression. These diversities may turn on all sorts
of questions—economic, religious, racial, historical; any of these
can produce in a certain group within the population a demand
for self-expression. Furthermore, these diversities may be distributed among the members of a society in such a fashion that
certain attitudes are found in particular territorial areas, or they
may be scattered widely throughout the whole of the society. *If
they are grouped territorially*, that is geographically, then the
result *may* be a society that is federal. If they are not grouped
territorially, then the society cannot be said to be federal.[15]

Why *may* be? Clearly because it is not just diversity, or any
diversity as such that matters, even if it is territorially located,
but only if it is a *significant* diversity, if it makes some demand
for recognition and protection by some *instrumentality*, and if
the rest of the society agrees to satisfy this demand. Thus:

> Component states exist because of some *great significant* diver-
> sity of such importance that it is felt that only a federal organi-
> zation can offer it sufficient protection.[16]

The notion of "instrumentality" is important to Livingston's thesis. He repeatedly argues that if we wish to discern the
genuine face of federalism we must neither look to the clauses
of a constitution alone, though "the provisions of the constitution are a good rough guide to the pattern of instrumentalities," nor even to the practice of the constitution. We must also
search among the

> . . . many things that are far from constitutional in importance
> in the ordinary sense of the word. *It includes such things as
> habits, attitudes, acceptances, concepts and even theories*. It in-
> cludes perhaps the rules of the American Senate, the makeup of
> the Canadian cabinet, the zeal of the Baptist Karens in Burma.
> All these may serve as *instrumentalities* for the expression of the
> diversities within a society, and whether a country is federal or
> not may best be determined by examining *the pattern of these*

15. *Ibid.* (My italics.)
16. *Ibid.*, p 38. (My italics.)

instrumentalities and not by checking its constitution against an *a priori* list of the characteristics of a federal constitution.[17]

What does this mean in applied terms? It means, for example, that:

> It is meaningless to insist that the Union of South Africa is unitary and not federal because of certain characteristics of its constitution. . . . The fact is that in many instances South Africa operates its institutions as though its constitution were federal.
> . . .
>
> A similar argument may be advanced in regard to Great Britain, a country whose constitution is most often cited as being typically unitary. Many elements of British public life are witness to the vitality of the federal principle in British society. Indeed there would seem to be an operative right to secede from that community, exemplified by the withdrawals from it in recent years of such elements as Burma and Ireland. Scotland has its own courts and legal systems. . . . Scotland, furthermore, is especially protected in the House of Commons by a Scottish committee which deals with questions pertaining to that area.[18]

And so, on to France, and presumably Italy. In sum, his thesis is:

> Federalism is a function not of constitutions but of societies. Viewed in this way, it will be seen that federalism is not an absolute but a relative term; there is no specific point at which a society ceases to be unified and becomes diversified. The differences are of degree rather than of kind. All countries fall somewhere in a spectrum which runs from what we may call a theoretically wholly integrated society at one extreme to a theoretically wholly diversified society at the other. . . . But there is no point at which it can be said that all societies on one side are unitary and all those on the other are federal or diversified. If a society contains territorial groups that are so different from the rest of the society that they require some instrumentality to protect and articulate their peculiar qualities, then the society is

17. *Ibid.*, p. 43. (My italics.)
18. *Ibid.*, pp. 43-44.

likely to provide some means for the creation of such an instrumentality.[19]

To those wearied of the elaborate classificatory sophistries of the "constitutionalists," Livingston's essay first came as a breath of fresh air. In one stroke the coils that had enveloped federal theory appeared to dissolve, and thus, freed from symbols and fictions, the federal inspector could now look at the true face of reality. Exhilarating and promising as this essay is, however, it is one thing to be free, and another to know what to do with one's freedom. If, as it appears, the covenantal roots are cut away so radically, what's left in the name? Is this the true representation of federalism, the true heir of "foedus," or is it a new genetic diversion unlike anything known before? If the federal aspects of a polity is to be found in instrumentalities that reflect "significant" territorially organized social diversities, will any instrumentality do, or only "significant" instrumentalities? And what is a Livingstonian to do with the question: "Is system X more/less federal than system Y?" Ignore it, argue its inappropriateness, or assess the number, range, practice, and significance of the "instrumentalities" in the manner of the "Federalism is a matter of degree" school?

Livingston is most certainly not a dogmatist nor an arithmetician. He constantly warns against drawing sharp lines, weighing or measuring.[20] But valuable as his insight is, his terms are slippery, arbitrary, and incorrigible. It is a theory without a tool-kit. Eschewing empirical precision for subjective intimation, it becomes metaphysics; and once again, different federal inspectors are fated to yield different results. For example, if diversity is the quality of any society, is it at all likely that there can be any territory within it where there are no "significant" social, economic, or cultural elements? Livingston takes the point by arguing that if the diversity is *signifi-*

19. *Ibid.*, p. 40.
20. *Ibid.*, pp. 40-41. "It cannot be said that when a society is just so diversified, it requires a federal constitution. In the first place, we are unable to quantify social and political forces to the degree necessary to warrant such a demarcation; and secondly, the forces themselves are incommensurable."

cant, then the "society is likely to provide" some instrumentality to satisfy it. But what is the test of significance? Success, or what? If, as it appears from his examples, it is success, then we are presented with an *ergo hoc propter hoc* argument. Thus: "The fact that Scotland has its own legal system, its own courts, and a Scottish Committee in the House of Commons, is evidence that the territorially organized social diversity is significant. For were it not so, if there were no strong Scottish Nationalist feeling, it is unlikely that 'instrumentalities' would exist." Indeed, such is Livingston's faith in this hypothesis that he predicts that:

> If . . . Scotland, or perhaps even other elements, were to seek
> actively for secession, it seems most unlikely that the right would
> be challenged.[21]

Doubtless if the Scottish Nationalist Party chose to follow the urban guerilla techniques of contemporary liberation movements, in the face of English obduracy, it might succeed in cancelling even the Act of Union with Scotland. But how could one prove him wrong? Would the Scottish failure to secede, for example, or to convert the United Kingdom to an American-model federation instead of a pallid system of Westminster "devolution," signify the insignificance of the Scottish diversity in Great Britain, the insignificance of the Scottish arguments, or the insignificance of the Scottish arms? Or, does the Basque or Catalan failure in Spain, for example, or the failure (to date) of the Kurdish National movement in Iraq, suggest that the Spanish and Iraqian society lack federal qualities? Or are the federal qualities of a society sufficiently attested by the continued agitation of a territorial movement for some recognition, even if resisted by the rest of society? Again, would the 1974 meeting of the Cornwall Stannary Parliament in England, the first in 220 years, reinforce the federal qualities of English society or not? We are free, it seems, but we are also put out to sea without a map, a compass, or a sextant, with only our eyes to fix on the stars and gauge the drift of the waves.

21. *Ibid.,* p. 44.

"FEDERALISM AS A PROCESS": FRIEDRICH ET AL.

Carl Friedrich's work on federal theory constitutes an impressive corpus of writing over some forty years. It has undergone a good deal of refinement and restatement in numerous sources over this period. But the most recent formulation is in the first and last chapters of his *Trends of Federalism in Theory and Practice*.[22] Let me quote two passages from these chapters. They characterize his position singularly well.

> The rapid expansion of federal regimes and proposals has led to a steady broadening of the theoretical scope of federalism. Nearly thirty years ago one could write that "from an empirical standpoint, an effectively centralized government, a federation, a confederation or league of governments (states), an alliance, an alignment, a 'system' of independent governments (states) and finally completely unrelated governments—all these could be represented as differences of degrees in the relation of governments to the persons subject to their rule." This was the beginning of the end of the traditional juristic notions, preoccupied with problems of sovereignty, of the distribution of competencies, and of the structure of the institutions. As for the latter, the emerging pragmatic and behavioural view recognized that a federal system (or state) could be characterized simply by the fact that its structure "resembles a league in one or more of its organizational features." Federal theory has come a long way since then, and the decisive turn is the recognition of its dynamic aspect: that federalism implies a *process* of federalizing, as well as a pattern or structure. It is the core of such a theory that a federation is a union of groups, united by one or more common objectives, rooted in common values, interests, or beliefs, but retaining their distinctive group character for other purposes. It unites without destroying the selves that are uniting and is intended to strengthen them; it constitutes organized cooperation of groups as groups. The nature of the particular groups which federate will have a decisive impact upon the particular system. Understood as *implying the process of federalizing*, an emergent

22. Friedrich, *Trends of Federalism*, Chap. 1, "The Theory of Federalism as Process," pp. 3-10, and Chap. 23, "Approaches and Conclusions," pp. 173-184.

federal order may be operating in the direction of both integration and differentiation; federalizing being *either* the process by which a number of separate political units, be they states or other associations (churches, trade unions, parties, and so forth), enter into and develop arrangements for working out solutions together, that is to say, making joint decisions and adopting joint policies on common problems, *or* the reverse process through which a hitherto unitary political community, as it becomes differentiated into a number of separate and distinct political subcommunities, achieves a new order in which the differentiated communities become capable of working out separately and on their own decisions and policies on problems they no longer have in common. Federalism refers to this process, as it does to the structures and patterns which the process creates. . . .

And:

. . . federalism should not be seen only as a static pattern or design, characterized by a particular and precisely fixed division of powers between governmental levels. Federalism is also and perhaps primarily the process of federalizing a political community, that is to say, the process by which a number of separate political communities enter into arrangements for working out solutions . . . on joint problems and, conversely, also the process by which a unitary political community becomes differentiated into a federally organized whole. Federal relations are fluctuating relations in the very nature of things.[23]

In some respects there is considerable empathy between Friedrich's and Livingston's perspectives. Both wish to place the federal concept in what Bryce called the concrete world of facts rather than constitutional theory; and both wish to train the federal inspector's eyes to focus on the "dynamics" of the system as well as its epiphenomena, viz., its "structure," "pattern," "design," or "instrumentalities." But like Livingston's formulation, Friedrich's attempt to reconstruct federal theory in the light of the "new facts" is burdened with ambiguity and tension. The ambiguity lies in Friedrich's notion of the *"federalizing process"*; the tension is created between his desire to

23. *Ibid.,* pp. 176-177 and p. 7.

explore the new frontiers of federal theory and his desire to keep some faith with the past; between his desire to divest himself of traditional juristic notions and his desire to maintain the relevance of structure; between his desire to focus simultaneously on federalism as a dynamic process and federalism as a design. Together they pose dilemmas enough to strain the heart of the boldest federal inspector. Let me explain.

The unfolding of a process in time, change, metamorphosis, fluctuation, integration, differentiation, progression, and retrogression is the language of dynamics, and the experience of all political systems. In drawing attention therefore to what Bryce in 1901 called "political dynamics"[24] or what Laski in 1925 termed the "kinetics" of life, Friedrich has rightly pointed to an imperative of analysis, description, and explanation which contemporary—and perhaps all past—students of politics imbibe (or should imbibe) with their mother's milk. Thus, Friedrich notes that the Federalists understood this well when they devised ways of amending the constitution, and he gives instances of this dynamic process in the history of the changing relations between the federal and state governments in America.[25] The same phenomenon can, of course, be instanced in a thousand other examples: in the changing relations of Rome to Byzantium, the Holy Roman Emperor to his kings and princes, Westminster to its colonies and dominions, in the tightening or loosening of alliances, in the formation of alliances where none existed before, in the relations of nations which are not formally allied, in the relations of central to local governments, and so on. Truly nothing is static except in the graveyard, and even there the metabolism of nature continues to do its work.

All this, doubtless, is what Wheare and Livingston mean to

24. James Bryce, *Studies in History and Jurisprudence*, Vol. I, pp. 257-258. See also Harold J. Laski, *A Grammar of Politics*, p. 284. If the notion of a "static" condition is part of the language of politics, it draws its meaning from the analogy of classical physics rather than society. Nevertheless, in classical physics the static situation can always be regarded as a special case of the dynamic situation.

25. Friedrich, p. 18. "They were, in fact, the first who realized, at least in part, that federalism is not a fixed and static pattern, but a process."

convey by referring to the importance of examining the changing "practice" of a federal system. And if Friedrich is drawing
our attention to this simple fact, it is a perfectly unexception-
able observation. The difficulty begins, however, with the first
question: What kind of changes in what relations fall within
the compass of the "federalizing process"? All changes or particular changes? If, for example, the "federalizing process" embraces any and every change in the relations of two or more
tribes, cities, states, empires, and regions, whatever these relations may be at any given moment, then the term "federalizing"
possesses no special meaning to distinguish it from a host of
other terms. One might just as well speak of these changes in
such terms as the process of centralizing/decentralizing, con-
centrating/deconcentrating, centralizing/devolving, unifying/
dispersing, integrating/disintegrating, collectivizing/individ-
ualizing, integrating/diversifying, solidifying/liquefying, or
any other play on the synonyms and antonyms of coalescing,
amalgamating, socializing, agglutinizing, assimilating, fusing,
merging, composing, fraternizing, banding, etc. Though cast
in an uncommon usage, "federalizing" would simply become
one of many descriptive terms to denote any and every process
of change in the relations of any two or more entities, and one
may choose to designate the process as one pleases. However,
Friedrich does not seem to intend this result, and the question
then is, what does he intend by the "federalizing process"?

The brief answer is: "Federalizing [is] *either* the process
by which a number of separate political units . . . enter into and
develop arrangements for working out solutions together . . . *or*
the reverse process through which a hitherto unitary political
community . . . achieves a new order."[26] But this answer can
hardly settle the matter. Why not? Consider, first, the term
"federalizing" itself. If we take its normal grammatical usage, it
simply suggests the process of *becoming* federal, by either one
or both of the two routes that Friedrich speaks of, and this
process entails all those activities involved in the *making,
bringing about,* or *moving toward* a federal end, by contrast

26. *Ibid.*, p. 177.

with the completion of the process—i.e., "federalized"—or arrival at the point of destination which someone may be disposed to call "federal."[27] And as such, therefore, we can only properly use the notion of a "federalizing process" for those changes in the relations of two or more entities where the direction is clearly federal. Thus, for example, it cannot be sensibly used to describe any and every cooperative relationship between two or more states simply because it *may* lead to a "federal" end (e.g., building a tunnel under the English Channel to facilitate traffic between England and France, or abolishing visas between Western European countries), unless one wishes to argue that all cooperative relationships between countries lead to this end, as indeed one may wish to argue that all courtship leads to marriage. And similarly, it cannot be used to describe all those changes in the relations of two or more entities which clearly lead or tend away from the condition of being federal. For how can one speak of, say, a secessionist movement (e.g., 1860 in the United States, or 1933 in Western Australia, or Quebec in recent times), or a federal takeover of the governance of a state (e.g., Kerala in India), or any tendency which contributes to the hegemony of a central government (e.g., the central monopolization of income taxation), or the dismemberment of a system, as part of the "federalizing process"? Indeed, to use the notion of "federalizing" for what may be a reverse or defederalizing process (e.g., the process of unifying, or the process of confederalizing) is as confusing as if we were to describe the process of, say, socializing, liberalizing, communizing, collectivizing, or centralizing, and their *opposite* tendencies, by the one and the same term.

In a word, it does not help the matter to use the one notion, the "federalizing process," to describe all the varied and fluctuating changes which take place in the relations of central and regional governments, or indeed the international relations of two or more cooperating states; and this because some changes

27. Cf. the idea of socializing, decentralizing, collectivizing, civilizing, liberalizing, etc. See also Dusan Sidjanski, "Will Europe be United on Federal Lines?"

(however expressed, whether in institutional or symbolic terms) lead away from and others lead towards, some weaken and others reinforce, the condition of being "federal." The only way we could make sense of this notion, therefore, is to use it to describe only those changes which go to the making, maintenance, or reinforcement of a federal system (e.g., the choice of tax-sharing in preference to a federal monopoly of the income-tax field)—assuming, of course, that we could agree on what the nature of being federal was like. But if we use it for this purpose, it would reduce the notion of the "federalizing process" to a description of the obvious.

Far more serious than the complications of grammar, however, is the question which is at the heart of the matter: What precisely does Friedrich think federalism is about? What is its "structure" or "design," and what is the nexus between federalism as a "process" and federalism as a "design" or "structure"? How can we tell whether the beginning of a cooperative relationship will or won't lead to a federal end, or tend away from it? We may be able to infer such a direction, for example, in cases where there are specific declarations of intent to become federal (e.g., the Indian Constituent Assembly in 1946, or the Australian Constitutional Conventions from 1890 to 1899, or perhaps even the activity of the European "federalists"). But this may not be possible, either because one cannot always rely on declared intentions (e.g., "We intend to go federal, but by federal we simply mean a common market or zollverein arrangement, no more"), or because the actors themselves may have no long-term sense of the direction they are likely to travel, and are simply responding to specific problems as and when they arise.[28] Again, we may be able to infer such a direction from the kind of arrangements made, or from some kind of objective signposts. But what are these signposts, what are these kinds of arrangements that entitle one to assume a "federal" direction? For example, how could one know at the moment when the Articles of Confederation were signed in 1778 that the

28. See Andrew Shonfield, *Europe: Journey to an Unknown Destination*, p. 96.

American colonies were engaged in or had committed themselves to a "federalizing process"? Or why should one assume
that the first glimmerings of cooperative arrangements between
the Australian colonies in the mid-nineteenth century were destined to express themselves in the terms of 1901? Or why should
one assume that the first meeting of the Cornwall Parliament in
220 years, or the resurgence of the Scottish Nationalist Party,
betoken the beginning or the continuation of a "federalizing
process"? Or, indeed, why should one presume that the EEC,
NATO, SEATO, etc., are set on a "federal" course? Because
they are "cooperative" arrangements, because of their decision-
making or executive structure, or because the declared aim, in
one or another case, is "federal"?

These doubts arise precisely because, while Friedrich formu-
lates a theory, it is difficult to get a firm purchase on it: he
oscillates between "federalism as a process" and "federalism as
a structure or design"; he shies off from a close account of what
a federal "structure" is about; and he gives little or no indication of what the link between the "process" and the "structure"
is. For example, in a paper he read to the International Political
Science Association conference at Geneva in 1964, "New Tendencies in Federal Theory and Practice," he stated:

> As new nations have emerged, as international organizations
> have multiplied, and the study of the politics of various groups
> and organizations beyond the governmental level, not only par-
> ties, but interest groups, churches, trade unions have been en-
> compassed, federalism has been more dynamically interpreted as
> the effective organizing of diversity and comprehensively related
> to the pluralism of modern industrial societies. . . . *Federalism is
> thus seen to be a process rather than a design*, as had been the
> prevailing outlook in the past. *Any particular design* or pattern
> of competencies or jurisdictions *is merely a phase*, a short-run
> view of a continually evolving political reality. *This does not
> mean, of course, that the former view is devoid of meaning; at
> any particular moment, the task of describing a federal order is
> still definitely a matter of ascertaining its design*. But the once
> crucial distinction between a federal state and a confederation of

states has become blurred, though it may still have significance
in law and political practice.[29]

But four years later, in a footnote to the concluding chapter of
Trends, Friedrich corrected himself by saying:

> I overstated the issue by insisting that the dynamic aspect of
> federalizing replace the static aspect of patterning and structur-
> ing; I believe the present formulation to be more appropriate.[30]

Plainly, had Friedrich simply equated the "federalizing process" with *any* process whereby *any* groups (territorial or nonterritorial) come together (cooperate) to work out *some* of their
common problems in *any* kind of association (or arrangement),
without regard to the nature, pattern, or design of their association, most of the difficulties would have been put to rest. He
would have found an historical haven for himself in the Greek
idea of *koinon*, or in Althusius' idea of *consociatio symbiotica*.
But his current formulation hardly removes the doubts either
about the perimeters or the operational value of his theory. For
in trying to link the process whereby groups cooperate as
groups with a particular "pattern" of association, he creates a
problem to which his theory gives no clear answer. And the
problem is this: If the "task of describing a federal order is still
definitely a matter of ascertaining its design," then what is his
"design"?—for there are many schools of "design." For example: there are those who, like Wheare et al., assert the distinc-
tiveness of the federal "pattern" or organization and pose
"tests" to determine how much or how little, how real or how
false, the "pattern" is; there are those who assert that it is not a
distinctive pattern or structure, that the so-called "tests" are
crude and subjective, and that the difference between the relations of decision-making units in federal states and the relations between decision-making units in any other state—e.g.,
confederal, decentralized unitary state, etc.—is simply a matter
of degree, not kind; and there are those who, like Livingston,

29. C. J. Friedrich, "New Tendencies in Federal Theory and Practice."
30. Friedrich, *Trends of Federalism*, p. 184, n. 10.

appear to argue that any instrumentality which recognizes a "significant" territorially based "social diversity" (e.g., the Scottish legal system) betokens the federal quality of a society. Which of these, or what combination of these positions, does Friedrich support? And even if we knew his "design," is it to become some sort of magnetic pole, Greenwich Mean Time, or center of gravity by which all federal inspectors can set their compasses or watches to measure the process of moving towards, maintaining, or moving away from the condition of "federalism"?

The answer is not clear, for his focus constantly shifts. In analyzing existing federal systems, purported federal (e.g., U.S.S.R.), or regional systems (e.g., Italy) his alignment is with the traditional questions: How much autonomy does each state or region enjoy, and by what means? Whereas with international, or supra-national systems (e.g., EEC, UNO), it is the evidence of groups entering arrangements to work out solutions in common that preoccupies him. At one place he has traditional constitutional factors before his eyes,[31] or cites Wheare's testing procedure with approval;[32] at another he would relax these tests to include systems that Wheare totally rejects from his federal collection—e.g., the British Commonwealth of Nations. In sum: Friedrich would, if he could, reach for the best of all possible worlds: to find a formula that would harmonize the voices of the past and the voices of the present; to bring federal studies into the whole body of "community," "association," "alliance," "integration," or nation-building theories; to retain the terminology and the tests of post-1787

31. "Effective separate representation of the component units for the purpose of participating in legislation and the shaping of public policy, and, more especially, effective separate representation in the amending of the constitutional charter itself, may be said to provide reasonably precise criteria for a federal as contrasted with a merely decentralized order of government." Or "No sovereign can exist in a federal system; autonomy and sovereignty exclude each other in such a political order. . . . No one has the 'last word.' The idea of a compact is inherent in federalism, and the 'constituent power,' which makes the compact, takes the place of the sovereign." (Friedrich, *Trends*, pp. 6 and 8.)

32. *Ibid.*, p. 178.

federalism; to speak of a "federalizing process" which embraces the becoming, the maintaining, or the disappearing of federalism, and more. But if this is possible, it is not on his terms.[33]

We have already remarked upon the twin tendencies that have overtaken contemporary federal systems. Whether we call them integration or centralization, however we explain their cause, and however long the centripetal phase will dominate the erratic oscillation of power in these, as in all, societies, the common phenomenon is the emergence of a distributive, all-influential, Leviathan central government. And the recent impact of it all in the United States, the birthplace of the 1787 idea of federalism, has precipitated nothing less than a second, albeit bloodless, crisis of identity. Thus while there was a time when one could speak of federalism and America in the one voice, this easy equation is no longer possible. Because for some, federalism in America is dead; for some, it is dying; for some, it is only ailing but far from dead or dying; for some, a new-style federalism (creative, cooperative, higher, national) has arisen in the place of the old style (dual federalism); and for some, only the death of the "old" is certain, while the character of the "new" is still as vague and uncertain as its future.

Indeed, *quot homines, tot sententiae*—there are as many opinions as there are men. But American scholars seem broadly agreed upon two things: *first*, in pronouncing the demise of "dual federalism" (i.e., the "old" federalism)—that tidy ornament of jurisprudential fiction which envisaged a dual world of sovereign, coordinate, coequal, independent, autonomous, demarcated, compartmentalized, segregated, and distinct constitutional personae, the federal and the state governments; and *second*, in affirming in its place the idea of something like a

33. Speaking of the vicissitudes of American federalism, and the different theories used to describe the changes, he concludes that "All this can be meaningfully interpreted when the federalizing process is given central attention." (*Ibid.*, p. 27.) I wish it were that easy!

vast cooperative of all governments of all levels, together with all group and individual interests of society, in a complex pluralistic relationship of sharing, reciprocity, mutuality, and coordination, as the true face of American federalism.[34]

Let me convey something of this position by three excerpts from the work of two of the best-known exponents of the "sharing" view of American federalism: the late Morton Grodzins and Daniel Elazar, the editor of Grodzins' major work, *The American System.* The first group of extracts will give Grodzins' exposition of the sharing thesis in the setting of his argument that "the structure of the United States government is chaotic"; the second group restates Grodzins' thesis in the metaphor of a "marble cake"; and the third group is one of a number of Elazar's expositions of the "sharing" thesis, in this instance with reference to the fallacies of "dual federalism."

First, Grodzin's thesis:

. . . *government in the United States* is *not simple,* either in structure or process.

The structure of the United States government *is chaotic.* In addition to the federal government and the 50 states, there are something like 18,000 general-purpose municipalities, slightly fewer general-purpose townships, more than 3,000 counties, and so many special-purpose governments that no one can claim even to have counted them accurately. At an educated guess, there are at present some 92,000 tax-levying governments in the country.

. . . The multitude of governments does not mask any simplicity of activity. There is no neat division of functions among them. If one looks closely, it appears that *virtually all governments are involved in virtually all functions.* More precisely, there is hardly an activity that does not involve the federal, state, and some local government in important responsibilities. *Functions of the American governments are shared functions.*

. . . This view of chaos in government is not one of despair. The system of American government flaunts virtually all tenets of legislative responsibility and administrative effectiveness. It appears always to be wasteful of manpower and money. At times

34. For example, see J. L. Sundquist, *Making Federalism Work,* pp. 6-10.

it threatens the very democracy it is established to maintain. But it works, it works—and sometimes with beauty.[35]

Sharing defined:

The significance of "sharing" depends upon the meaning given the word. In using the word, we will restrict its meaning. "Sharing" or "shared functions" will designate *one or more* of the following conditions:

a. In the formulation of any given program, *significant decision-making* power is exercised *both* by those in the federal government and those in state and local governments.

b. Similarly, where *officials of all governments* exercise *significant responsibilities* in the administration of a given activity, this will be called a "shared" function.

c. Finally, where *representatives of all governments* exert *significant influence* over the operations of a given program, it will be considered a form of sharing.[36]

Second, Grodzins' restatement of the "sharing" thesis in the much-quoted metaphor of the "marble cake":

. . . the general view [of the American political system] is the view of the three-layer cake of government, the institutions and functions of each "level" being considered separately.

In fact, the American system of government as it operates is not a layer cake at all. It is not three layers of government, separated by a sticky substance or anything else. *Operationally, it is a marble cake,* or what the British call a rainbow cake. *No important activity of government in the United States is the exclusive province of one of the levels,* not even what may be regarded as the most national of national functions, such as foreign relations; not even the most local of local functions, such as police protection and park maintenance.

If you ask the question "Who does what?" the answer is in two parts. One is that officials of all "levels" do everything together. The second is that where one level is preponderant in a given activity, the other makes its influence felt *politically* . . . or through *money* . . . or through *professional associations.*

35. Morton Grodzins, *The American System,* pp. 3-4 and 7. (My italics.)
36. *Ibid.,* p. 11.

> *The central hypothesis . . . of this book, stated in its extreme form, is this: all levels of government in the United States significantly participate in all activities of government.*[37]

Third, Elazar:

> The central hypothesis of this study is that the traditional picture of nineteenth-century American federalism is unreal, that federalism in the United States, in practice if not in theory, has traditionally been cooperative, so that virtually all the activities of government in the nineteenth century were shared activities, involving federal, state, and local governments in their planning, financing, and execution. The pattern of sharing in American federalism was established, in its essentials, in the first decades after the adoption of the Constitution.
>
> . . . [The] central conclusions [of this study] are that the theory of dual federalism was not viable when applied to concrete governmental problems in specific situations even in the early days of the Republic; that dual federalism when interpreted to mean demarcation of responsibilities and functions has never worked in practice; and that, while the amount of governmental activity on all planes in relation to total activity of American society . . . has increased, the governmental activity that existed in the nineteenth century was shared in much the same manner as governmental activity in the twentieth century. All this is true despite formal pronouncements to the contrary, made by the political leadership of the day who spoke in terms of demarcation but practiced cooperation.[38]

What precisely is the status of the "sharing hypothesis" as a theory of federalism? Does the "federalism of sharing," like "cooperative federalism," simply betoken an adjustment in our vocabulary to pacify the "ghost" of a dead federalism—as Landau may have suggested[39]—or is the federal spirit of 1787 still alive and well, though clothed in other dress? Let us approach the matter by considering how the federalism of "shar-

---

37. *Ibid.*, pp. 8 and 13.
38. See Elazar's essay, "Federal-State Collaboration in Nineteenth-Century United States," in his book *Cooperation and Conflict*, p. 84.
39. Landau, "Baker v. Carr and the Ghost of Federalism," p. 244.

ing" answers to the two imperative requisites of "traditional" federalism: the division of power, and its corollary, the *independence* of each member to conduct its affairs as it thinks best, without responsibility to anyone but its own electors.

To begin with, one might suppose that in a true fraternity of states, or in some kinds of partnership, or indeed in most marriages, it is more appropriate to speak of a "division of functions" or "division of labor" rather than a "division of power"; for where the notion of "division" or "demarcation" is put aside in favor of joint or shared action, where a situation becomes analogous to the sharing of "common property," there is no longer a "mine" or a "thine" implied by demarcation, but only "ours." And in such truly sharing situations, there is no place for the conventional idea of a "division of power."

But the sharing hypothesis of Grodzins and Elazar is not like this, even though the faint sounds of the purest federal fraternity may be occasionally heard in their work. Neither of them has suggested that sharing entails the pooling of all powers, whether legislative, administrative, or fiscal, as one might share common property. Nor have Grodzins or Elazar suggested that the idea of sharing displaces or is in conflict with the conventional notion of a "division of power." On the contrary, if Grodzins does not speak to the matter directly, Elazar repeatedly stresses that if federalism is to survive and prosper, then the practice of sharing must function side by side with the constitutional diffusion of power. For just as decentralization implies a center from which functions can be decentralized, so the idea of cooperation and sharing between territorially based governing units, implies units with power to cooperate and share. One can hardly speak of cooperation between master and slave, except in the voice of poetry.

However, if it is clear that Grodzins and Elazar accept the principle of a "division of power" as a continuing ingredient in their federalism of sharing, it is far from clear precisely what they have accepted; for example, what their acceptance implies in regard to the content of the division, or in regard to the minimum number of exclusive powers that Wheare insists is necessary to the idea of federalism,[40] or, indeed, the great over-arching question of independence. The matter of content and exclusivity need not detain us. Intriguing as these questions may be, it is hard to see whether it greatly matters now how we divide the infinite world of political activity, or between what number of governmental levels (two or more), when the ethos of the sharing system is to play down demarcation and exalt partnership. Equally, it is hard to see whether it is necessary (except perhaps for a purely scholastic or juridical theory of federalism) to preserve a minimum of one head of exclusive authority for each of the two principal governments, when, as Grodzins tells us, in practice no important activity of government is the exclusive preserve of any government. The vital question that defines the character of the "new" federalism, and to which all other questions are linked, is: Where do the "new" federalists of sharing stand on the question of independence?

Now the catechisms of old-style federal theory run like this: Within their respective "ambit" of power (however foggy or uncertain the perimeters) and the terms of the bargain, the members of the federal state are each masters of their own destiny, free to initiate and pursue what ends they choose, rational or irrational, and in what manner they choose, politics and the constitution permitting. They may cooperate or not cooperate, reciprocate or not reciprocate, share or not share, fraternize or not fraternize; they may even lease or permanently alienate their sovereign birthright for a mess of federal pottage, if they choose; but unless they choose of their own free will, they cannot be made to share, to cooperate, to negotiate, to fraternize, or to reciprocate against their will.

Question? Which of these ideas does the "sharing hypothesis" retain and which does it abandon? If, for example, as Aaron Wildavsky argues, "the operational meaning of federalism is

40. "There must be some matter, even if only one matter, which comes under the exclusive control, actual or potential, of the general government and something likewise under the regional governments. If there were not, that would be the end of federalism." (Wheare, *Federal Government*, p. 79.) Also see Sawer, *Modern Federalism*, pp. 166-168.

found in the degree to which the constituent units disagree
about what should be done, who should do it, and how it
should be carried out,"[41] then how far can one member of a
community living by the faith of sharing disagree? How far can
one state hold a national program to ransom, for instance, by
refusing to cooperate? Conversely, how far can and how far
should the national government go to isolate, neutralize, or
nullify the "independence" of a deviant state by creating or
threatening to create alternative modes of delivering its services
or manipulating its grants as a punishment? Indeed, if it is now
true that the federal initiative is unlimited, and its constitutional resources ample for whatever it wants to do (with or
without the help of other states), does the new federalism still
sanctify the consent and participation of all parties as the
highest federal virtue, or is it more kindly disposed to the
coercion or circumvention of the states in the name of the
national interest? In sum, is the voice of the new federalism of
sharing the voice of Esau or the voice of Jacob? For if it is the
voice of Jacob, then the new federalism is not new; but if it is
the threatening voice of Esau, then it is neither new nor old, it
is simply American "federalism" in want of a less brotherly
name than "sharing."

The federalists of sharing speak of "independence" in different measures and in different voices. Compare and contrast
Grodzins' and Elazar's positions. Grodzins takes the view that
in an interdependent world, it is unrealistic and undesirable to
speak of "independence" any further.

> State and municipal strength thus must be viewed from the per-
> spective of a tightly geared economy and a highly interdepen-
> dent culture. In this context, "independence" in the traditional
> sense becomes a relatively unimportant and highly unrealistic
> attribute. It is unimportant because it is undesirable in the con-
> text of modern society. It is unrealistic because it is impossible to
> achieve. Independence is impossible and unrealistic for states
> and municipalities in the same manner and for roughly the same

41. Aaron Wildavsky, *A Bias Toward Federalism*, p. 1.

reasons that the national government cannot be independent of events in Europe or Vietnam.[42]

If not old-style "independence," however, in what language shall we speak of their "new" status, and how shall we measure their "new" relations? Grodzins' answer is: the *"strength"* or *"vitality"* of the *various units in the federal system.*

> A far more valid measurement of the strength of states and municipalities is the extent to which these governments are constructively involved in the great public service functions. From this point of view, no one can doubt that the states and municipalities are strong. They are spending more money, doing things more effectively, touching more people in more important ways than ever before in their history. And they are doing this in fruitful collaboration with the national government. Virtually all functions of government in America are shared functions. And the sharing of the states and localities in these functions is not simply passive participation. One sees, at every turn, states and localities contributing to planning, policy, and administration.[43]

And further on:

> *Whatever governmental "strength" or "vitality" may be, it does not consist of independent decision-making in legislation and administration.* Federal-state interpenetration here is extensive. . . .[44]

What of Elazar? Elazar's writing on federalism is considerable, but his position on this question is not developed as directly or as explicitly as Grodzins'. Like Grodzins, he argues that the "strength and vitality" of the states continues to flourish and grow[45] as never before; and like Grodzins he mobilizes much the same evidence to illustrate this tendency. But unlike Grodzins he does not confront the question of "independence" directly; he neither renounces the concept nor argues, even

42. Grodzins, p. 381.
43. *Ibid.*
44. *Ibid.*, p. 388. (My italics.)
45. Elazar, *American Federalism: A View from the States*, pp. 197-216.

indirectly, that it may be an inappropriate way of talking about the relations between the federal and state governments. Why not? The answer could hardly be that the evidence needed to establish the existence of state "independence" is precisely the same as the evidence of their "strength and vitality." If it were so, then much of the anticolonialist or secessionist rhetoric of liberation would dissolve with the counter-demonstration of rising GNP figures, expenditure on local schools and welfare, increasing local participation in colonial welfare programs, etc. And indeed, when Grodzins joins the states and municipalities together in the one phrase, and evidences their strength and vitality in the same way, he is surely not equating the two ideas! What then is Elazar's position here?

To begin with, Elazar's conception of American federalism is virtually coextensive with American society—its spirit, its way of life, its politics, its economy, and its constitution.[46] Just as it was for the Founding Fathers, so it is now: the symbol is freedom, the diffusion of power is its instrument, and the foundation stone of the noncentralized partnership of the federal government and the states is the idea of an indestructible union of indestructible states. What "independence" or "freedom" is to be enjoyed by the partners, however, is to be gleaned from a number of suggestive phrases and sentences scattered throughout his writing. Thus, in one place he speaks, for example, of "partnership" as the distribution of "*real* power among several centers which must negotiate cooperative arrangements with one another in order to achieve common goals."[47] In another, he refers to "*negotiated cooperation*" as the central theme of the American federal system. Elsewhere he puts it, "The political principles that animate federal systems emphasize the *primacy of bargaining* and *negotiated coordination* among different power centers which exist by *right*. . . ."[48] At another place he refers to "cooperative relationships which do not involve the loss of *integrity* of the general or constituent governments." Or,

---

46. Elazar, *The Meaning of American Federalism.*
47. Elazar, *American Federalism*, p. 3. (My italics.)
48. Elazar, "First Principles," *Publius*, Vol. III (Fall 1973), p. 3.

". . . it has always been the *prerogative* of the states to decide whether or not to accept any federal aid. . . ."[49] Or he speaks of the emergent pattern of cooperative relations which the states, and increasingly the localities, operate as *equal partners.*

What do these two positions reveal? As a preliminary, one may infer that while both Grodzins and Elazar subscribe to the "sharing hypothesis" as a descriptive fact and a desired goal of the American federal system, they appear to differ on the value of autonomy in the age of interdependence, on the relative importance of federal and state autonomy, and on the permissibility of national coercion. Elazar, it would seem, mainly reaffirms the traditional view in a way that appears to draw him more closely to Wheare's mix of constitutional doctrine, political sentiment, and political practice than Grodzins does. For Elazar, consent and equality are as of old, the stuff of "negotiated cooperation," and coercion in any shape or form is a total denial of the spirit of partnership. Grodzins' position is less clear. While he does not explicitly say so, it could be inferred from his philosophy of an "interdependent" world that in some situations, and for some purposes, some measure of some kinds of pressure, dominance, compulsion, or duress would not offend the credo of sharing.[50]

49. Elazar, *Cooperation and Conflict,* p. 19.
50. "When the consequences of free activity may result in dangers to the whole society, then freedoms must be limited. This is true for the constitutional freedom of individual American citizens. It is no less true for social institutions. The controls exercised over businesses, labor unions, and lobbying groups are a case in point. The decline in the discretion of cities and states is a related case. *If state or city freedoms result in social policies that are inimical to the national economy or in public health programs that endanger the lives of whole population groups, then it is quite clear that those freedoms should not be exercised.*" (Grodzins, p. 380; my italics.) The question of "coercion" permeates much of the argument in contemporary American writing about the kind of organizational relations that are appropriate to different brands of "sharing." And doubtless it is precisely the consequences of these differences in devising and operating intergovernmental programs that Aaron Wildavsky had in mind when he wrote: "Where conflict is viewed as functional, consent is considered essential. Where cooperation is normative, coercion is deemed legitimate. Because units should cooperate, they ought to be coerced when they conflict. When units ought to differ, they can only resolve their differences by consent." (Wildavsky, *A Bias Toward Federalism,* p. 22.)

Now the difference between Grodzins and Elazar may be represented simply as a mild difference of values or emphasis or both. But whether one represents the differences between them (or, for that matter, between other American students of the "sharing" school) in these terms or not, the fundamental obstacle in coming to grips with both Grodzins and Elazar is the same problem that has haunted a great deal of contemporary theory the moment it left the relative safety of federal jurisprudence for the messy world of politics: viz., *the generality, the ambivalence, and the uncertainty of their analytical and operational code.* For example, it is fairly plain that if Grodzins has rejected the reality and desirability of *"near-absolute independence"* for the states, he did not reject the idea that some version of independence or autonomy is indispensable to every brand of federalism—dual, cooperative, new, permissive, etc. On the contrary: the common-day inspectoral questions of "who shares in what" and "how much and when," "who is consulted," "how great and how willing is the involvement," etc., are as much before his eyes (and obviously Elazar's) as they are in Wheare's mode of analysis.[51] Given this, it would follow for Grodzins, albeit broadly, that if the states were denied either a *significant* decision-making role or *significant* administrative responsibility or *significant* operational influence in any joint federal-state program, or if in Elazar's terms "negotiated cooperation" is the euphemism for a "Godfather's" duress ("Washington has made the states an offer they can't refuse"),[52] or if the credo of "partnership" is translated not in the relationships of "equals" but in the dominance of one and meekness of the other, then the relationship is patently offensive to Grodzins and more emphatically to Elazar.

51. Richard Lehne has rightly argued that both the "dual" and "cooperative" concepts are narrowly constructed on the autonomy dimension of state-national relations. See Lehne, "Benefits in State-National Relations."

52. See James A. Maxwell: "The danger to be avoided in use of specific-purpose grants is covert coercion of state governments. A state government, when confronted with a *fait accompli* in the form of a 'new' federal grant with conditions which are fiscally oppressive, cannot readily refuse the grant. It will bear its share of the cost of the grant whatever its priorities may be." (Maxwell, *Specific Purpose Grants in the United States: Recent Developments*, p. 86.)

But as Mr. Doolittle might have said, a "translation in the broad does not dispose of the problem in the deep," and this because Grodzins' and Elazar's operational concepts are even less capable of precise analysis or instrumentation than Wheare's. Wheare at least had a comparatively simple task of it. Of his five criteria that we noted earlier, at least two (co-equal jural status of the national and state governments, and the possession of self-sufficient governmental machinery) are relatively easy to check for breaches. It is only when the probe enters his third, fourth, and fifth criteria (the fiscal autonomy of the national and state governments, a viable balance in the division of power, and the "good" type of party system) that federal inspectors, in search of conformism and deviance, enter a twilight world which bares the softness of their tools.

And precisely such a world is Grodzins' "chaotic," "crazy-quilt" world of intergovernmental relations. For instance, what exactly does Grodzins look for in a relationship when he is testing whether federal, state, or local participation is "significant" or not? What Grodzins' study makes brilliantly clear, of course, is the *fact* of cooperation, joint action, involvement, participation, and mutual aid, together with all the legislative and executive techniques that make it possible. Whether he uses the example of the "national" police system, or the "national" recreation system, or the "bundles" of federal services offered in small towns throughout the United States, the evidence of intergovernmental relations is striking. What Grodzins does not reveal, however, is how he distinguishes "significant" from "insignificant" (or "peripheral") involvement in either the planning, formulation, or administration of intergovernmental policy. He assumes significance in all his examples, but he does not explain, direct, or argue its use. Indeed, just as Livingston is silent on the meaning of "significant diversity,"[53] as distinct from "insignificant diversity," so Grodzins is silent about "significant and insignificant involvement" and thereby exposes himself to precisely the same analytical difficulties.

53. See pp. 171-172 above.

Plainly, the opportunities for whim and fancy in using such highly personal analytical tools are so great that it must affect the consistency, reliability, and comparability of the results we can expect from two or more inspectors testing Grodzins' special thesis. And though we may offer the obvious instance— e.g., federal grants-in-aid—to illustrate the "significant" kind of involvement, the fact is that the "significant" basis of cooperation may not be (and is not) always "cash," the cash component may not always be "significant" for every or any party, and other forms of involvement may not always be "significant," nor their "significance" obvious.

Grodzins, of course, was acutely aware of the untidiness, tentativeness, and complexity of the matter. As he wrote immediately after formulating the three conditions which defined his notion of sharing:

> *All three statements are deceptive in their simplicity, and none is easy to test against actual events.* They are further complicated because sharing can take different forms.

And again:

> There are difficulties of analysis that cannot be completely solved. *The tactic of the following chapters is to make minimum claims: the real contribution of both federal and state-local views to a given decision must be apparent* before it is labelled a shared decision; and the real participation of both sets of officials must be apparent before a given activity is labelled a shared function. . . . what is revealed in the nature of sharing from this sort of evidence is not the whole picture. . . .[54]

But rich as his documentation is, the solidity and particularity of his data stand in marked contrast to the fragility, generality, and arbitrariness of his sharing hypothesis.[55]

54. Grodzins, pp. 11-12. (My italics.)
55. For a valuable critical essay on Grodzins' thesis, albeit from a different approach, see A. Lee Fritschler and Morley Segal, "Intergovernmental Relations and Contemporary Political Science: Developing an Integrative Typology," *Publius*, Vol. I (Winter 1972), pp. 95-122, esp. 101. Also see Reagan, *The New Federalism*, p. 160.

And this, in substance, is the case with Elazar also; whether we are trying to analyze his varying formulations of the "sharing" hypothesis (e.g., "bargaining"/"open bargaining," "integrity"/"fundamental integrity," etc.), or whether we are trying to reconcile Elazar's and Grodzins' views (e.g., where Elazar gives primacy to the doctrine of "open bargaining" between equal partners in the federal process, Grodzins is concerned with the concept of "significant involvement" in intergovernmental relations rather than "independence"). For instance, it is not at all clear how we can operate effectively with the idea of "open bargaining" unless we are told what parameters of "openness" are realistic for the various bargainers; whether they are operating in something analogous to a classical free-market economy (which is unlikely to be as true for local government agencies as for the states or the federal governments in some types of grant-in-aid programs), a monopolistic economy, or an oligopolistic economy. Nor is it clear how we can operate effectively with the concept of "negotiated cooperation" unless we are told how to identify the disguises in which coercion masquerades as consent, or "control" as "supervision" in intergovernmental relations.[56] Nor is it clear what we can regard as the "integrity" (or "fundamental integrity") of, say, the states, unless we are told whether Elazar is concerned with their political "prestige," their "economic viability," their "constitutional posture," their role in intergovernmental programs (as Grodzins understands it), "their capacity to resist federal duress," "their effectiveness as governing machinery," etc. Nor is it clear, further, how we are to determine these matters; for plainly, none of the conceptual particles that go into the making of Elazar's particular compound of "sharing" federalism is so clear that it can be easily recognized when it comes walking down the street. And it is at least questionable whether Elazar's

56. See exchange of views between Representative Charles E. Goodell of New York and Anthony J. Celebrezze, Secretary of Health, Education and Welfare: "'What makes me tear my hair in frustration is when you say there are no controls,' Mr. Goodell said. 'Mr. Goodell, you call it controls, I call it objectives,' Mr. Celebrezze replied quietly." (Quoted in George F. Break, *Intergovernmental Fiscal Relations in the United States*, p. 79.)

"bargaining" tool can stand up to the test of a rigorous analysis any better than Grodzins' three "ideal" modes of sharing.

The task of analysis is even further compounded if we try to run both Grodzins' and Elazar's "theories" in tandem. Let me illustrate: First observe that in theory there are many possible ways of combining federal, state, and local governments in cooperative schemes which would fall within any one or more of Grodzins' "ideal" types of sharing, and many that would not. Grodzins does not clarify the widely different relations that may be built from his "ideal" types or their deviants. But if we remember that Grodzins' hypothesis will be satisfied if at least one of the three conditions is present, then here, for example, are two hypothetical cases which may be negotiated between the parties. The first consists of an arrangement which satisfies *one* of Grodzins' three conditions—where all three governments (federal, state, and local) "share" a significant responsibility *only* in the administration of a joint project, and in no other respect (e.g., policy-making). The second consists of an arrangement which does not satisfy any of Grodzins' three conditions.[57] We may represent the two cases in the following way:

Case 1: a. significant decision-
              making power   = federal and state
                                               governments
          b. significant administrative
              responsibility   = federal, state, and local
                                               governments
          c. significant operational
              influence   = state and local governments

Case 2: a. significant decision-
              making power   = federal government
          b. significant administrative
              responsibility   = state and local governments
          c. significant operational
              influence   = state and local governments

57. How real is Case 2 (or any other version of it), and how often does it occur in the total complex of ongoing intergovernmental arrangements? For if it

Now secondly, observe that "sharing" (or "significant" involvement) as Grodzins understands it, and "bargaining" as Elazar proposes it, are values and conditions which will not always, or necessarily, coincide. Bargaining, in other words, however free and open, cannot guarantee that any of Grodzins' conditions will be satisfied, simply because the parties may have other aims in mind. Indeed, the outcome of Elazar's "negotiated cooperation" may be the very opposite of what Grodzins stipulates as sharing. And if this is correct, then it follows that there will be a number of combinations that may satisfy Grodzins' notion of sharing, but offend Elazar's idea of bargaining (e.g., either because the "bargaining" was not "open," or under duress, or indeed because a state may have been persuaded to "bargain" away its "integrity" through a political misjudgment on its own part!); or conversely, there are combinations that may satisfy Elazar's idea of bargaining but breach every one or any combination of Grodzins' "ideal" types of sharing; and of course, there are patterns of cooperation that may fall neither within Grodzins' meaning of sharing nor Elazar's prime condition of open bargaining.

If we were now to draw a mental diagram for the purpose of fixing and comparing coordinates for each intergovernmental arrangement on the intersecting axes of Grodzins' idea of "sharing" and Elazar's idea of bargaining,[58] it becomes very plain again that the opportunity for personal divination in adjudicating degrees of "significance" in sharing, and degrees of "freedom" in bargaining is compounded by more than a mere factor of two! To illustrate, simply permutate and reclassify all the possible ingredients with all their possible variations in a case such as this: The federal government decides policy and supplies the money in a grant-in-aid program; the local govern-

---

occurs at least as often as Case 1 (or any other version of it), then the utility of a theory which covers only half the known cases of "cooperation" is, like any .5 correlation, highly questionable.

58. See, for example, Daniel Elazar's attempt to fix coordinates on the twin axes of "federalism as structure" and "federalism as process" in "The Ends of Federalism" (working paper prepared for the founding conference of the Joint Center for Federal and Regional Studies, Basel, June 1975).

ments face the administrative and operational problems; and
the state government, if involved at all, reluctantly goes along
with the whole thing.

Clearly, with operational criteria such as these, the road to
judgment can be little different from that of those whose analytical procedure relies on mathematical analogies and person-
ally tailored slide-rules to estimate precisely where a political
system, an institution, a piece of legislation, a financial
arrangement, or any intergovernmental "bargain" is to be located on some metaphoric *continuum* or *spectrum*. Still less
ought we to be surprised that criteria as fluid and imprecise as
this can be responsible, in whole or in part, for the divergence
between those who assert that federalism in the United States is
alive and well, and those who deny it.

Thus, for example, in the mid-sixties, Grodzins could contest
those "prophets of doom . . . so fashionable today" who declared the end of American federalism, by pointing to the
strength and *vitality* of the states and the cities in the "fruitful
collaborative system" that emerged in the "past half-century"
alongside "the inevitable growth to primacy of the central government."[59] And in the same period Elazar could give a similar
assurance:

> There are few cases of federal expansion at the expense of on-
> going state operations. While the states may have had the
> authority to act in any given field from the first, federal involve-
> ment has generally come about where the states have not acted or
> have been unable to do so. . . .
>   . . . It is the American commitment to noncentralization that
> has forced the federal government to seek ways to develop na-
> tionwide programs with minimum national requirements
> within the framework of the cooperative system.
>   . . . It has always been the prerogative of the states to decide
> whether or not to accept any federal aid proferred under formal
> grant programs. And, despite the prevalent idea that no state can
> resist federal subsidies, few, if any, states have taken advantage of
> every grant offered them.[60]

59. Grodzins, pp. 390-391.
60. Elazar, "Federalism and Intergovernmental Relations" in *Cooperation and
    Conflict*, pp. 5 and 19.

And Landau could argue to the contrary that federalism had fulfilled its purpose; and by its "dramatic success" in enabling a nation to evolve, had signalled its own demise:

> This is the "crisis of the states." They have had to yield to a "system dominated by the pervasiveness of federal power." They have lost status, prestige, and power. They have lost so much, Leonard White stated, "that competent observers at home and abroad have declared that American federalism is approaching its end." Roscoe Drummond put it more directly: "Our federal system no longer exists."
>
> Drummond's conclusion is not sensational. A system so dominated by central power cannot, by definition, be classified as federalist. If, analytically, we stop the system at various times—ranging from 1800 to the present—and if we examine the state of the system at each of these times, i.e., if we compare the operations of government with the classical or constitutional models, we are bound to find less and less correspondence. As a matter of fact, this is what our researches have unquestionably demonstrated. Our findings are of such order that it becomes increasingly difficult to represent our governmental system as federalist.[61]

It is an endless contestation, and an endless polemic.[62] But it is important to note that the differing diagnoses among the "doctors" of twentieth-century American federalism do not necessarily stem from ambiguous facts or fuzzy criteria of what federal life or death is about; nor from any differences about the kind of criteria we should use to test federal life or death; nor even from the precise way we apply agreed criteria to any given situation.[63] Obviously, any one or all of these may explain the

---

61. Landau, "Baker v. Carr and the Ghost of Federalism," p. 244.
62. For example, see I. Sharkansky, *The Maligned States*, esp. p. 105; and Reagan, *The New Federalism*, esp. pp. 159-164. Also Elazar, "Cursed by Bigness"; and Vincent Ostrom, "Can Federalism Make a Difference?" Again, see argument between "Publius," "Cato," "Althusius," and "Polybius," in *Publius*, Vol. II (Spring 1972), pp. 98-147.
63. For example, Wheare draws attention to the fact that Freeman adopted a similar method to his own in distinguishing "constitution" and "government." (Wheare, *Federal Government*, p. 16, n. 2.) What is probably more interesting, however, is that the use of the same method could yield a different classification. Thus note (p. 29) where he joins issue with Freeman on

differential diagnoses. But they are, as it were, the epiphenomena. For however we dissect the literature, the questions constantly and fundamentally at issue, on or below the surface, are:
What was *American* federalism intended to be? What is it now?
What can it be in the new age? And ultimately: What do the
contending and changing voices want it to be about?

This is the crisis of identity, and, as always, the constant
attendants of such a crisis are beliefs, ends, and values. These
are the unseen interests which fashion the criteria, condition
the expectations, issue the diagnoses, and write the reform proposals. And if this is so, then we can scarcely expect a similar
diagnosis of federal life, illness, or death from one who proposes the thesis that "American federalism is not strictly speaking a federal system, but is rather a *national system* that is
profoundly tilted towards decentralization"; or one who asserts
the noncentralist, nonhierarchical character of the American
system, who speaks of the "prerogatives," "integrity," and
"rights" of the states, alongside the language of "sharing,"
"partnership," and cooperation; or one who speaks in the pure
voice of classical "dual federalism"; or one who lays the Constitution aside to project a society of "higher federalism" where
there is no demarcation, no separation, only a fluid multi-
faceted partnership of all with all, all organizations of state
with all the associations of society.[64]

the classification of the Constitution of the United Netherlands. Indeed, the
whole dispute over the classification of the state form of the German Empire is as much a conflict between different conceptions of federalism as it
is over the use of different methods in the application of the same conceptions, or even the different value given to the same institutions by the use of
the same analytical methods.

64. Note, for example, Martin Diamond in a discussion with Nelson Rocke-
feller on American federalism: "When people think of Federalism, they
think of enumerated powers in the Constitution or mechanical division of
authority between the central government and the states. But it's a much
richer textural thing than that. Federalism in our country is closely involved, for example, with voluntary associations, private groups of individuals. . . . In a way, what you say about the association of formal governmental Federalism with informal, private association reminds me of the
origin and meaning of the word. Federalism derives from the Latin for
'faith': 'fides,' as in bona fides, or confidence; and Federalism is, to some ex-

What price, then, the theory of "sharing federalism"? There can be little question that much of the contemporary American attempt to explain their own federal experience, much of the effort to reconcile, revise, modernize, extol, or vindicate their system, has been no less ingenious and rigorous, nor indeed less proud and ethnocentric, than the labors of the Germanic "doctors" to clothe the Germanic Empire with a fitting identity. Nevertheless, the intensive work of recent years has not only confirmed the inadequacy of the "dual federalism" model, but it has made it increasingly plain that the "crazy-quilt" of the "new" intergovernmental relations cannot even be explained by the model of "sharing federalism."[65]

The new focus on "sharing," "intergovernmental cooperation," or "partnership" has, to be sure, all the simple imagery and seductive tidiness of "dual federalism." And more: by approving and enjoining the fraternization of all governments with all private and communal bodies, it takes on something of the same evangelical and moral enthusiasm with which the voices of "dual federalism" once preached the credo of intergovernmental celibacy. But if sharing is to be the new way of understanding the nature of American federalism, if "open bargaining," "negotiated cooperation," "constructive involvement," and "significant participation" have become the insignia, the paths, and the goals of the "new" federalism, then the simplicity of sharing, whether as system, procedure, objective, or ethic, is grossly deceptive. It conceals a veritable bog of difficulties; and to traverse the ground between Grodzins' concept of sharing and its practice may prove as treacherous as crossing the gulf between the fictional world of "dual federalism" and reality. And this is so not simply because of the prob-

---

tent, a faith system. . . . It's a relationship of individuals associatively or of units of government associatively, but not under coercion, not under necessary sovereignty, but out of a kind of volition—out of a faithful compliance with the terms of the association." (From the transcript of a videotaped discussion made for USIA; by courtesy of the U.S. Consulate General, Melbourne.)

65. Wildavsky, *A Bias Toward Federalism*. His review makes this point amply clear.

lematic way that political theories are distanced from the grub-
by facts of life, but also because neither Grodzins nor Elazar
really presents a fully developed theory of "sharing" or "partnership" to guide their followers through all the changing sea-
sons,[66] any more, indeed, than the system devised by the Founding Fathers in 1787 gave their heirs a clear theory of intergovernmental relations to light their way. Indeed, where "dual
federalism" was progressively elaborated in a juristic, albeit
doomed, theory of "non-interference" and a political theory of
separatism, the "new" federalism (except for an occasional hint
in Elazar's work) does not offer a precise operational, still less a
normative, code of conduct befitting the federalism of sharing
—unless, of course, it is the code of ethics implied in the "open
bargaining" of the free marketplace: *caveat emptor*.

The paradox, in truth, is that the closer microanalysis has
brought scholars to the untidy facts of intergovernmental life in
America (as indeed elsewhere), the greater the conundrum of
identity, the wider the net to catch deviant behaviour, and the
greater the disposition to new mythologies. Worse: the theory
of "dual federalism" always was (and still is) an impeccable
theory of constitutional authority and status, even if it was also
an unnatural and somewhat paranoic theory of intergovernmental relations. But in seeking to erase the last vestiges of
"dual federalism," and in their concern to substitute the politics of fraternity, or a modern version of Althusius' *consociatio
symbiotica universalis*, for the politics of celibacy, many schol-

66. To have done so would have involved them in composing a normative and
    descriptive theory of cooperation, touching such matters as: What, if any,
    obligations to cooperate should govern the relations of governments? What
    considerations should pass between cooperating parties? What should be
    the proper rules of bargaining? What should be just or equitable considera-
    tion between "equal" partners? What is permissible and what impermis-
    sible conduct between partners in the formulation of specific kinds of coop-
    erative agreement? Etc. Perhaps such a theory could be composed now,
    unlike 1787, out of the myriad of cooperative arrangements, institutions,
    practices, and understandings that have accumulated over time. But ob-
    viously, a normative theory of intergovernmental cooperation is political
    prescription and, as such, it can only be cast in the context of a theory of
    federalism—which, if we agree with Diamond, emerges from a general the-
    ory of political ends!

ars have been thrust into a deep ambivalence: whether to proclaim the end of the legal division of power and acclaim the federal government as the dominant, if not sole, arbiter of how power will be diffused; whether to acknowledge the omnicompetence of the federal government but acclaim the American political process, in its entirety, as the proper and effective heir to this decision; whether to acknowledge the traditional contributory roles of federal/state authority but set them within the changing limits of political circumstance; whether to acknowledge the possibility of all these and other variations on the theme of "diffusion" and proclaim that, however chaotic, contradictory, varied, or incoherent federal/state relations may be, all belong to the house of federalism, so long as most parts are left with some dignity for most of the time; or indeed, whether to weave all this, together with doctrines of pluralism, liberalism, individualism, the philosophy of Montesquieu, Locke, Mill, and Adam Smith, into a nontransferable theory of federalism unique to the American culture. Such ambivalence is scarcely surprising. In the very nature of an open polity, in what moves it to action and defines its relations, in what generates its tensions and expresses its doubts, it could not be otherwise.

7

In the End?

Or, towards the year 4000 A.D.

How is the subject to continue its days? Is it to be brought back to its humble beginnings, calibrated on a spectrum of "more or less," slowly poisoned by increasing doses of qualifications and rechristenings, or enlivened by fresh ideas on the ways human beings associate with each other? Here are some of its present names:

dual	federalism	coercive	federalism
orthodox	federalism	competitive	federalism
classic	federalism	centralized	federalism
polis	federalism	decentralist	federalism
traditional	federalism	peripheralized	federalism
cooperative	federalism	fused	federalism
bargaining	federalism	corporate	federalism
integrated	federalism	national	federalism
interdependent	federalism	social	federalism
creative	federalism	oligarchic	federalism
new	federalism	unitary	federalism
permissive	federalism	constitutional	federalism
functional	federalism	international	federalism
pragmatic	federalism	military	federalism
organic	federalism	political	federalism
pluralistic	federalism	monistic	federalism
monarchic	federalism	polar	federalism
perfect	federalism	total	federalism
imperfect	federalism	partial	federalism
direct	federalism	contract	federalism
private	federalism	feudal-functional	federalism
"picket-fence"	federalism	incipient	federalism

204

Are these all similitudes, flowing from the same generic source, or are some so distant, the resemblance so faint, that they are alien to all others?

There has rarely been a time in the history of the subject when it has been in a more depressing and uncertain condition than it is now.[1] And this is not because we know less about the facts of federal life; on the contrary, there has never been a time when so much has been known about the subject, nor indeed an awareness of what more there is to know.[2] Only the more we have come to know about it, the less satisfying and the less reputable has become almost the whole of our legacy of federal theory. Virtually all the perspectives of politics have contributed to the decline of the federal Humpty-Dumpty. And it is not clear how we can put him together again, in what shape we can put him together again, whether we ought to put him together again, or, indeed, whether the new kings of Macedon and the emperors of Rome will let us put him together again in any shape or form which threatens to bridle their zeal.

The greatest disenchantment has come with the discovery that, throughout history, the repeated mix of culture-bound, time-bound theorems of constitutional rationalism and political sentiment have not prepared statesmen and electors for the facts of federal life, nor have they explained their experience as they lived it. Whether it is the method of Bodin, Althusius, Pufendorf, the later practitioners of nineteenth-century German *staatslehre* and Anglo-Saxon constitutional jurisprudence, or the bias of the Federalist Papers, Freeman's interpretation of the Achaean League, or Dicey's comparision of unitary and federal states, the result is the same—the manipulation of reality to serve a new rationalism or a new cause, or both. Indeed, it is difficult to do even a modest guided tour of the federal literature through Sobei Mogi without wonderment at the magisterial confidence with which successive generations of scholars set the conditions, diagnosed the ills, and prognosed the fate of those who chose to live the federal life.

1. In this section I have relied on my chapter, "The Federal Principle Revisited," in D. P. Crook (ed.), *Questioning the Past.*
2. Richard H. Leach, "Federalism: A Battery of Questions."

Observe, for instance, this passage in Dicey:

The distribution of all the powers of the state among coordinate authorities *necessarily* leads to the result that no one authority can wield the same amount of power as under a unitarian constitution is possessed by the sovereign. A scheme again of checks and balances in which the strength of the common government is so to speak pitted against that of the state governments leads, on the face of it, to a certain waste of energy. *A federation therefore will always be at a disadvantage in a contest with unitarian states of equal resources.*[3]

How quaint and how transparent it all seems now; this constitutional rationalism, this excess of ideologized federal theory. Yet how understandable for any generation (e.g., John Stuart Mill, Bagehot, Maine) nurtured in the political jurisprudence that one head was the law of nature and two heads a freak, a mutant, an abomination. And how especially understandable that Dicey, who opposed the federalization of the British Empire, should write about federalism as if it were simply a bastard child of a political passion for union without unity, a genetically inferior departure from the single Westminster order. But if this is the portrait of a British unitarian of 1885, is Harold Laski, historian, political theorist, and British Labor party activist, so different in 1939? Remember his epitaph to the "Obsolescence of Federalism" where he indicted the American federal system, and indeed federalism everywhere, because of its inability to "cope with their outstanding problems," "to satisfy living demands," "to keep pace with the tempo of the life giant capitalism has evolved."[4] Yet again, how else? Given Laski's acceptance of the Marxist theory of the state,

3. A. V. Dicey, *Introduction to the Study of the Law of the Constitution*, pp. 171-172. (My italics.) See also G. A. Denison, *The Power and Stability of Federal Governments*, discussed by J. H. Burns in "An English View of Federalism in 1829." Denison's thesis is an extreme formulation of Dicey's proposition that "federal government means weak government." In Denison's own words, federal government is a form "whose tendency, unless counteracted by the operation of more prevailing causes, is disunion and decay."

4. Harold J. Laski, "The Obsolescence of Federalism."

especially in the 1930's, could we expect him to separate the "federal principle" from the very particular way that American society chose to live its federal life?

The tradition which gave impetus to these ideas is not wholly spent. If it is crumbling on one side of the Atlantic, it is alive and well on the other. While Grodzins and Elazar may write in the language of "sharing" and "partnership," Wheare and the Kilbrandon Commission still translate the federal vision in terms of sovereignty, coordinate status, and independence. Indeed, the Kilbrandon view of what federalism is about might well have been taken directly from the pages of Dicey.[5] And as for Wheare, is there any difference in the way he distributes the categories of federal/quasi-federal from the nineteenth-century style of arranging unions or leagues of states in a dichotomous federal scheme of perfect/imperfect, pure/impure, or total/partial? Or is there any difference in the way he searches for federal deviants—for example, the disallowance power of the Canadian Governor-General, the unusual power of amendment in the Swiss Constitution, the federal monopoly of income taxation in Australia—from the way German scholars wrangled over the majoritarian principle, the role of the Emperor, the possibility of dividing functions fairly, or the necessity for independent administrative organs?

But if we have not all been freed from the hypnotic comfort of traditional scholasticism, there is little left to guide us through a rapidly changing world of new shapes and endless variations but a few harmless maxims (e.g., "unity in diversity," *imperium in imperio*, "union not unity," etc.), the structural shell of 1787 U.S. federalism, a set of constitutional fictions, a universal history of covenant, an increasing volume of diverse "federal" practice, and ultimately a personal vision of individual and communal autonomy. Almost all the older propositions attributing universal qualities to federalism are either emasculated, surviving in a new language, or defended by new rationaliza-

5. *The Report of the Royal Commission on the Constitution, 1969-1973*. For the Commission's view of what "federalism" is about, see the "short description" in Chap. 13, pp. 152-161.

tions. What has cast us forth from the Garden of Eden, what we have learned from the sheer force of historical experience is this: *first*, that the informational, explanatory, and descriptive value of the federal symbol is very much less than it was once thought to be; *second*, that the language of traditional analysis offers us little security; and *third*, that the structure of a federal system is simply the designation of the visible, never the invisible.

At base, the federal symbol may still tell us that there are territorial groups (communities, states, nations, regions, etc.) which desire to draw together, or reconstitute themselves in a particular form of association, constitutionally and structurally nearly distinct from all other forms of association. Outside of this, however, it can tell us nothing at all about a vast number of things that critically shape the life of any political system. For example:

> the reasons why states wish to unite in the federal form;
> the precise division of functions;
> the potential range, status, and influence of these functions in a given society;
> the manner and the conditions in which these functions can and are likely to be exercised in each system;
> the area, population, wealth, and its socio-geographic distribution;
> the social composition, diversity, cohesion, habits, skills, institutions, and traditions of its politics;
> the party system, its dispersion or concentration, its "federal" and other ideas, its inner power structure, and its bases of support;
> the centrifugal and centripetal factors which play upon and within the system;
> the valuation and experience of local institutions;
> the official perceptions and expectations of the "federal" system;
> the texture of federal-state relations in peace, depression, and war;
> etc.

And because nothing of this is communicated in the statement "This country has a federal system of government," because nothing of the personality, texture, color, taste, or smell of a political system is conveyed, two things follow:

First, we cannot infer that a political system by virtue of being "federal" *is* or *is not* likely to be (by comparison with a unitary or any other system)

> strong or weak in war;
> adaptive or maladaptive in crisis;
> flexible or rigid, fast or slow, in constitutional adjustment;
> potent or impotent in satisfying "living" demands;
> conservative or progressive in its politics;
> legalistic or political in resolving its conflicts;
> efficient or inefficient in the provision and delivery of its basic services;
> faithful or faithless to the pursuit of liberty;
> "ecumenical" or "parochial" in intergovernmental relations;[6]
> centralist or decentralist in disposition;
> etc.

Nothing, indeed, but that which strictly flows from the kind of society it is.[7]

Second, if we cannot presume more than a formal identity (for a division of power is by itself only a partial rather than a total identification), then we should *not* expect to profit from the pursuit of such comparative questions as:

> Why do federations succeed or fail?
> Do federal systems inhibit economic growth?
> Do federal systems frustrate economic planning?
> Are federal systems appropriate to underdeveloped countries?
> Are federal systems costly forms of government?
> Do federal systems promote or inhibit freedom?
> Do federal systems achieve a higher rate of performance in the delivery of goods and services than unitary states?

6. I am indebted to Ivo Duchacek for this delightful contrast.
7. G. E. Lavau, *Les Partis Politiques et Les Realités Sociales.* Lavau's critique of Duverger's *Les Partis Politiques* is a valuable parallel study for students of federalism. Note for example: "L'element decisif qui explique le 'Wafd' ce n'est ni sa structure, ni le systeme partisan ou electoral où il s'inscrit, c'est l'Egypte." (Lavau, p. 9.)

Do federal systems produce a higher rate of citizen participation
in decision-making than unitary states?

Are federal systems subject to "higher levels of conflict and
political controversy" than unitary states?

Do federal systems require "larger expenditures of time and
effort on public decision-making than a unitary system of
government"?[8]

Etc.

Indeed, it is little wonder that the findings of these pursuits
are so often ambivalent, strained, and cast at such vaguely
guarded levels of generality (e.g., "highly" federalized political
system) that they have little power to instruct or enlighten.
Consider, for example, the conclusions of the study *Why Federations Fail: an Inquiry into the Requisites for Successful Federalism.*

Were there common factors which brought each of the four
federations to this end? [East Africa, Malaysia, Central Africa,
and the West Indies] . . . The principal cause for failure, or
partial failure, of each of the federations studied cannot, it thus
seems, be found in an analysis of economic statistics or in an
inventory of social, cultural, or institutional diversity. *It can
only be found in the absence of a sufficient political-ideological
commitment to the PRIMARY concept or value of federation
itself.*[9]

8. Some of these questions are simply conversions of fifteen propositions formulated by Vincent Ostrom to illustrate the "difference" a federal system
can make. (See his "Can Federalism Make a Difference?," esp. 229-232.)
Ostrom's view is reminiscent of Dicey's classic contrast between federal and
unitary states, and it commits the same fallacy of attributing unwarranted
universal qualities to partly homogeneous systems. Not only is it highly
improbable that any of the fifteen ways in which federalism can make a difference can be proved, it is even easier to think of ways of refuting each and
every proposition. For example, take his proposition that "citizens in a
highly federalized system will be able to exercise greater voice in the conduct of public affairs (than citizens in a unitary political system)." (P. 229.)
Can one presume that a federal system of low literacy, low GNP, and poor
liberal traditions, compared to a unitary system similar in size and population but with high literacy, high GNP, and rich liberal traditions, will (by
virtue of being federal) rank higher on the "participation" scale than the
unitary system?

9. Thomas M. Franck (ed.), *Why Federations Fail*, Chap. 5, pp. 167-199, esp.
177.

Would we be more surprised if we had asked "Do federal systems promote freedom?" and were told "They promote freedom
when they value freedom"? Or consider a parallel question:
Why do unitary systems of government such as Great Britain,
Japan, Denmark, Iceland, Egypt, Spain, etc., survive, while
other unitary systems, such as Estonia, Latvia, Armenia, Tibet,
did not survive? Would it surprise us to be told that "unitary
political systems survive when there is sufficient commitment
to the primary concept or value of the unitary state, and in the
absence of a sufficient commitment, the unitary state will probably fail"? Or again, consider a classic instance of special pleading, the Federalists' case against "confederal" systems of
government. Madison's and Hamilton's arguments were constantly sustained by the proposition that all ancient and
modern confederations had come to grief because the central
government lacked the strength to cope with their internal and
external enemies. Ergo—to avoid this historic fate let the center
be strengthened. The advocate's purpose is always plain—to
win a cause. But it was only some eighty years later that Edward
Freeman gave the fitting reply:

> The fact that no state can resist a power which is physically
> stronger than itself proves nothing as to the merits of particular
> forms of government. Aristocratic Rhodes, democratic Athens,
> federal Achaea, and kingly Macedonia were all alike, as their
> several turns came round, swallowed up by the universal power
> of Rome.[10]

The truth of the matter is—and experience has been the
teacher—that some "federal" systems fail, some do not; some
are able to resist aggression, some are not; some inhibit economic growth, some do not; some frustrate *some* kinds of
economic planning, some frustrate *other* kinds; some develop a
great diversity of public services, some do not; some promote a
great measure of civil liberty, some do not; some are highly
adaptive, some are not; some are highly efficient in servicing
the needs of a modern state, some are not; some gratify values

10. Edward A. Freeman, *History of Federal Government*, Vol. I, p. 54.

that others do not. Indeed, over a long or short span of time, some are always something (socially, economically, politically, administratively, constitutionally) which other federal systems are not. But whatever their condition at any one time (e.g., adaptive/maladaptive, conservative/progressive, efficient/inefficient, etc.), it is rarely clear that it *is* so because of their federalness, or the particular character of their federal institutions, or the special way they practice federalism, or in spite of their federalness. And further: when at some moment federal systems resemble or differ from each other in some respect or other (e.g., efficiency or inefficiency in the delivery of public services, tepidity or zealotry in the pursuit of civil liberties), the reasons, though sometimes traceable to similarities or differences in their constitutional structure, flow more often than not from the things they share in common as societies or the things that distinguish them as societies.

In a word, we are dealing with things that are only partly the same. And if there is, as Macmahon suggests,[11] a common "logic" running through all federal systems, it lacks the force to transcend their different political cultures and impose a common political direction. This is the massive fact we have come to learn. To expect to give a common explanation for, say, the failure of the Weimar Federal Republic and the Central African Federation in any other than trivial generalizations, or to expect that political performance will necessarily differ because states are federal or unitary, is to exaggerate the limited potentialities of contemporary federal theory and mistake the limited value of the distinction between federal and unitary systems.

The central implication of all this for the future of federal theory is plain enough. If the credo of unity in diversity still flourishes, it wears many more faces than five, eight, fourteen, eighteen, or twenty-seven.[12] And this because no one or a thousand relationships of groups of men, whatever their shape or basis, can exhaust their associational potentials. Put directly, it may be doubted whether it is possible to make any further

11. Arthur W. MacMahon, *Federalism*, p. 6.
12. See Appendix, listing the "federal" states according to six authors.

progress with the term "federal," or any of its variants. Phylo-genetically senile, these terms have become crackly, dry, and scattered among the tribes. We have worked them to the bone, and saddled them with burdens they were not built to endure. Indeed, to try to salvage the term "federal" by such qualifying prefixes as "quasi-federal" does not resolve the matter any more than if we tried, with similar logic, to refresh the terms "con-federal" or "unitary" with similar prefixes (e.g., quasi-con-federal, quasi-unitary), or with similar new refinements (e.g., "integrated unitary/confederal," "pragmatic unitary/confeder-al," etc.), or with entirely new compounds (e.g., "quasi-oli-garchic-confederal"). Only the dissonant tonal sound of the compound chord could disqualify some of the choices.[13]

In this condition, it is tempting to fantasy the possibility of retiring the "federal" concept from active duty, granting it a grace-and-favor residence (in Athens, Rome, or Philadelphia), and declaring a public search for its successor. We are, after all, at a familiar crossroads in political conceptualization, having been there many times before—with "imperialism," with "sov-ereignty," with "constitution," and a host of other constructs of political communication. And given that "all classifications, no matter how natural they appear, are invented,"[14] then what man creates, man can put aside.

---

13. The logic of the current situation is brilliantly caught by Martin Landau. It is not true, he argues, that we are inescapably the prisoners of our con-cepts, because "... each of us continually *tests against* experience—that we probe, experiment, investigate, try out, feel our way—all the time *learning* that our conceptualizations are not intractable." And he illustrates "the way in which experience alters even the most durable of our categories" by taking the concept of "separation of powers" as a case in point. The federal concept is similarly a case in point. (Landau, *Political Theory and Political Science*, Chap. 2, "Objectivity, Neutrality, and Kuhn's Paradigm.") Thus, once we admit that the properties of this concept are no longer dichoto-mous, it is doubtful whether we can resort to the idea of a spectrum to cure our problems; unless, that is, we can create some clearly defined dimensions that will permit the construction of rating scales. But heaven forbid an "F" scale on which the federal property of the United States is .75 in 1974 com-pared to .55 for India!!
14. Landau, p. 50.

Yet this is the purest fantasy. No one, and perhaps not even a lexicographer Caesar, can rule over the domain of etymology. We cannot stem the momentum of two thousand years of usage, nor can we sensibly deny that the longevity of the concept is some testimony to its continuing need, expressive, symbolic, or instrumental. For concepts live, wither, or die as needs must; and over great stretches of time different societies have satisfied their different needs for preferred relations with others through the mutual commitment of *foedus*—a concept that by repeated encounters with different experiences has become interwoven not with one thing, but many things. Therefore, according to our needs, we could choose from the many ways that the federal concept has revealed itself in the past, and conceivably may reveal itself in the future.

We may, for example:

1. Employ a possible early signification of the concept—which is the widest use of it, connoting simply *any* cooperative association of groups, whether *territorial or not*. Like the Greek *koinon* or Althusius' notion of *consociatio symbiotica*, it would embrace all forms of association, whether leagues, alliances, temporary or permanent, simple or complex, or whatever their purpose—political, social, economic, etc. It would embrace all confederacies, as understood prior to 1787 and after 1787; all versions of the "federal" state after 1787; and all forms of international association—UNO, NATO, EEC, the World Federation of Trade Unions, etc.

2. Apply the term to any cooperative association of groups as in (1), but limit the genus by any one or combination of elements: e.g., territoriality, purpose, organization, operation, etc. In this way we may include or exclude such bodies as, for example, the World Federation of Trade Unions, the International Federation of Oil Consumers, the EEC, the International Chess Federation, the British Commonwealth of Nations, etc.

3. Retain the term for any state formation where "power is divided" in accordance with the "U.S. model." And thus, according to the way this model is read, one would either include or exclude, by reference to the constitutional structure alone, states such as India, Malaysia, etc.

4. Retain the term for state formations where "power is divided" on the lines of any of the existing "federal" or purportedly "federal"

systems, and where constitutional/political practice sustains a "signi-ficant" measure of "independence" (autonomy) in at least one field of activity. Significance being treated as a matter of degree, individual judgment can then allow for a "strict" or "loose" interpretation; for example, whereas some might admit Malaysia to the federal club, others would not.

5. Apply the term to any state formation where, though power is divided constitutionally between two or more jurisdictions (i.e., fed-eral/state, federal/state/local, federal/state/regional/metropolitan, etc.), all levels of government are given "significant" responsibilities in virtually all activities.

6. Retain the term for any state formation where any "instrumental" or "institutional" recognition is given to any "significant" territori-ally organized diversity—e.g., the Scottish legal system. In Living-ston's words, "We must treat this group of people living in that specific region differently in this particular matter from the way we treat all other groups."

7. Extend the term to any state formation where "power is divided" between two or more levels of authority, all acting directly on the citizen in those matters pertaining to their responsibility, but there is no constitutional presumption of co-equality, and only custom and political practice sustains the "integrity" of each level of government —for example, South Africa, Italy(?).

8. Apply the term to any state formation where "power is divided" and practiced strictly in accordance with the separatist notions of "twin-stream" or "dual federalism."

9. Identify "federal" with any system where "power is divided," but qualify the term by national categories: thus, American federalism, Swiss federalism, Indian federalism, etc., implying a series of separate and distinct political systems with a partial formal identity which is no more significant than the notion "unitary" or "confederal" consti-tutional system.

10. Treat the evolution of the "federal" concept in paradigmatic terms—for example, Grecian federalism, Roman, Germanic, Ameri-can, nineteenth-century Western, post-colonial, Afro-Asian, etc.

The tie that binds all these is *foedus*: this is the heart of the matter. Whatever its institutional mutations in history, it is the primary cell of all relationships wherever individuals, families, tribes, communities, societies, nations have come together to promote both personal and common interests. It knows no degrees, it is indifferent to forms, it is blind to everything but the promise of communality and individuality, and to this it demands fidelity. Without this there can be no association, no cooperation, no treaty, no leagues, no constitution.

If *foedus* is there, then one may choose not only from ten ways of perceiving the subject, but from all the possible variations and combinations of these alternatives. Some of these ways have a more recent etymological license than others, some have greater theoretical coherence, some greater empirical verifiability, some more fashionable appeal, some greater coverage than others, some greater operational value. But historically, none has a greater legitimacy than any other. And as descriptive or explanatory modes, all are imperfect. No single perception of the subject will provide us with an accurate means of decoding and translating the transactions of any single federal culture; nor will any combination of the known ways of looking at the matter enable us to decode and translate the transactions of all the heterogeneous phenomena that move about in the "federal" galaxy.

This is where the federal idea stands after 2,500 years. Its future rests with those who can resist the urge to tidy the matter, while continuing to play out the limitless potentialities of its diverse history, its diverse progeny, its diverse practices, and its diverse purposes. If there are now ten ways of looking at the subject, how many more will there be by the year 4000 A.D.?

APPENDIX:

THE FEDERAL STATES,
according to six authors

A. B. HART (1891)	K. C. WHEARE (1951)	B. M. SHARMA (1951)
(a) *The Four Great Existing Federations:* U.S.A., 1787 Switzerland, 1874 Germany, 1871 Canada, 1867 (b) *Latin-American Federations:* Mexico, 1824-1935 1867-1890 Central American Confederation, 1824-1839 Venezuela, 1830-1890 Argentine Republic, 1860-1890 United States of Colombia, 1863- 1886 Brazil, 1889-1890	(a) *Genuine Federal States:* U.S.A. Canada Switzerland Australia (b) *Quasi-Federal, Insufficiently Known, Not Genuine:* Argentine Constitution, 1853 Brazilian Constitution, 1891 German Empire Constitution, 1871-1918 Weimar Republic, 1919-1933 Austrian Constitution, 1920 U.S.S.R. Constitution, 1936 Mexican Constitution, 1917 Indian Constitution, 1935	U.S.A. Switzerland Canada Australia South Africa Mexico U.S.S.R. Yugoslavia Pakistan China Malaya Czechoslovakia Indonesia India

R. L. WATTS (1966)	C. J. FRIEDRICH (1954 and 1968)	I. D. DUCHACEK (1970)
(a) *Classic Federations:*	*Bowie and Friedrich, 1954*	"21 of the existing Nation-States are
U.S.A.	U.S.A.	considered or claim
Switzerland	Switzerland	to be federal":
Canada	Canada	
Australia	Australia	U.S.A.
(b)	West Germany	Switzerland
Purported	*Friedrich, 1968**	Canada
Federations:	*Case Studies:*	Australia
West Germany	Australia	Soviet Union
Yugoslavia	Brazil	Mexico
Brazil, 1946	Canada	Argentina
Venezuela, 1947	Cyprus	Brazil
Argentina, 1949	Germany	Venezuela
(c)	India	West Germany
New Federations:	Switzerland	Yugoslavia
India	Yugoslavia	Austria
Pakistan		Czechoslovakia
Malaya and	*Note: "The above	India
Malaysia	systems are only a	Pakistan
Nigeria	selection from	Burma
Rhodesia and	among the large	Malaysia
Nyasaland	number of federal	Nigeria
The West Indies	systems now oper-	Libya
(d)	ating or emerging."	Tanzania
Recently Attempted		Camerouns
but Now Failed		
Federations:		
South Arabia, 1959		
Indonesia, 1949		
French West Africa		
French Equatorial		
Africa		
Mali Federation		
Union of Central		
African Republics,		
1960		

R. L. Watts (1966) *Continued*	
Cameroun Republic, 1961 Arab Federation of Jordan and Iraq United Arab Republic (Egypt, Syria, Yemen), 1958	

Bibliography of Works Referred to, and Other Select Reading

I have compiled this bibliography with two objects in mind: first, to facilitate reference to the principal texts cited in the footnotes; and second, to indicate the principal accessory sources that I have used but not referred to in the footnotes. In general, I have given prominence only to the major comparative texts that have been published over the past thirty years instead of attempting to list studies of particular federal systems. For a comprehensive bibliography, one may well begin with, and build upon, Albert Liboiron's 231-page bibliography, *Federalism and Intergovernmental Relations in Australia, Canada, the United States and Other Countries* (Institute of Intergovernmental Relations, Dunning Hall, Queen's University, Kingston, Ontario, 1967).

I. THE LEAGUES: ANCIENT AND MEDIEVAL

Allen, J. W. *A History of Political Thought in the Sixteenth Century.* London: Methuen, 1957.

Althusius, Johannes. *Politica Methodice Digesta.* Reprinted from the 3rd ed. of 1614. Edited, with an Introduction, by C. J. Friedrich. Cambridge, Mass.: Harvard University Press, 1932.

Badian, E. *Foreign Clientelae (264-70 B.C.).* Oxford: The Clarendon Press, 1958.

Barker, Ernest. *From Alexander to Constantine.* Oxford: The Clarendon Press, 1956.

Bentwich, N. *The Religious Foundations of Internationalism: A Study in International Relations Through the Ages.* London: Allen & Unwin, 1933.

Bodin, J. *Method for the Easy Comprehension of History.* Translated by Beatrice Reynolds. New York: W. W. Norton, 1945. (English translation of *Methodus ad Facilem Historiarum Cognitionem.* Paris: Apud Martinum Juvenem, 1566.)

―――. *The Six Bookes of a Commonweale.* A Facsimile reprint of the English translation of 1606. Corrected and supplemented in the light of a new comparison with the French and Latin texts. Edited with an Introduction by Kenneth Douglas McRae. Cambridge, Mass.: Harvard University Press, 1962.

―――. *Six Books of the Commonwealth.* Translated and abridged by M. J. Tooley. Oxford: Basil Blackwell, 1955.

Botsford, G. W., and E. G. Sihler, editors. *Hellenic Civilisation.* New York: Columbia University Press, 1915. Chap. 12, "Hellenic Interstate Relations," and Chap. 17, "Politics of the Greek Homeland: The Federal Unions (323-146 B.C.)."

Bowie, R. R., and C. J. Friedrich, editors. *Studies in Federalism.* Boston: Little, Brown, 1954.

Bright, John. *A History of Israel.* 2nd ed. London: Westminster Press, 1972.

Bryce, J. *The Holy Roman Empire.* London: Macmillan, 1902.

von Busolt, Georg. *Griechische Staatskunde.* 2 vols. Edited by Heinrich Swoboda. Munich: C. H. Beck, 1926.

Cambridge Ancient History. Vol. VII. *The Hellenistic Monarchies and the Rise of Rome.* Cambridge: The University Press, 1969. "The Large State and the Polis," pp. 22-40.

Cambridge Medieval History. Vol. VII. *Decline of Empire and Papacy.* Cambridge: The University Press, 1964. Chap. 7, "The Swiss Confederation in the Middle Ages."

Cambridge Modern History. Vol. II. *The Reformation, 1520-1559.* Cambridge: The University Press, 1968. Chap. 10, "The Empire of Charles V. in Europe."

Carlyle, R. W., and A. J. Carlyle. *A History of Medieval Political Theory in the West.* Edinburgh: Blackwood, 1950.

Cary, M. *The Geographic Background of Greek and Roman History.* Oxford: The Clarendon Press, 1950.

―――. *A History of the Greek World from 323 to 146 B.C.* 2nd ed. London: Methuen, 1972.

Cary, M., and H. H. Scullard. *A History of Rome Down to the Reign of Constantine.* 3rd ed. London: Macmillan, 1974.

Clarke, M. V. *The Medieval City-State: An Essay on Tyranny and Federation in the Later Middle Ages.* Cambridge: Speculum Historiae, 1966.

Dunning, W. A. *A History of Political Theories, Ancient and Medieval.* 3 vols. London: Macmillan, 1902.

Ehrenberg, Victor. *The Greek State.* 2nd ed. London: Methuen, 1969.

Elazar, D. J. "Government in Biblical Israel." *Tradition,* Vol. 13 (Spring-Summer 1973), pp. 105-123.

Eulau, Heinz H. F. "Theories of Federalism Under the Holy Roman Empire." *American Political Science Review,* Vol. 35 (August 1941), pp. 643-664.

Eyre, E., editor. *European Civilization: Its Origin and Development.* 7 vols. London: Oxford University Press, 1934. Vol. I, Chap. 2, "The Greek Expansion and the Formation of Greek Society," and Chap. 5, Athens, "The Attempt at Unity in Greece." Vol. VII, Chap. 9, "Some Features of Medieval Institutions."

Figgis, J. N. *Political Thought from Gerson to Grotius, 1414-1625.* New York: Harper Torch Books, 1960.

Francotte, H. *La Polis Grecque: Recherches sur la Formation et l'Organisation des Cités, des Ligues et des Confédérations dans la Grèce Ancienne.* Rome: L'Erma di Bretschneider, 1964. Esp. Chap. 12, "La Sympolitie ou Confédération."

Freeman, Edward A. *History of Federal Government,* Vol. I. London: Macmillan, 1863.

von Gierke, Otto. *The Development of Political Theory.* New York: Howard Fertig, 1966.

_____. *Political Theories of the Middle Ages.* Translated, with an Introduction, by F. W. Maitland. Cambridge, England: The University Press, 1900; reprinted 1968.

Giovannini, A. *Untersuchungen über die Natur und die Anfänge der bundesstaatlichen Sympolitie in Griechenland.* Gottingen: Vandenhoeck & Ruprecht, 1971.

Grotius, Hugo. *The Law of War and Peace.* 2 vols. New York: Oceana Publications for the Carnegie Endowment for International Peace, 1964.

Hayes, C. J. H. *Historical Evolution of Modern Nationalism.* New York: Crowell-Collier-Macmillan, 1937.

Hinsley, F. H. *Sovereignty.* London: C. A. Watts, 1966.

Hopper, R. "Interstate Juridical Agreements in the Athenian Empire." *Journal of Hellenic Studies,* Vol. 63 (1943), pp. 35-51.

Hughes, C. J. "The Theory of Confederacies." Paper read to the Sixth World Congress, International Political Science Association, Geneva, 1964.

Hugo, Ludolph. *De Statu Regionum Germaniae.* 1661.

Jeffery, L. H. *Archaic Greece: The City-States, c. 700-500 B.C.* London: Ernest Benn, 1976.

Kitto, H. D. F. *The Greeks.* Edinburgh: Pelican Books, 1957.

Larsen, J. A. O. "Federation for Peace in Ancient Greece." *Classical Philology,* Vol. 39 (July 1944), pp. 145-161.

————. *Greek Federal States.* Oxford: The Clarendon Press, 1968.

————. *Representative Government in Greek and Roman History.* Berkeley and Los Angeles: University of California Press, 1966.

Laski, Harold J. *A Grammar of Politics.* 4th ed. London: Allen & Unwin, 1941.

Leibniz, G. W. *De Suprematu Principum Germaniae.* 1678.

Locke, John. *Second Treatise of Civil Government.* Book II, Chap. 12, any edition.

Marshall, F. H. *The Second Athenian Confederacy.* Cambridge: The University Press, 1905.

McIlwain, C. H. *The Growth of Political Thought in the West: From the Greeks to the End of the Middle Ages.* New York: Macmillan, 1957.

Mogi, Sobei. *The Problem of Federalism.* 2 vols. London: Allen & Unwin, 1931.

de Montesquieu, Baron. *The Spirit of the Laws.* Vol. 1, Book IX, in *The Complete Works of M. Montesquieu,* translated from the French. Dublin: printed for W. Watson et al., 1777.

Nussbaum, Arthur. *A Concise History of the Law of Nations.* New York: Macmillan, 1947.

von Pufendorf, Samuel. *An Introduction to the Principal Kingdoms and States of Europe.* 8th ed. English translation, London, 1719.

————. *Of the Law of Nature and Nations.* 4th ed. London: J. Walthoe et al., 1729.

————. *De Officio Hominis et Civis Juxta Legem Naturalem.* 8th ed. 2 vols. Cambridge: Typis Academies, 1715.

Rhyne, C. S. *International Law.* Washington, D.C.: C. L. B. Publishers, 1971.

Rostovtzeff, M. *The Social and Economic History of the Hellenistic World.* 3 vols. Oxford: The Clarendon Press, 1953.

Ryder, T. T. B. *Koine Eirene: General Peace and Local Independence in Ancient Greece.* London: Oxford University Press, 1965.

Sandys, John. *A History of Classical Scholarship.* 2 vols. London: Hafner, 1967.

Schwarzenberger, G. *A Manual of International Law.* 5th ed. London: Stevens & Son, 1967.

Sealey, R. "The Origin of the Delian League." In *Ancient Society and Institutions: Studies Presented to Victor Ehrenberg,* pp. 233-255. Oxford: Basil Blackwell, 1966.

Spencer, Herbert. *The Principles of Sociology.* London: Williams & Northgate, 1882.

Tarn, W. *Hellenistic Civilization.* London: Edward Arnold, 1951.

Ullman, W. *A History of Political Thought in the Middle Ages.* Baltimore: Penguin Books, 1965.

Vaughan, C. V., editor. *The Political Writings of Jean-Jacques Rousseau.* 2 vols. With Introduction and Notes. Oxford: Basil Blackwell, 1962.

Weeramantry, C. G. *The Law of Contracts.* Colombo, Ceylon: Mortlake Press, 1967.

West, A. B. *The History of the Chalcidic League.* Bulletin No. 969. Madison: University of Wisconsin, 1912.

Zimmern, A. *The Greek Commonwealth: Politics and Economics in Fifth-Century Athens.* 5th ed., rev. London: Oxford University Press, 1961.

II. THE AMERICAN MODEL

Bassett, J. S. *The Federalist System, 1789-1801.* New York: Cooper Square Books, 1968.

Bennett, William H. *American Theories of Federalism.* University, Ala.: University of Alabama Press, 1964.

Benson, G. C. S., editor. *Essays in Federalism.* Claremont, Calif.: Institute for Studies in Federalism, 1961.

Borden, M., editor. *The Antifederalist Papers.* East Lansing: Michigan State University Press, 1965.

Bowen, Catherine Drinker. *Miracle at Philadelphia: The Story of the Constitutional Convention.* Boston: Little, Brown, 1966.

Brown, R. E. *Reinterpretation of the Formation of the American Constitution.* Boston: Boston University Press, 1963.

Chinard, Gilbert. "Polybius and the American Constitution." *Journal of the History of Ideas,* Vol. I (1940), pp. 38-58.

Corwin, E. S. "The Progress of Constitutional Theory Between the Declaration of Independence and the Meeting of the Philadelphia Convention." *American Historical Review,* Vol. 30 (1925).

Crosskey, W. W. *Politics and the Constitution.* 2 vols. Chicago: University of Chicago Press, 1953.

Curti, M. *The Growth of American Thought.* 3rd ed. New York: Harper & Row, 1964.

Diamond, Martin. "The Federalist's View of Federalism." In *Essays in Federalism,* edited by G. C. S. Benson, pp. 21-64. Claremont, Calif.: Institute for Studies in Federalism, 1961.

Dietze, G. *The Federalist: A Classic on Federalism and Free Government.* Baltimore: Johns Hopkins Press, 1960.

———, editor. *Essays on the American Constitution.* Englewood Cliffs, N.J.: Prentice-Hall, 1963.

Elazar, Daniel J. *American Federalism: A View from the States.* New York: Crowell, 1966.

———. *The American Partnership.* Chicago: University of Chicago Press, 1962.

Elliot, Jonathan, editor. *The Debates in the Several State Conventions on the Adoption of the Federal Constitution as Recommended by the General Convention at Philadelphia in 1787.* 2nd ed. 5 vols. New York: Burt Franklin, from the edition of 1888.

Farrand, Max. *The Framing of the Constitution of the United States.* New Haven: Yale University Press, 1967.

———, editor. *The Records of the Federal Convention of 1787.* 4 vols. New Haven: Yale University Press, 1938; rev. ed. 1966.

Fenno, R. F. Jr. *The Power of the Purse.* Boston: Little, Brown, 1966.

Goldwin, R. A., editor. *A Nation of States: Essays on the American Federal System by Morton Grodzins and Others.* Chicago: Rand McNally, 1966.

Grodzins, Morton. *The American System: A New View of Government in the United States.* Edited by D. J. Elazar. Chicago: Rand McNally, 1966.

Hunt, E. M. *American Precedents in Australian Federation.* New York: A. M. S. Press, 1968.

Jensen, M. "The Idea of a National Government During the American Revolution," *Political Science Quarterly,* Vol. 58 (1943), pp. 356-379.

———. *The Making of the American Constitution.* Princeton, N.J.: Van Nostrand, 1964.

Kenyon, Cecelia M. "Men of Little Faith: The Anti-Federalists on the Nature of Representative Government." *The William and Mary Quarterly,* 3rd series, Vol. XII (1955), pp. 3-46.

———, editor. *The Antifederalists.* Indianapolis: Bobbs-Merrill, 1966.

Koch, Adrienne. *The American Enlightenment*. New York: Braziller, 1965.

_____. *Power, Morals and the Founding Fathers*. Ithaca, N.Y.: Cornell University Press, 1961.

Leach, Richard M. *American Federalism*. New York: Norton, 1970.

Lewis, J. D. *Anti-Federalists versus Federalists*. San Francisco: Chandler, 1967.

Madison, James. *Notes of Debates in the Federal Convention of 1787*. With an Introduction by Adrienne Koch. Athens, Ohio: Ohio University Press, 1966.

Main, J. T. *The Anti-Federalists*. Chapel Hill: University of North Carolina Press, 1961.

Mason, A. T. *The States Rights Debate: Antifederalism and the Constitution*. With selected documents. Englewood Cliffs, N.J.: Prentice-Hall, 1964.

Mason, A. T., and R. H. Leach. *In Quest of Freedom*. Englewood Cliffs, N.J.: Prentice-Hall, 1959.

Miller, Perry. *The New England Mind: From Colony to Province*. Cambridge, Mass.: Harvard University Press, 1953.

Mitchell, B., and L. P. Mitchell. *A Biography of the Constitution of the United States*. New York: Oxford University Press, 1964.

Morison, Samuel, and Henry Steele Commager. *The Growth of the American Republic*, Vol. I. New York: Oxford University Press, 1962.

Parrington, Vernon Louis. *Main Currents in American Thought*. New York: Harcourt, Brace & World, 1958.

Patterson, J. T. *The New Deal and the States: Federalism in Transition*. Princeton, N.J.: Princeton University Press, 1969.

Prescott, A. T. *Drafting the Federal Constitution*. New York: Greenwood Press, 1968.

Ranney, John C. "The Bases of American Federalism." *The William and Mary Quarterly*, Vol. III (January 1946), pp. 1-35.

Robinson, J. H. "The Original and Derived Features of the Constitution." *Annals of the American Academy of Political Science*, Vol. 1 (1890), pp. 203-243.

Rossiter, Clinton. *1787—The Grand Convention*. New York: Macmillan, 1966.

Rottschaefer, H. *The Constitution and Socio-Economic Change*. New York: Da Capo, 1972.

Scheiber, N. *The Condition of American Federalism: An Historian's*

View. A study submitted by the Committee on Intergovernmental Relations to the Committee on Government Operations, U.S. Senate, October 15, 1966 (89th Congress).

Schuyler, Robert L. *The Constitution of the United States*. New York: Macmillan, 1923.

Sharkansky, I. *The Maligned States: Policy Accomplishments, Problems, and Opportunities*. New York: McGraw-Hill, 1972.

Smith, David G. *The Convention and the Constitution: The Political Ideas of the Founding Fathers*. New York: St. Martin's Press, 1965.

Stolberg, W. V. *The Federal Convention and the Formation of the American States*. New York: Liberal Arts Press, 1958.

Sundquist, J. L., with D. W. Davis. *Making Federalism Work*. Washington, D.C.: Brookings Institution, 1969.

Swisher, C. B. *American Constitutional Development*. Boston: Houghton Mifflin, 1943.

_____. *The Growth of Constitutional Power in the United States*. Chicago: University of Chicago Press, 1946.

de Tocqueville, Alexis. *Democracy in America*. Translated by Henry Reeve. 2nd ed. London: Saunders & Otley, 1836-1840.

Van Doren, Carl. *The Great Rehearsal*. New York: Viking Press, 1948.

Vile, M. J. C. *The Structure of American Federalism*. London: Oxford University Press, 1961.

Warren, Charles. *The Making of the Constitution*. New York: Barnes & Noble, 1967.

White, L. D. *The Federalists: A Study in Administrative History*. New York: Macmillan, 1959.

Wildavsky, Aaron, editor. *American Federalism in Perspective*. Boston: Little, Brown, 1967.

Wright, Benjamin F. *Consensus and Continuity*. New York: W. W. Norton, 1967.

_____, editor. *The Federalist*. Cambridge, Mass.: Harvard University Press, 1961. Chap. 5, "The Idea of Federalism."

III. MODERN THEORY AND PRACTICE

Aiyar, S. P. "The Federal Idea in India." In S. P. Aiyar and U. Mehta, *Essays on Indian Federalism*. Bombay: Allied Publishers, 1965.

_____. *Federalism and Social Change: A Study in Quasi-federalism*. Bombay: Asia Publishing House, 1961.

Babcock, Kendrick C. *The Rise of American Nationality, 1811-1819*. New York: Harper, 1906.

Birch, A. H. "Approaches to the Study of Federalism." In *American Federalism in Perspective*, edited by Aaron Wildavsky, pp. 65-76. Boston: Little, Brown, 1967.

————. *Federalism, Finance and Social Legislation in Canada, Australia and the United States*. Oxford: The Clarendon Press, 1955.

————. "Opportunities and Problems of Federation." In *Federation in East Africa: Opportunities and Problems*, edited by C. Leys and P. Robson. Nairobi: Oxford University Press, 1965.

Black, E. R. *Divided Loyalties: Canadian Concepts of Federalism*. Montreal: McGill-Queen's University Press, 1975.

Boorstin, D. J. *The Americans: The National Experience*. New York: Random House, 1965.

Bowie, R. R., and C. J. Friedrich, editors. *Studies in Federalism*. Boston: Little, Brown, 1954.

Break, George F. *Intergovernmental Relations in the United States*. Washington: Brookings Institution, 1967.

Brugmans, H. *La Pensée Politique du Fédéralisme*. Foreword by Raymond Aron. Leyden: Sijhoff, 1969.

Bryce, James. *Studies in History and Jurisprudence*. 2 vols. Oxford: The Clarendon Press, 1901. Vol. I, Chap. 3, "Flexible and Rigid Constitutions," and Chap. 4, "The Action of Centripetal and Centrifugal Forces on Political Constitutions."

Burns, J. H. "An English View of Federalism in 1829." *Political Studies*, Vol. IV (1956), pp. 312-315.

Currie, David P., editor. *Federalism and the New Nations of Africa*. Chicago: University of Chicago Press, 1964.

Davis, Rufus. "The Federal Principle Reconsidered." *Australian Journal of Politics and History*, Vol. 1 (1955), Part I, pp. 59-85, and (1956), Part II, pp. 223-244. Part I also appears in *American Federalism in Perspective*, edited by Aaron Wildavsky, pp. 3-33. Boston: Little, Brown, 1967.

————. "The Federal Principle Revisited." In *Questioning the Past*, edited by D. P. Crook. Brisbane: University of Queensland Press, 1972.

Deutsch, K. W., et al. *Political Community and the North Atlantic Area*. Princeton, N.J.: Princeton University Press, 1957.

Diamond, Martin. "The Ends of Federalism." *Publius*, Vol. 3 (Fall 1973), pp. 129-152.

Dicey, A. V. *Introduction to the Study of the Law of the Constitution*. 10th ed. London: Macmillan, 1964.

Duchacek, Ivo D. *Comparative Federalism: The Territorial Dimension of Politics.* New York: Holt, Rinehart & Winston, 1970.

Earle, V., editor. *Federalism: Infinite Variety in Theory and Practice.* Itasca, Ill.: F. E. Peacock, 1968.

Elazar, Daniel J. "Cursed by Bigness." *Publius,* Vol. III (Fall 1973), pp. 239-298.

————. *The Meaning of American Federalism.* Public Education Paper No. 7. Philadelphia: Temple University Center for the Study of Federalism.

————, editor. *Cooperation and Conflict.* Itasca, Ill.: F. E. Peacock, 1969.

————, editor. *The Federal Polity: A Symposium.* Entire issue of *Publius,* Vol. III (Fall 1973). Philadelphia: Temple University Center for the Study of Federalism.

Franck, Thomas M., editor. *Why Federations Fail: An Inquiry into the Requisites for Successful Federalism.* New York: New York University Press, 1968.

Friedrich, C. J. "International Federalism Theory and Practice." In *Systems of Integrating the International Community,* edited by E. Plischke. Princeton: Van Nostrand, 1964.

————. "New Tendencies in Federal Theory and Practice." Paper read to the International Political Science Association at Geneva, 1964. Published in English, in *Jahrbuch des Offentlichen Rechts,* New Series, Vol. 14 (1965).

————. *Trends of Federalism in Theory and Practice.* New York: Praeger, 1968.

Haas, Ernst B. "The Study of Regional Integration." In *Regional Integration,* edited by L. N. Lindberg and S. A. Scheingold. Cambridge, Mass.: Harvard University Press, 1971.

————. *The Uniting of Europe—Political, Social and Economic Forces, 1950-1957.* Stanford, Calif.: Stanford University Press, 1968.

Hay, P. *Federalism and Supranational Organizations: Patterns for New Legal Structures.* Urbana: University of Illinois Press, 1966.

Hicks, W. K., et al. *Federalism and Economic Growth in Underdeveloped Countries.* London: Allen & Unwin, 1961.

Hofstadter, R. *The American Political Tradition and the Men Who Made It.* New York: Knopf, 1948.

Hughes, C. J. *Confederacies.* An Inaugural Lecture. Leicester, England: Leicester University Press, 1963.

LaNauze, J. A. *The Making of the Australian Constitution.* Melbourne: Melbourne University Press, 1972.

Landau, Martin. "Baker v. Carr and the Ghost of Federalism." In *Reapportionment*, edited by G. Schubert, pp. 241-248. New York: Scribner's, 1965.

_____. *Political Theory and Political Science*. New York: Macmillan, 1972.

Laski, Harold J. "The Obsolescence of Federalism." *New Republic*, May 3, 1939, pp. 367-369.

Lavau, G. E. *Les Partis Politiques et les Réalités Sociales*. Paris: Fondation Nationale des Sciences Politiques, 1953.

Leach, Richard H. "Federalism: A Battery of Questions." *Publius*, Vol. III (Fall 1973), pp. 11-47.

Lehne, Richard. "Benefits in State-National Relations." *Publius*, Vol. II (Fall 1972), pp. 75-94.

Leys, C., and P. Robson, editors. *Federations in East Africa: Opportunities and Problems*. Nairobi: Oxford University Press, 1965.

Livingston, William S. *Federalism and Constitutional Change*. Oxford: Oxford University Press, 1956.

_____. "A Note on the Nature of Federalism." In *American Federalism in Perspective*, edited by Aaron Wildavsky. Boston: Little, Brown, 1967.

_____, editor. *Federalism in the Commonwealth: A Bibliographical Commentary*. London: Cassell, 1963.

Maas, A., editor. *Area and Power: The Theory of Local Government*. Glencoe, Ill.: Free Press, 1959.

MacMahon, Arthur W., editor. *Federalism, Mature and Emergent*. New York: Doubleday, 1955.

Matthews, R. L., editor. *Fiscal Federalism: Retrospect and Prospect*. Research Monograph No. 7. Canberra: Australian National University Centre for Research on Federal Financial Relations, 1974.

Maxwell, James A. *Specific Purpose Grants in the United States: Recent Developments*. Research Monograph No. 12. Canberra: Australian National University Centre for Research on Federal Financial Relations, 1975.

May, R. J. *Federalism and Fiscal Adjustment*. Oxford: The Clarendon Press, 1969.

Mentschikoff, Soia. "Federalism and Economic Growth." In *Federalism and the New Nations of Africa*, edited by David P. Currie. Chicago: University of Chicago Press, 1964.

Menzies, R. G. *Central Power in the Australian Commonwealth*. Melbourne: Cassell, 1968.

Morris-Jones, W. H. *The Government and Politics of India.* London: Hutchinson University Library, 1967.

Morton, W. *The Critical Years: The Union of British North America.* Toronto: University of Toronto Press, 1969.

Ormsby, W. G. *The Emergence of the Federal Concept in Canada, 1839-1854.* Toronto: University of Toronto Press, 1969.

Ostrom, Vincent. "Can Federalism Make a Difference?" *Publius,* Vol. 3 (Fall 1973), pp. 197-232.

——. *The Political Theory of a Compound Republic.* Blacksburg, Va.: Public Choice, VPI & SU, 1971.

Ostrom, Vincent, and E. Ostrom. "A Behavioral Approach to the Study of Intergovernmental Relations." *Annals of the American Academy of Political Science,* Vol. 359 (May 1965), pp. 137-146.

Popper, Karl. *Objective Knowledge: An Evolutionary Approach.* Oxford: The Clarendon Press, 1972.

Reagan, Michael D. *The New Federalism.* New York: Oxford University Press, 1972.

The Report of the Royal Commission on the Constitution, 1969-1973 (The Kilbrandon Report), Vol. 1 (October 1973). London: Her Majesty's Stationery Office.

Riker, W. H. *Federalism: Origin, Operation, Significance.* Boston: Little, Brown, 1964.

Rothschild, D. A. *Toward Unity in Africa: A Study of Federalism in British Africa.* Washington, D.C.: Public Affairs Press, 1960.

Sawer, G. F. *Modern Federalism.* London: C. A. Watts, 1969.

——, editor. *Federalism: An Australian Jubilee Study.* Melbourne: Cheshire, 1952.

Schlesinger, R. *Federalism in Central and Eastern Europe.* New York: Oxford University Press, 1945.

Serle, Geoffrey. "The Victorian Government's Campaign for Federation, 1883-1889." In *Essays in Australian Federation,* edited by A. W. Martin. Melbourne: Melbourne University Press, 1968.

Shonfield, Andrew. *Europe: Journey to an Unknown Destination.* London: Allen Lane, 1973.

Short, Lloyd M. *The Development of National Administrative Organization in the United States.* Baltimore: Johns Hopkins University Press, 1923.

Sidjanski, Dusan. "Will Europe Be United on Federal Lines?" *Futuribles,* Vol. II (1965), pp. 189-245.

Simeon, R. *Federal-Provincial Diplomacy: The Making of Recent Policy in Canada.* Toronto: University of Toronto Press, 1972.

Tarlton, Charles D. "Symmetry and Asymmetry as Elements of Federalism: A Theoretical Speculation." *Journal of Politics*, Vol. 22
(November 1965), pp. 861-874.

Trudeau, P. E. *Federalism and the French Canadians*. New York: St.
Martin's Press, 1968.

Watts, R. L. *New Federations: Experiments in the Commonwealth*.
Oxford: The Clarendon Press, 1966.

Wheare, K. C. *Federal Government*. 4th ed. London: Oxford University Press, 1963.

Wildavsky, Aaron. *A Bias Toward Federalism: A Review Essay on
Planning, Organization Theory, and Governmental Structure*.
Working Paper No. 40. Berkeley: University of California Graduate
School of Public Policy, 1975.

Wilson, A. W. *Political Integration by Jurisprudence*. Leyden: A. W.
Sijthoff, 1969. Chap. 1, "Political Integration and Federalism."

Index

233

Design: Theo Jung
Composition: University of California Press
Lithography: Edwards Brothers, Inc.
Binding: Edwards Brothers, Inc.

Text: Compset/500 Baskerville
Display: Compset/500 Baskerville
Paper: EB Book Natural, basis 50

DATE DUE